MW00850041

Global Fitness for Global People
How to Manage and Leverage Cultural Diversity at Work

Global Fitness for Global People is for all those wanting to thrive in today's global workplaces and to flourish in culturally diverse contexts. For this you need Global Fitness. Such competence does not develop by chance; individuals and organisations each need to foster it deliberately. This book explains why and how. Global Fitness results from tackling three key areas—establishing your Global Fitness goals, mastering your Global Fitness toolkit, and moulding the Global Fitness environment. The approach of *Global Fitness for Global People* is in line with the Chinese saying "If you give a man a fish, you feed him for a day. If you teach a man to fish, you feed him for a lifetime." In today's rapidly changing and uncertain environment, people need sound insights and guiding principles to shape their actions—whatever the situation and whenever or wherever it occurs. *Global Fitness for Global People* prepares you for this challenge, providing you with a set of core principles and tools that you can apply flexibly and dynamically to meet your own and your organisation's needs—now and in a changing future.

Helen Spencer-Oatey is Managing Director of GlobalPeople Consulting Ltd. (GPC) and Emeritus Professor of Intercultural Communication at the University of Warwick. She is internationally renowned for her work on intercultural rapport, relationship management, and communication.

Professor Peter Franklin focuses on intercultural communication and intercultural management in his work at Konstanz University of Applied Sciences, Germany. He also helps organisations and their employees to handle cultural complexity and use it as a resource.

Domna Lazidou has a PhD in Culture and Communication and a background in Internal Communication Management in complex, intercultural workplaces. She works internationally to support culture change and to design and deliver global leadership and diverse team development programmes.

Praise for *Global Fitness for Global People*

Inspiring! Profound and insightful without being too academic. The authors use new and powerful tools to describe culture and its impact. I particularly liked the positive approach of Global Fitness. The authors take us on a learning journey and make it clear that the ability to deal with intercultural issues has a lot to do with one's own inner attitude towards leveraging diversity.
—*Monika Krause, Intercultural trainer and coach, Vice-President, SIETAR Germany*

Global Fitness for Global People is brimming with cutting edge research that is illuminated with real-world case studies and extensive activities for reflection and application. I highly recommend this resource to global workers everywhere who are looking for practical solutions for building a more culturally intelligent world.
—*David Livermore, PhD, author and thought leader on cultural intelligence and global leadership*

This book will help people who want to be successful working or leading in multi-cultural contexts to accurately diagnose what "cultural muscles" they need to strengthen and the most effective way to do that.
—*Zhou Ning, CEO of Daimler Northeast Asia Parts Trading and Services Co., Ltd.*

This book provides a treasure trove of insights and practical applications based on real-life case studies for succeeding within diverse workplaces as well as in daily living—this is a must-read for all those desiring to successfully navigate differences!
—*Darla K. Deardorff, author and Founding President,*
World Council on Intercultural and Global Competence

In an ever-changing world where the most vulnerable often lose out, *Global Fitness for Global People* provides compelling solutions to challenges at home and abroad. Global interconnectivity is here to stay and this book provides the tools with which to make it work for all of us.
—*Rt Hon David Lammy MP, Member of Parliament for Tottenham and*
Shadow Secretary of State for Foreign and Commonwealth Affairs, UK

The beauty of this book is that it is so practical—dozens of case studies, numerous helpful charts and diagrams, down-to-earth prose—and so engaging that it will appeal even to people who may not be sure they need more cultural awareness. And for those keen to improve their cross-cultural skills, there are honest-to-goodness treasures on every page.
—*Craig Storti, Intercultural trainer and author of The Art of Doing Business across Cultures*

Global Fitness is a thorough and practical guide to managing cultural diversity at work.
—*Andy Molinsky, PhD Professor at Brandeis University, USA, and author of Global Dexterity*

This comprehensive book really captures cultural diversity at work, and how to navigate and bring together different perspectives to succeed and thrive.
—*Anne Marie Graham, Chief Executive, UK Council for International Student Affairs*

Praise for *Global Fitness for Global People*

This is a gem of a book on so many levels!

The authors have skilfully disentangled the complexity of the many aspects and components of cultural diversity; by transforming high-brow and outdated concepts into updated and easily comprehensible frameworks for reflection and action, they have created a refreshing and highly accessible approach that will attract everyone engaged or interested in international and intercultural interactions.

Most importantly, in contrast to so many prescriptive "how-to" books on individual cultural competence development, *Global Fitness for Global People* places the reader firmly at the core of the global cultural experience. Gently, yet consistently, the authors encourage us to reflect on ourselves and our belief systems, thereby raising not only our self-awareness but also developing much more objective and differentiated lenses through which to consider "otherness."

At a time of renewed geopolitical shifts and global turbulence, this book provides a truly vital contribution to understanding diversity from different perspectives and preventing the development of deeply ethnocentric lenses and actions.

A must-read for students, managers, educators, trainers, and coaches worldwide.

—Anke Middelmann, Director, Global Executive MBA, SKEMA Business School, France

Why do I find this invitation to enhance Global Fitness so exciting? By stressing a positive attitude towards diversity, while taking account of the organization and the context, this book offers a forward-looking and encouraging approach with practical examples for all those who want to develop their communicative and relational skills in global settings.

—Julika Baumann Montecinos, Professor of Intercultural Management at the HFU Business School, Hochschule Furtwangen University, Germany

In addition to practice-oriented theories, models, toolkits and case studies, this book provides practical solutions applicable to diverse workplace scenarios. It broadens the reader's understanding, triggers thoughts for in-depth reflection, and inspires actions that bring positive changes. This book achieves that and more. I truly appreciate its comprehensive and exceptional insights on such a complex topic as cultural diversity.

—Anni Wang, Certified Coach and HR Training & Development Manager— Daimler Greater China

This original and inspiring book takes us on a professional development journey towards Global Fitness. Drawing on their extensive experience in teaching, training and research, the authors engage the reader in a wide variety of authentic case studies of handling cultural diversity, which are underpinned by solid insights into communication, psychology, management and cultural studies. With great clarity yet avoiding any oversimplification, the authors have thus laid out an attractive comprehensive program that is suited for self-study, training, and for teaching upcoming global professionals.

—Jan Van Maele, PhD Professor at Faculty of Engineering Technology, KU Leuven, Belgium, and specialist in language and communication

Global Fitness for Global People

How to Manage and Leverage Cultural Diversity at Work

Helen Spencer-Oatey
Peter Franklin
Domna Lazidou

Melbourne – London – Tokyo – New York

www.castledown.com

Level 9, 440 Collins Street, Melbourne, Victoria 3000, Australia

4th Floor, Silverstream House, 45 Fitzroy Street Fitzrovia, London W1T 6EB United Kingdom

2nd Floor Daiya Building, 2-2-15 Hamamatsu-cho, Minato-ku, Tokyo 105-0013, Japan

447 Broadway, 2nd Floor #393, New York NY, 10013 United States

First published 2022 by Castledown Publishers, Melbourne

Information on this title:
www.castledown.com/professional-books/view-title/?reference=9780648184430
DOI: 10.29140/9780648184430

Global Fitness for Global People: How to Manage and Leverage Cultural Diversity at Work

© Helen Spencer-Oatey, Peter Franklin, & Domna Lazidou, 2022

Typeset by Castledown Design, Melbourne

ISBN: 978-0-648184-43-0 (Paperback)

Contents

Acknowledgements

Many people have helped to make this book possible, and we are sincerely grateful to them all for their various contributions. First, we would like to express our thanks to the numerous colleagues, clients, friends, family members, writers, researchers and students—known to us personally or through their published work—who have contributed to our thinking through sharing their experiences and ideas. Some of them feature in the book—referenced if their work is published, or otherwise with pseudonyms. All have made a very valuable contribution to the book, stimulating our thinking and helping us develop new insights.

We are particularly indebted to a number of people and would like to mention them by name. We're very grateful to the team at Castledown Publishers, who have taken a very personalised and supportive approach to the creation of this book; in particular, Blake Tanner, our editor, for his patience, encouragement, flexibility, and responsiveness as we discussed the whole project and developed the manuscript; Anne Skehan for her willingness to produce multiple versions of the book cover and flyer, until all of us were satisfied; and Samantha Fischer for her support over financial aspects.

In addition, we'd like to thank the following colleagues: Sophie Reissner-Roubicek and Daniel Dauber at the University of Warwick for their input into early discussions on the concept of Global Fitness and their support in developing and testing related tools; and Eva Jordans for her PhD research at the University of Warwick that inspired our conceptualisation of the Interaction Compass. We would also like to thank Brian Switzer of Konstanz University of Applied Sciences and Sophie Reissner-Roubicek for their design suggestions on the book cover.

We are particularly grateful to each other for the countless stimulating discussions that we have enjoyed and for each person's detailed feedback on the ever-changing drafts. We experienced in real-time some of the issues we were writing about—how disagreement can lead to new insights when each person's perspective is truly engaged with. This was enormously inspiring for each of us.

Finally, we are thankful to our families and friends for their patience as we sat in front of our computers for hours on end, drafting the chapters or participating in endless online discussions with each other. Without their support, the book would never have been possible.

Introduction

1

Becoming global: Mapping your development journey

Introduction

"I was very surprised to find people here keep dogs as pets. It made me excited and happy, and really curious to find out why. In my country, dogs are mostly kept for security purposes and rarely as pets, let alone taken for walks or on buses."
—A musician after his arrival in a foreign country.

"I find small talk with strangers difficult—I'm afraid they'll ask me about my family and that I'll have to reveal my sexuality."
—A young businesswoman who works internationally.

"Recent moves to control education have had very obvious negative consequences for the English teaching industry and the field of language education."
—Language teacher working in a foreign country.

"They made fun of my way of praying—mocking me."
—Young woman, sharing accommodation with others from a faith different from her own.

"Sustaining smooth communication is a real challenge as the majority of the buyers here are very emotional, whereas my colleagues on the manufacturing side may not be very emotional."
—An international salesman.

Colleagues, clients, and friends of ours have recently made the above comments. All of these people were sharing their experiences of cultural diversity. Some were finding it challenging, some were finding it interesting and exciting, others were experiencing prejudice and discrimination. The sources of the differences were varied: governmental policies, personal beliefs and attitudes, patterns of communication, societal practices, to mention just a few.

This book has been written for all those living and working in situations where differences such as these come to the fore. If you experience this kind of diversity in your working life and are curious to handle it with greater understanding, pleasure and success, this book will take you on a professional development journey, leading—via reflection and self-reflection—to insights and skills that will enable you to achieve greater satisfaction and success not only at work but also in other areas of life.

This book is different from others which claim to have similar goals. It doesn't mainly offer advice—dos and don'ts, tips and tricks—to handle cultural differences and difficulties. Nor does it attempt to hide the complexity of working and interacting across cultures behind over-simplified and wrongly applied dimensions and dichotomies illustrated in simple stories.

Rather, using numerous authentic cases and examples drawn from our own experience and the research literature,[1] we unpick this complexity: we present digestible insights and describe the qualities and skills you need to handle it and make the most of it. We use authentic case studies as an indirect way of illustrating difference; we also include many activities that ask you to reflect on the case studies and/or to apply the learning points from them to your own situations. This approach may necessarily make it a longer learning path, but it is one we are convinced will lead to more sustainable learning and professional development.

Global People and cultural diversity at work

In Marshall McLuhan's 'global village'[2], potentially everybody can count themselves among the group of Global People. The Internet, the social and classical media, access to cheap travel and easily passable frontiers—despite Covid restrictions and increasingly inward-looking foreign policies of some states—all make it much easier than only twenty years ago to have contacts with people and organisations around the world.

---

[1]   Where the case studies come from published or public sources, we provide the relevant references. If no reference is given, this means that the case study comes from our own professional interactions or unpublished research data.

[2]   McLuhan, M. (1962): *The Gutenberg galaxy.* Toronto: University of Toronto Press.

But by the word *global* we mean more than this ease of contact with others elsewhere on the globe. We are interested in the personal changes that this contact brings. To gain some insights into this, we talked with a range of people who have experienced the global in different contexts. We asked them to reflect on their encounters with cultural diversity in their daily work, and to comment on the changes they have seen in themselves. The small sample below illustrates several of the different contexts and aspects this book addresses.

Brand consultant, Michael, for example, experiences a global work context in his home environment. He explains how encounters with other country cultures have triggered a learning process (Mini-bio 1.1).

Mini-bio 1.1: Michael—brand consultant

"I am a British young man who works as a brand consultant in a global research agency in the UK. My organisation is very large, so my colleagues come from many different cultural backgrounds. As a global agency we also work with lots of different countries, so we often need to consider the impact of cultural differences on markets for particular goods. For instance, when we are interpreting data on alcohol sales, we need to consider the impact of local cultural practices and beliefs. Initially, a primary challenge for me, both internally and externally, was not assuming everyone thinks in the same way as me and learning to take cultural differences into account when building rapport. From my experiences I have learned to be more open-minded and not to make hasty judgements about people."

We deal with features he mentions in later chapters—personal qualities, such as open-mindedness, in Chapter 2 and building rapport in Chapters 5 and 7.

Michael refers to country cultures, yet as we explain below, cultural diversity is not restricted to this. The insights, skills, and qualities we explore in this book apply equally to interactions with any kind of social group diversity. Take Femi, for example. Like Michael he's working 'at home', but in an environment in which he conceives of the cultural context as one impacted by politics, tribal affiliation, and religion (Mini-bio 1.2).

Mini-bio 1.2: Femi—management consultant

"I was born and brought up in Akure, the capital city of Ondo state, Nigeria. It's home to people from many different parts of the country and they are all warmly welcomed. Industry and commerce are thriving, but politically the situation is more challenging for Akure Indigenes. Several of them have lost governorship elections in recent years, despite often presenting better and more equipped candidates. This has made it difficult to take forward indigene agendas. I myself am a managing partner of a consulting company, working as part of a team of 10 consultants from different tribes, religions, and backgrounds. We operate out of four of Nigeria's six regions. Most of our clients are from Nigeria, but recently we've had more enquiries from other parts of Africa. Often, I've just wanted to get things going quickly, but then realise that without understanding people's contexts properly, problems can arise. I have had to learn to take things more slowly and to be open to learning about the diverse perspectives of my team and clients. By doing this, it's broadened my understanding of different issues, enabling me to respond to their needs more effectively."

Many of you reading this book are likely to be working away from home, maybe similar to Saskia, who leads diverse teams like Femi but does so in many different parts of the world (Mini-bio 1.3). She describes the need to adjust to different communication styles, and to be able to interpret them, something we explore in Chapter 4.

Mini-bio 1.3: Saskia—senior project manager in international development

"Growing up in The Netherlands I have always been curious and interested in other countries and cultures, which led me to study for an agricultural engineering degree and a career in international development. Currently I am doing consultancy work for the United Nations to support rural and agricultural development projects. My work is to advise and support national project teams in several countries in Africa and Asia on issues related to water management and farmers' organisations. This involves working with, and leading teams of, colleagues from Africa, Europe, and Asia. Initially I had to get used to more indirect communication styles and learn how to interpret what people say. Over the years, I have learned to not make assumptions, but instead to be open and curious about how we all view the work and how best to reach our goals. Working in this diverse context inspires and energises me."

Some of you will not only be travelling like Saskia for work but also living abroad—in what is, or was, a foreign country. Living and working abroad for a long time can bring an adjustment so enjoyable and so complete that a person feels uncomfortable with the behaviour of his or her culture of origin, as Jason does.

Mini-bio 1.4: Jason—Learning and development manager

"I'm originally from Manchester, UK. I came out to Japan upon graduation from university and have been living here since, working in a variety of public and private sector roles related to education and learning. I am currently the head of the regional learning function in a major global pharmaceutical company. I very much enjoy life here in Japan and particularly appreciate the respect and manners people display towards one another—the vast majority of people here are very considerate. I feel really acclimatized to living and working here—to the extent that I sometimes find it challenging working with colleagues from other countries who have different styles of communication! For example, in global team meetings I often find myself not able to get a word in edgeways because I am more used to Japanese-style meetings where there are gaps in the discussion for people to reflect and add their view. I think I've become much more patient over the years towards cultural differences such as this—things that previously I would have found frustrating / annoying."

Adjusting to cultural difference and the notion of one's behavioural comfort zone are among the topics of Chapter 6.

We suggest you take a moment to think about your own experiences of cultural differences.

Activity 1.1: Personal reflections on cultural diversity

Think back on your own life.
1. How and in what context(s) have you experienced cultural diversity?
2. How has it affected you?
3. How similar or different are your experiences to the ones reported above?

All the people mentioned above refer to the learning that has resulted from their encounters with cultural diversity. So, the next section explores what cultural diversity encompasses.

Cultural diversity—What does it cover?

A thread running through all the personal reflections above is the notion of social groups. People talked of different nationalities, different regions, and different religious groups, mentioning attitudes and behaviours that they needed to adjust to. Putting it more formally, we can explain cultural diversity and its impact like this:

Cultural diversity exists when people who are working or living together in some kind of community are members of two or more different social groups. This can impact on interaction in two main ways: (a) people's attitudes (e.g., positive, negative, competitive, or neutral) towards members of other social groups ('them' and 'us' phenomenon), and (b) people's preferred and 'usual' ways of doing things, along with their underlying beliefs and values, all of which can influence (but not determine) how they behave. When social group members develop considerable resemblances in their attitudes and behaviours, they can be regarded as a cultural group.

Very often, especially in the intercultural field, people link cultural diversity with national group membership and differences between countries; in other contexts, it is often associated with ethnicity. In fact, there are numerous different types of social groups and so there are multiple sources of cultural diversity.

Figure 1.1 illustrates this. Culturally diverse workplaces are thus those in which interaction takes place between people who are from different social groups. (See Chapter 3 for a discussion of the notion of culture).

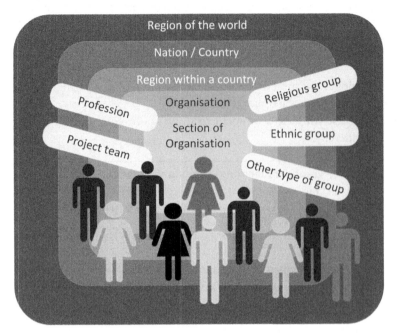

Figure 1.1: Potentially relevant social groups for members of a workplace

We will be picking up on these various points throughout the book, but here we draw attention to two important ways in which social groups—and associated cultural characteristics—affect interactions among people from different backgrounds.

Social group membership and its impact

Social group membership has two very important impacts on people: their sense of identity and their ways of thinking and behaving.

Social group membership and identity

Social group membership gives people a sense of belonging, and associated with that, a sense of identity—that is, a sense of who they are and where they fit. In other words, people's sense of identity is closely intertwined with their group memberships.

Psychologists distinguish between two fundamental types of identity: personal identity (people's sense of themselves as a unique individual) and group identity (people's sense of themselves that comes from their group memberships).[3]

Cultural diversity is particularly associated with group identity. From their group identities, people easily develop a 'them' and 'us' mentality—favouring members of their own group (often known as the in-group) and ignoring, disfavouring or discriminating against members of other groups (often known as the out-group). This is summarised in Figure 1.2. We consider the impact of identity in many chapters in the book, and especially in Chapters 5, 7 and 11.

It is useful to note here (and as indicated in Figure 1.2) that everyone is a member of multiple social groups. In other words, each person belongs simultaneously to, for example, a geographical region of the world, a nation (or more than one nation) and a particular province or district, as well as to other social groups such as a workplace organisation, a professional group, a religious group, a sports group, an ethnic group, and so on. This means that the impact of culture on people's attitudes, thinking and behaviour is always complex.

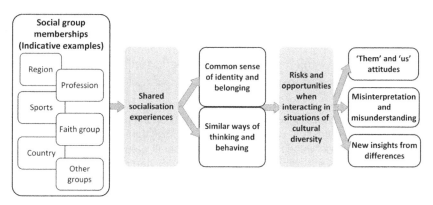

Figure 1.2: Social group memberships and their impact on situations of cultural diversity

Social group membership and ways of thinking and behaving

A second important feature of social group membership is its impact on ways of thinking and behaving. Similarities emerge from people's exposure to shared experiences. These include a similar educational system, similar media channels, similar induction processes at work, and so on. Although everyone responds to

---

3   E.g., Simon, B. (2004). *Identity in modern society. A social psychological perspective.* Oxford: Blackwell.

these shared experiences in different ways, they nevertheless lead to a certain amount of regularity or patterning in people's thinking and behaviour. We call these the 3Ps of culture—products, practices, and perspectives—and explain them in Chapter 3.

These shared patterns of thinking and behaving give rise to expectations, so when different patterns are encountered, this can lead to misinterpretation and misunderstanding (see Figure 1.2). We consider many examples of this throughout the book.

Despite the multiple types of social group memberships that give rise to cultural diversity, many of the case studies in this book concern people from different country-culture backgrounds. This is largely because of the greater ease with which such data can be collected. However, we believe the insights, skills, principles, and qualities we unpack in the book are equally applicable to all types of cultural diversity.

Handling diversity is complex, whatever the source, and requires Global Fitness for managing and leveraging it. We turn to that next.

Global Fitness—the key to success

Cultural diversity brings both challenges and opportunities. We believe Global Fitness is what is needed to overcome the former and make the most of the latter.

Global Fitness comprises all the features that enable a person or organisation to succeed in contexts of cultural diversity. It entails three key aspects: (a) the skills, qualities and values of individuals and small groups needed for global working, (b) the steps they take to develop these characteristics and grow as individuals and teams, and (c) the environment or context that supports and fosters their development. Taken together, these features enable people and organisations to function effectively when they face differences of many kinds.

The organisation of our book corresponds to these three aspects. Part 1 focuses on the skills and qualities needed for global working; Part 2 explores how these skills and qualities can be acquired and developed; Part 3 examines the features of the environment that can foster and support the development process.

Why use the term 'Global Fitness'?

You may be wondering why we use the term Global Fitness. There are several reasons.

- People often want a 'quick fix' for handling cultural diversity challenges—a speedy solution to problems encountered when communicating and working in culturally heterogeneous settings. However, like physical fitness, Global Fitness is not built overnight; it requires ongoing attention. In other words, we all need to keep working at the skills and qualities needed for handling situations of diversity. We need to keep learning and developing on a regular, ongoing basis. We need to 'work out' regularly in the Global Fitness 'gym'.

- The name Global Fitness hints at the need to 'fit in', drawing on the psychological concept of Person-Environment Fit, or P-E Fit. This does not mean that one person should change and 'fit in' with others; rather, psychologists identify two types of fit, both of which are important for Global Fitness.

  Complementary Fit. Firstly, organisations can benefit from individuals with different skills and qualities so that they can complement each other; they each contribute their differing strengths, ideas, and expertise to a task. This is known as Complementary Fit. It is particularly important for delivering synergistic outcomes characterised by creativity and innovation. In other words, diversity acts as a crucial resource for fostering new practice.

  Congruence Fit. Secondly, organisations can also benefit from individuals who are from diverse backgrounds to be able to work together harmoniously, finding compatible ways of communicating and relating. This is known as Congruence Fit. This second interpretation of Global Fitness means stepping out of one's comfort zone to engage with people who are different from oneself. In doing this, people also look for points of compatibility so that the benefits of diversity can emerge through ways of working and interacting that go well together.

The importance of context

Importantly, throughout the book we maintain and show that there is no single, set or pre-determined best way of handling cultural diversity in all circumstances; what is best—or what at least works—always depends on the possibly varied and numerous aspects of the context. The variability of context is thus a crucial factor and makes all recipes for behaviour and the dos and don'ts of cultural guides unreliable or incomplete at the very least.

The Global Fitness Development Cycle

As mentioned above, the three core aspects of Global Fitness form the organising principle for our book and we regard it as a development cycle (see Figure 1.3).

Part 1: What it means in real life—Global Fitness in Practice,

Part 2: What individuals and teams need to do to strengthen it—Global Fitness Engagement, and

Part 3: What kind of environment can help foster it—Global Fitness Environment.

Here we provide an overview of these three areas.

Figure 1.3: The Global Fitness Development Cycle

Understanding your goals: Global Fitness in Practice

Before starting any physical fitness training regime, it is important to know what you are aiming at, and the same applies to Global Fitness. Consider some more comments from colleagues, clients, and friends.

> *"I very much enjoy chatting with my patients, but I've found it difficult to handle small talk. It seems they all want to chat, whatever their background, and I'm not sure what to say. I need to find good ways of handling that."*
> —A doctor working internationally.

"I was very disappointed with the project leader. He focused on his own interests and viewpoints and was very closed to the wishes of the project members who were from a range of different backgrounds."
—A university researcher.

"I found it difficult to join in discussions at work. I couldn't find the space to join—everyone spoke quickly, one after another, and it seemed there was no gap."
—An engineer who had emigrated.

"We were running a sports event for young people from South-east Europe. In some publicity material, the word Macedonia was used instead of FYROM (Former Yugoslav Republic of Macedonia). A representative from the Greek Embassy was extremely upset and wanted to withdraw. We spent two days trying to resolve the issue."
—A cultural attaché.

These comments illustrate some key areas for Global Fitness development: personal qualities, background knowledge, communication, and management of relations. Part 1 of the book covers each of these areas in turn and thereby helps you understand and clarify your goals in terms of developing Global Fitness. They are summarised in Figure 1.4.

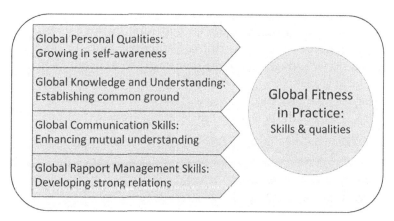

Figure 1.4: Outline characteristics of Global Fitness in Practice

At first glance, these skills and qualities may appear to be an easily reached set of goals. You may feel you know yourself well already, have a good general knowledge, that you successfully communicate every day, and get on well with other people. This may well be the case when you are operating in familiar contexts. However, the harsh reality is that none of us may be as 'fit' in a global context as we may assume.

Global Fitness in Practice is not different in nature from the skills and personal qualities that are needed in all interactions. Nevertheless, although there are obvious overlaps, cultural diversity adds a critical layer of complexity and uncertainty to all aspects of work, including project management, communication management, and relationship management. Moreover, underlying all those aspects are the personal qualities and attributes of the individuals concerned—how well individuals can flex and adapt to different needs and contexts.

Part 1 of the book thus introduces you to the key characteristics of Global Fitness in Practice, so that you can know what you are aiming at and start identifying your own priorities for development. Part 2 turns to practical steps to help you develop in those various areas.

Mastering your development toolkit: Global Fitness Engagement

Part 2 of the book deals with the 'How to ...' aspect of Global Fitness. There are no easy short-cuts to this—it requires active engagement and reflection. This development approach is in line with a theory of learning known as transformational learning, which guides our work and which we explain below.[4]

One of the most important features of transformational learning is the role of unexpected or stimulating experiences. These are important because they act as triggers for the 'transformation'—for the learning and development. If we stay in our comfort zones, rarely encountering anything unusual or different, our opportunities for experiential learning are much reduced. It is for this reason that we place great emphasis on engagement in our Global Fitness Development Cycle.

As Figure 1.5 shows, such engagement can be of many different types. The chapters in Part 2 of the book reflect the different types of engagement shown in this figure.

---

[4]   Mezirow, J. (1990). How critical reflection triggers transformative learning. In J. Mezirow (Ed.), *Fostering critical reflection in adulthood. A guide to transformative and emancipatory learning* (pp. 1–20). San Francisco, CA: Jossey-Bass Publishers.
    Taylor, E. W. (1994). Intercultural competency: A transformative learning process. *Adult Education Quarterly*, 44(3), 154–174.

Figure 1.5: Indicative examples of Global Fitness Engagement

These engagement opportunities, which all involve unfamiliarity and difference in some way, each have the potential to stimulate the new learning and behaviour that can lead to Global Fitness in Practice.

Nevertheless, encountering unexpected or unusual situations is insufficient in itself. The brief comments and mini-bios reported above all suggest that active effort is required. People need to pay careful attention to the key features of any new or unexpected situation they are facing, to find out more about it, think through the issues, and consider what they should or should not do.

We summarise this transformational learning approach with the acronym E4A and illustrate it in Figure 1.6. We explain it more fully in Part 2 of the book, including in the introduction to Part 2. Here we can simply note that reaping the benefits of unfamiliar situations requires active engagement. People need to pro-actively involve themselves in the new, different, or unknown aspect of the situation, trying to find out more about it and applying their new insights to what they do or say or think.

In Part 2 of the book, we explore many of the unfamiliar situations that cultural diversity can bring, as illustrated in Figure 1.5, and offer case studies and activities to help you along your journey towards Global Fitness. In this, you will not only learn from the materials and resources, but also from becoming familiar with the transformational learning process itself. We believe that it will provide you with strategies for learning and development that you can apply to your own personal experiences and situations.

E4A Transformational Learning

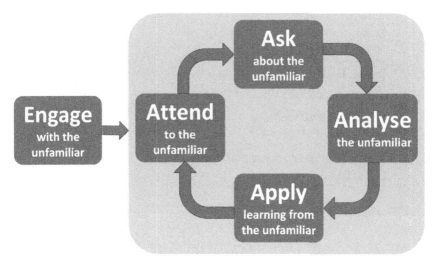

Figure 1.6: Transformational learning steps for developing Global Fitness

Moulding the organisational context: Global Fitness Environment

Very often there is an assumption that if there is a performance problem (i.e., insufficient Global Fitness in Practice), it is the 'fault' of the individuals concerned. While individuals obviously play a key role, the responsibility is not only theirs. The organisational context, or more broadly the environment they are working in, also plays a crucial role, and yet this is often overlooked. For example, we were recently asked to advise on the following situation.

> Company X with operations worldwide had started receiving complaints from customers on a range of issues. The company decided that what was needed was intercultural customer service training for all employees who dealt with customers. We were approached to provide this intercultural training. During our discussions it emerged that there were a number of senior management responsibilities that had been completely ignored (e.g., they had no customer service policy). We advised that without addressing these, the intercultural training would only provide a partial or one-sided solution.

This example makes clear that if an organisation wants high-quality performance (e.g., in this case, in customer service), top-management and decision-makers need to clarify and define exactly what this means for their particular organisation. This entails a range of factors, including drawing up detailed plans as to what it will mean for the organisation in terms of strategic and operational procedures and adjustments.

Part 3 of our book thus deals with the Global Fitness Environment—the contextual and organisational factors that set the framework conditions for developing Global Fitness. These conditions affect the ease with which employees can develop Global Fitness and display it in their performance and are matters senior management and decision-makers thus need to address. Figure 1.7 provides a summary of them, each of which are dealt with in the chapters in Part 3.

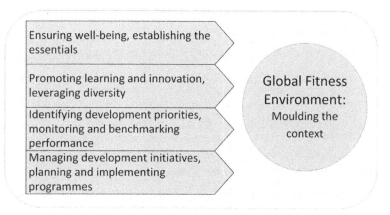

Figure 1.7: Indicative examples of Global Fitness Environment

Key takeaways

- Global People with Global Fitness are better able to manage and leverage cultural diversity at work and to succeed in culturally complex contexts.
- This book presents the three elements of a journey of conscious learning, the Global Fitness Development Cycle, which can support individuals, teams, and organisations to build Global Fitness.
- This development cycle consists of 1) Global Fitness in Practice—what it means in real life, 2) Global Fitness Engagement—what people need to do to strengthen it and 3) the Global Fitness Environment—what kind of environment can help foster it.
- The development cycle of these three elements involves 1) understanding your goals, 2) mastering your toolkit, and 3) moulding the environment.
- Together the three parts of this book show you how to acquire Global Fitness and manage and leverage cultural diversity at work.

Part 1

Understanding your goals: Global Fitness in Practice

Introduction to Part 1

Understanding your goals: Global Fitness in Practice

Before starting any physical fitness training regime, it is important to know what you are aiming at, and the same applies to Global Fitness. Part 1 of the book introduces you to the four key elements of Global Fitness.

First, everyone needs to start by looking at themselves. The better people understand themselves, the firmer their foundation for understanding and working well with others. We explore this in Chapter 2.

Second, if people are to interact and work well with others, they need to understand their contexts and preferences. This entails building common ground with them and this is achieved by enhancing Global Knowledge and Understanding. We examine this in Chapter 3.

Third, communication is crucial for effective working. Without it, people can misunderstand messages and get annoyed with each other. So, Chapter 4 focuses on Global Communication Skills.

Fourthly, staff well-being and project success are closely related to positive workplace relationships. Chapter 5 therefore explores Global Rapport Management Skills.

These four elements of Global Fitness are summarised in Figure P1.1 below.

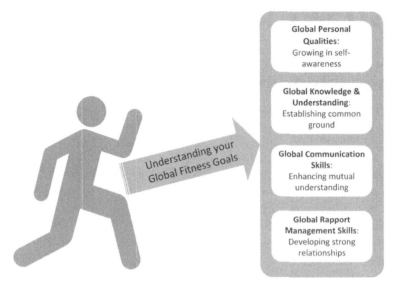

Figure P1.1: Global Fitness Goals: The four key elements

We introduce a number of key concepts and frameworks within these chapters, which we also draw on in Parts 2 and 3 of the book. These include:

- The **Interaction Compass:** to help you consider relationships and rapport management across different cultural groups.
- The **3Ps of culture—Products, Practices, and Perspectives:** to help you grasp the different types of impact that culture can have.
- **The Communication Process:** to help you understand how meaning is negotiated and co-constructed.
- **The Rapport Management Process:** to help you be aware of factors that influence relationship management.

2

Global Personal Qualities: Growing in self-awareness

Introduction

A key Global Fitness goal is to develop Global Personal Qualities. A crucial starting point for this is self-awareness, which is particularly important for working in contexts of cultural diversity. The aim of this chapter is therefore to help you:

- Become more aware of your own personal qualities and how they relate to Global Fitness.
- Understand what aspects of self-awareness contribute to Global Fitness.
- Introduce you to the Interaction Compass for understanding the personal qualities needed for working with unfamiliar other people.
- Reflect on what your personal values and aspirations are.

Introductory case study

We start with a situation to reflect on.

Case Study 2.1: Initiating a project[5]

A few years ago, a British government body negotiated with a Chinese counterpart organisation to establish a set of collaborative projects to design shared professional development resources. British organisations were invited to bid and several of the top proposals were selected. An equivalent process took place in China. A Joint Steering Committee meeting was then held in Beijing and members of that government-level committee established which successful British organisations would be paired with which Chinese organisations, in a sort of 'arranged marriage'.

---

[5] Spencer-Oatey, H., & Tang, M. (2007). Managing collaborative processes in international projects: Programme management perspectives. In H. Spencer-Oatey (Ed.), *e-Learning initiatives in China. Pedagogy, policy and culture* (pp. 159–173). Hong Kong: Hong Kong University Press.

> Each partner pair was given a broad topic to focus on, informed of their two-year budget, and encouraged to make contact with their respective partner organisation to start planning and implementing their project.
>
> **Reflect**
> a. What challenges do you think each of the projects would face in getting their project off the ground?
> b. What personal qualities do you think would be particularly important for each project leader to show?

As we move through this chapter, we gradually explore each of these questions, looking at what actually happened and the personal qualities that the project leaders and members needed to demonstrate in order to implement their projects successfully.

A fundamental quality that underpins almost all other qualities is self-awareness, and so we start by considering that. Then we turn to the aspects of self-awareness that are particularly needed for Global Fitness.

Self-awareness: The key quality

The most crucial personal quality needed to achieve Global Fitness is self-awareness. It enables you to gain insights into your reactions to other people's behaviour and to your preferred ways of doing things. These insights are essential foundations to (a) understanding your strengths so you can build on them, (b) identifying and working on your weaknesses, and (c) considering the circumstances under which you may wish to modify your preferred behaviour.

The good news is that, according to research by Tasha Eurich, 'self-awareness is a surprisingly developable skill'.[6] Yet writing in the Harvard Business Review,[7] she reports that only 10%–15% of the people she and her colleagues studied were actually self-aware. So, what does self-awareness really mean? She explains it as "the ability to see ourselves clearly—to understand who we are, how others see us, and how we fit into the world around us." In line with this, she draws a distinction between two types of self-awareness, 'internal self-awareness' and 'external self-awareness', and explains them as follows:[8]

---

[6] Eurich, T. (2017). *Insight. How to succeed by seeing yourself clearly.* London: Pan Macmillan.

[7] Eurich, T. (2018). What self-awareness really is (and how to cultivate it). Harvard Business Review, 4 January 2018. Retrieved from https://hbr.org/2018/01/what-self-awareness-really-is-and-how-to-cultivate-it

[8] Eurich, T. (2018). What self-awareness really is (and how to cultivate it). Harvard Business Review, 4 January 2018. Retrieved from https://hbr.org/2018/01/what-self-awareness-really-is-and-how-to-cultivate-it

Internal self-awareness represents how clearly we see our own values, passions, aspirations, fit with our environment, reactions (including thoughts, feelings, behaviors, strengths, and weaknesses), and impact on others. We've found that internal self-awareness is associated with higher job and relationship satisfaction, personal and social control, and happiness; it is negatively related to anxiety, stress, and depression.

External self-awareness means understanding how other people view us, in terms of those same factors listed above. Our research shows that people who know how others see them are more skilled at showing empathy and taking others' perspectives. For leaders who see themselves as their employees do, their employees tend to have a better relationship with them, feel more satisfied with them, and see them as more effective in general.

In other words, internal self-awareness enables you to understand who you are, while external self-awareness enables you to perceive how others see you. Both are critical for Global Fitness in that they help you think over and decide how to respond to difference. In Part 2 of the book, which focuses on personal development, we'll return to the issue of gaining external self-awareness. In this chapter, we focus particularly on internal self-awareness, and we divide these into four broad areas: managing stress and negative emotions, engaging with the unfamiliar, working with others, and recognising personal values that mean the most to you.

Managing stress and negative emotions: How resilient are you?

We start by following up on Case Study 2.1. Marie was the programme manager for all the projects, and she relates what happened next as the projects got underway.

Case Study 2.2: Uncertainties and project beginnings

"The Joint Steering Committee recommended that the Chinese partners visit the UK as soon as possible to meet with their British partners, so they could get to know each other and start planning the details of their joint projects. As the UK Programme Manager, I attempted to facilitate this. However, despite emailing and phoning key people, I only got non-committal responses about such a visit. It seemed as though there was some kind of problem, but I had no idea what it was. I then phoned a senior Chinese professional whom I knew well, and who was closely involved in the projects, but he was not able to shed any light on the situation either.

After a few months, all of us in the UK had become very concerned about the delay and so we decided to visit China instead. This was a step into the unknown because the level of commitment on the Chinese side felt low, and we didn't know how we would be received. However, when we all arrived in Beijing, we were welcomed very warmly by our Chinese partners. We were treated to lavish banquets and were taken out on sightseeing visits. Everyone was delighted about this and some of our doubts about the Chinese partners' commitment were reduced. However, project members were also very keen to start planning their joint projects rather than spending the majority of their time on social events."

Reflect

a. What different emotions do you think the British team members, and especially the Project Directors and Marie, the overall Programme Manager, felt during this start-up phase of the initiative?
b. Why do you think they may have felt this way?
c. What emotions do you think the Chinese partners felt?
d. Why do you think they didn't respond to Marie's initial attempts to arrange for them to visit the UK?

What is very clear from this account is that all the British participants experienced a lot of uncertainty.

The British felt:

- Uncertain and confused as to why the Chinese partners did not respond to invitations to visit the UK.
- Uncertain about the level of commitment of their Chinese partners to the project.
- Uncertain about how they would be received by their Chinese partners when they took the decision to visit.

In fact, the British were not alone in experiencing high levels of uncertainty. The Chinese partners were experiencing it, too. Some of it related to administrative issues, as they were waiting for ministry-level approval for a visit to the UK; some was more project-specific. The Chinese felt:

- Uncertain when they would receive ministry-level approval for the visit.
- Uncertain how their British partners would react to the delay.
- Uncertain how much the British partners would appreciate their hospitality.

Uncertainty can easily lead to worry and anxiety on the one hand, and irritation and anger on the other. For instance, Marie reported that everyone experienced anxiety during the team's visit to China. Many had continual headaches from worrying over how things would turn out and from the general stress of the whole situation.

Triggers of uncertainty

Uncertainty arises from three main sources:

- Ambiguity: difficulty in interpreting a situation with complete clarity.
- Unpredictability: lack of control over the nature and volatility of future events.
- Complexity: difficulty handling complicated situations.

All three of these challenges frequently occur when working across cultures and that is one reason why people can easily experience tension and stress.

A key first step is to understand the kinds of situations that trigger uncertainty in yourself, because that is fundamental to finding ways of managing those triggers. Some people, by personality, are more likely than others to experience uncertainty as stressful, yet no one is completely immune. For that reason, it is extremely useful to reflect on the issues that trigger uncertainty in yourself personally and cause you to worry.

Activity 2.1: Reflecting on uncertainty and stress

1. Think about a particular business trip. When travelling abroad for your work, how worried do you feel about the following potential uncertainties?

	Very worried					Not at all worried
Travel disruption	1	2	3	4	5	6
Illness	1	2	3	4	5	6
Eating local food	1	2	3	4	5	6
Hygiene	1	2	3	4	5	6
Language & communication challenges	1	2	3	4	5	6
Fully understanding the local situation	1	2	3	4	5	6

| Managing partner/ client relations | 1 | 2 | 3 | 4 | 5 | 6 |
| Negotiating a successful outcome | 1 | 2 | 3 | 4 | 5 | 6 |

2. What situations of uncertainty do you find most difficult to cope with?

In other words, building self-awareness of the issues that trigger high levels of personal uncertainty is the first step in learning to deal with it and to develop a key facet of Global Fitness: resilience.

Reactions to uncertainty

Interconnected with building this particular self-awareness is being aware of any negative reactions you may have to uncertainty. Uncertainty in itself may not be problematic; it is how you or people think, feel and behave in response to it that is key. Responses in these three areas can be positive or negative. Some possible reactions are shown below. Resilience is associated with the positive reactions, and we need to foster these as much as we can.

Table 2.1: Responses to uncertainty

Type of uncertainty	Type of impact	Response/Reaction	
		Negative	**Positive**
Ambiguity **Unpredictability**	Feelings ⟷ Thinking	Anxiety Worry Irritation Self-doubt Denial Threat	Calmness Courage Excitement Confidence Curiosity Spirit of adventure
Complexity	**Behaviours**	Avoidance Postponed decision-making Inaction	Information-seeking Decision-making Trying new things Action

We have already noted that one very common emotional response to uncertainty is worry and anxiety; another is irritation and anger. It is particularly common for a person to experience annoyance when they have been hindered in some way from achieving a goal that is important to them, such as when negotiations don't go well or when others don't understand or disagree with their position on an issue.

In global contexts, it is particularly important to manage how that emotion is handled, because there can be cultural differences in what is considered acceptable when talking about or displaying emotion. These include expectations as to how far emotions can be made explicit non-verbally or need to be concealed, or whether it should be masked by conveying a different emotion such as by smiling. If individuals hold different display rules, this can cause problems as Case Study 2.3 illustrates. This example reports the experience of a young Greek woman, Angelina, who worked in a British organisation in Greece.

Case Study 2.3: A boss's criticism

I found myself receiving criticism from my British boss—that I should increase my self-awareness. At first, I didn't know what he meant, but it turned out that he didn't like the amount of passion I showed when discussing things with him. For me, it was a way of showing commitment, but he didn't like it and expected me to be more detached. It was probably partly a matter of personality differences combined with cultural differences.

Reflect

a. How far do you try to conceal the non-verbal signs of your emotions (e.g., your anxiety or anger) at work?
b. To what extent do you talk about your emotions?
c. What are the pros and cons of doing so?
d. How do you feel when others convey more emotions or fewer emotions than you are used to?
e. How far do your feelings influence your evaluations of the other person?
f. To what extent do you think cultural factors and/or personality play a role in all of the above?

In this particular example, Angelina was evaluated negatively—and probably unfairly—by her boss, because he didn't take cultural differences into account.

In international collaboration or negotiations, the management of emotions is equally important. Sometimes it may be used tactically for greater persuasive effect, but this can be risky when dealing with potential long-term partners. In such cases, it may cause lasting relational damage, especially when the cultural expectation is to control or conceal emotions. With established long-term partners, on the other hand, emotional display may be more readily accepted by those who know you.

In Part 2 of the book, we consider ways of handling the uncertainty that comes from challenging situations, so that unhelpful responses are minimised, and more fitting responses are nurtured. In Part 3, Chapter 11, we consider uncertainty from a management perspective and consider its links with well-being.

Embracing the unfamiliar: How curious are you?

The second major area associated with self-awareness and Global Fitness personal qualities is embracing the unfamiliar. This has links with the notion of unpredictability that we considered in the previous section. People working in conditions of cultural diversity need to be keen and willing to move out of their comfort zones and experience differences of all kinds; in other words, to embrace uncertainty rather than fear it and avoid it. This entails engaging with those experiences in multiple ways, reflecting on them and learning from them. Part 2 of the book focuses particularly on the developmental process; here we concentrate on the initial facets that stimulate that process.

A key starting point for engaging with the unfamiliar is a spirit of adventure—the type of attitude that stimulates people to move out of their comfort zones and participate in new and stimulating situations. For some, this means things like travelling to unusual places, taking up a challenging new hobby, or agreeing to participate in a 'scary' activity.

For Global Fitness, applying this kind of attitude can mean taking part in situations that are personally uncomfortable but important for others, including simple things like eating unusual food that a host wants you to try. Case Study 2.4 provides one such example, experienced by a French intern in Finland.

Case Study 2.4: Overcoming inhibitions[9]

David, a recent French engineering graduate, had gone to Finland as an intern in a Finnish subsidiary of a large non-French multinational located in a small Finnish town. After two weeks he was expected to take part in a sauna in order to build team spirit. He reported afterwards that it was a huge cultural shock and that he needed to 'force' himself to go along with it. Although he did not feel particularly modest, he nevertheless found it disconcerting to be naked with his boss and other team members. In addition, the heat burnt his nose and mouth, and then he had to plunge into the cold sea, where the temperature was around 12 degrees Celsius. The next day he wrote a long and detailed letter about it to all his friends in France.

Reflect

a. How would you have felt if you were in David's situation?
b. If David had not participated in the sauna, do you think it would have mattered? Why/why not?

In this example, David demonstrated a spirit of adventure and took part in an activity that was strange and disconcerting to him personally but was important to his colleagues. Saunas are very significant in Finnish life and from a work perspective, they play a key role in helping people bond together. So, it was

---

[9]   Fougère, M. (2008). Adaptation and identity. In H. Spencer-Oatey (Ed.), *Culturally speaking: Culture, communication and politeness Theory* (pp. 187–203). London: Continuum.

good that David overcame his inhibitions and participated. This was not the only positive step that he took, though. Afterwards, he wrote in detail to his friends about the experience. This not only helped him record and remember exactly what occurred, but probably helped him reflect on the whole event. As we shall explore in Part 2 of the book, reflecting on unfamiliar experiences and drawing out learning from them is as vital as participating in the first place.

David's attitude stands in stark contrast to that reflected in Case Study 2.5, where a British member of staff, Sarah, was unwilling to change her behaviour.

Case Study 2.5: Dress code

Sarah visited her organisation's office in Oman and because it was hot and humid, she wanted to wear very light clothing that left her shoulders bare. However, she and her colleagues had meetings with senior government officials, and the Omani staff insisted on her covering her shoulders with a shawl when attending those meetings. Sarah objected strongly, maintaining that the weather was far too hot for that and conveying bewilderment as to why it would be necessary. Her colleagues explained that dress code is important in Oman and that without the shawl she would appear unprofessional and disrespectful of Omani traditions. She could not understand this and was extremely unhappy about the situation, asserting that since she is hot, she shouldn't have to cover up in any way.

Reflect

a. When individuals wear clothes that are different from what you are used to (e.g., the full veil, or shorts in a place of worship), what is your reaction?
b. Why do you think Sarah was so unwilling to change her behaviour?

In this case, Sarah was not so much unwilling to engage in behaviour that was personally embarrassing or daunting, but rather simply wanted to follow her own preferences. In other words, she was more concerned about herself than her impact on others. In this, she showed a lack of self-awareness, or perhaps simply selfishness. Either way, she was not open to changing her behaviour. She wanted to stay in her own comfort zone, ignoring the norms and preferences of those around her.

Facing unfamiliar situations is thus insufficient in itself; it needs to be accompanied by curiosity and openness towards any unexpected situations that arise. These are key Global Fitness strengths that need to be fostered; they are vital for the E4A transformational learning approach that we introduced in Chapter 1 and discuss further in Part 2.

Some companies have recognised this explicitly. For instance, the pharmaceutical company, Novartis, arranged a 'curiosity month' in September 2019, arguing that curiosity "drives discovery, solves problems and powers innovation" and is needed "to work, to grow, to fail, to improve, to achieve, to extend people's lives, to re-imagine medicine".[10] In other words, curiosity sends us on a journey

---

[10] https://www.novartis.com/our-company/people-and-culture/we-are-instilling-curiosity

of discovery that can stimulate all kinds of new initiatives and inventions and is a valuable source of creativity. In terms of Global Fitness, certain types of information are particularly important, and we consider those in the next chapter.

Working with others: How flexible are you?

So far in this chapter, we have considered the types of personal qualities that function as independent characteristics of individuals. Such characteristics are complemented by important interdependent characteristics—in other words, the personal qualities that are closely associated with interactions between people. This is because whatever we do or say elicits some kind of reaction from others, and this needs to be as positive as possible, no matter whether the context is professional or personal.

Psychological research has revealed that there are two fundamental dimensions (or continua) underlying interpersonal interaction: a control dimension and a connection dimension. The control dimension relates to people's level of desire and/or need to pro-actively handle or control an interaction; in other words, to be directive and commanding at one extreme, and obedient and submissive at the other. The connection dimension relates to people's level of desire and/or need to connect with others, ranging from high collaboration at one end to independence and self-focus at the other (see Figure 2.1).

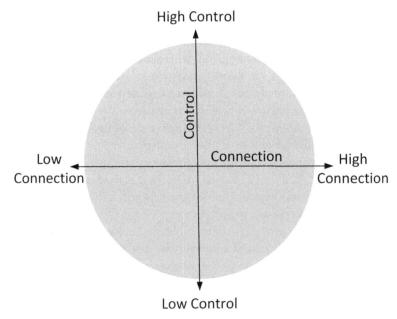

Figure 2.1: The Interaction Compass

Psychologists have identified these two dimensions as fundamental to analysing and understanding interpersonal relations across all social groups, so understanding them and their interconnections is of great importance when working with others and managing relations. Together they form an Interaction Compass that needs to be consulted (consciously or sub-consciously) on a regular basis so that power relations can be handled appropriately, along with levels of autonomy.

With regard to leadership, much effort has traditionally been directed at identifying the traits of 'good leaders'. In our view, however, it is more helpful to take a dynamic, more behavioural Interaction Compass approach. This proposes that all people, including leaders, need to adapt or flex appropriately and simultaneously along the two core dimensions of control and connection. In doing so, they need to take into account both their personal desires and preferences for connection and control, as well as the degree of connection and control that the situation requires or that the other participants want.

If we think back to the mini-bios in Chapter 1, we can see how these two dimensions were involved in people's comments on their Global Fitness challenges. For instance, Michael referred to the need to take cultural differences into account when managing the connection dimension in building rapport.

Others referred to the control dimension. For instance, Femi talked of his natural tendency to take control and move ahead quickly without consulting others, and how he found the need to slow down so that he could work more collaboratively with others.

Conversely, Jason found that others were controlling or dominant in meetings, such that he had difficulty joining in the discussion. In other words, the distribution of control among the members of the meeting was out of balance and he needed to find ways of handling this. Activity 2.2 encourages you to reflect on these issues.

Activity 2.2: Reflecting on the Interaction Compass

1. To what extent do you (like to) take control in meetings or projects? e.g., How far do you direct or dominate the discussion? How much do you like to control the agenda?
2. In what situations might you be happy for others to take control?
3. How do you think others react to the level of control you usually show? Do they think you're too controlling or too laid back or show an appropriate level of control? How do you know?
4. How easy or difficult do you find it to build connections with colleagues?
5. How easy or difficult do you find it to manage tasks on your own?
6. How far do you take/like a collaborative approach to projects or expect/prefer people to work individually on their own strands of the project? What are the strengths and weaknesses of these different approaches?

So far, we've discussed level of control and level of connection as independent dimensions; however, their interconnections also need to be managed so that there is an appropriate balance between control on the one hand and connection on the other. This can be made more difficult by culturally-based differences in expectations as to how the two dimensions 'should' be balanced.

For instance, in some contexts, employees want and expect to participate in decision-making and be consulted by their boss before a decision is made (i.e., medium control with high connection). In other contexts, they may interpret discussion as evidence of the leader's incompetence or simply as an opportunity to take advantage of the leader, as Case Study 2.6 illustrates. In subsequent chapters, we return on many occasions to this need to balance control and connection, as well as ways of doing so.

Case Study 2.6: Adjusting leadership style

A young Kenyan leader, Binti, reflected as follows on the challenge of balancing a high control style with a participative one:

> "Sometimes, people you lead are too relaxed, and they find it difficult to meet deadlines when no one is watching. An open leadership style does not apply to everyone, it depends on the people you work with—some need more guidance. I recommend giving your team members freedom, but you need to monitor, and you cannot use this style with everyone."[11]

Reflect

a. What challenges have you experienced as a leader in balancing the need for control with the need for connection, e.g. when introducing a new initiative?
b. How did you handle the challenges?

A further consideration, which is hinted at in Case Study 2.6, is that the two main dimensions (control and connection) bring out different types of responses from others. The control dimension tends to encourage *contrasting or opposite* behaviour; for instance, authoritative behaviour tends to induce responsiveness and/or (unwilling) submission, while indecisive behaviour often tends to induce directiveness from others.

In contrast, the connection dimension tends to elicit *similar* behaviour; for instance, friendliness tends to induce friendliness and collaboration tends to induce collaboration, while competitiveness tends to induce competitiveness and independence tends to induce independence and lack of collaboration.

---

[11] Mutooni, K., Ng'weno, B., & Jordans, E. (2020). Changing leadership perceptions: Leaders in the private sector in Kenya. In E. Jordans, B. Ng'weno, & H. Spencer-Oatey (Eds.), *Developing global leaders. Insights from African case studies* (pp. 211–257). London: Palgrave Macmillan.

Understanding your values: What is most important to you?

Tasha Eurich[12] argues that productive self-awareness is increased by asking 'what' questions rather than 'why' questions. For instance, instead of asking yourself 'why am I feeling dissatisfied with my job?' it is more helpful to ask, 'what do I dislike about my current job?'. Applying this insight to Global Fitness and self-awareness, it is useful to understand what your key values and aspirations are. These will often influence many aspects of your behaviour, and the more aware you are of those influences, the better you will be able to understand and manage your reactions and behaviour. So here we recommend you engage with Activity 2.3 and keep a note of your choices. We'll be returning to them on a few occasions in subsequent chapters.

Activity 2.3: Reflecting on personal values and aspirations			
a. Which of the following are key values or aspirations for you? Choose the 10 that mean the most to you. Then try to rank them from 1 to 10.			
1. Having authority		16. Achieving fame	
2. Being caring towards others		17. Being flexible	
3. Open to change		18. Serving others	
4. Being collaborative		19. Experiencing freedom	
5. Meeting social expectations		20. Being helpful	
6. Being thoughtful towards others		21. Being independent	
7. Being in control		22. Having influence	
8. Being polite / courteous		23. Acting with integrity	
9. Being decisive		24. Being loyal	
10. Being dedicated		25. Experiencing new things	
11. Being respectful		26. Doing what others want	
12. Being discerning		27. Being patient	
13. Showing empathy to others		28. Maintaining privacy	
14. Caring towards the environment		29. Minimising risk	
15. Acting fairly		30. Upholding social justice	

---

[12] Eurich, T. (2017). *Insight. How to succeed by seeing yourself clearly*. London: Pan Macmillan.

31. Having status		34. Being wealthy	
32. Being successful		35. Having wisdom	
33. Being tolerant		36. Acting with humility	

Reflect on how your chosen 10 values / aspirations may relate to the Interaction Compass.

a. Put them into the table below
b. What does that show you about your own preferences for relating to others?
c. Are there any that did not map easily onto the dimensions of the Interaction Compass? What do you think are the reasons for this?

Connection	High	
	Low	
Control	High	
	Low	
Unmapped		

Key takeaways

Core insights	**Applications for practice**
<ul><li>Self-awareness is a crucial quality for Global Fitness, including awareness of personal values and aspirations.</li><li>Three key personal strengths for Global Fitness:<ul><li>Resilience</li><li>Curiosity</li><li>Flexibility</li></ul></li><li>The Interaction Compass identifies two key relational tendencies—Control and Connection.</li></ul>	<ul><li>Which Global Fitness strengths do you most need to work on?<ul><li>Resilience—to deal with uncertainty and stress</li><li>Curiosity—to maximise learning from unfamiliar experiences</li><li>Flexibility—to adjust to different circumstances and requirements</li></ul></li></ul>

3

Global Knowledge and Understanding: Establishing common ground

Introduction

In the previous chapter we explained the importance of self-awareness for Global Fitness. In this chapter, we turn to a second key feature of Global Fitness—the need for shared Global Knowledge and Understanding of the people you are interacting with and the environments you and they are working in. It is needed for many aspects of global work, including wise decision-making, meaningful communication, and successful rapport management. This is because it helps build common ground and shared expectations between the parties, and thereby enhances the opportunities for developing mutual understanding.

As, of course, no one can know everything, it is necessary to build up Global Knowledge and Understanding gradually and in accordance with your needs. As with physical fitness training, goals concerning the knowledge to be acquired need to be set and then targeted. This chapter maps the field to help with this.

More specifically, the aims of this chapter are to:

- Increase your awareness of the different types of Global Knowledge and Understanding that are particularly important for working in culturally diverse contexts.
- Gain insights into the ways in which these various types of Global Knowledge and Understanding affect work situations.
- Reflect on the applications of the insights to your own situations and contexts.
- Acquire conceptual frameworks for thinking about culture and Global Knowledge and Understanding.

We start by considering this chapter's introductory case study and reflecting on the questions it raises about Global Knowledge and Understanding.

Introductory case study

Case Study 3.1 reports comments from Peter, a senior British member of a major international charity with offices throughout the world. He had recently been posted to the Republic of Ireland as Director of the office there, having previously worked in many different countries, including India, Indonesia, and Scotland.

Case Study 3.1: A posting to the Republic of Ireland

"I've just arrived in Ireland and my challenge is understanding what my predecessor calls the nuances of the relationship. There is a long history of hurt between Ireland and Britain and, as a British person, I have to communicate in ways that are sensitive. I've got to learn a lot about Irish history because I don't know all the things and you can very inadvertently say the wrong thing. It's doubly compounded in Ireland because Ireland is divided north and south."

Reflect

a. What was Peter concerned about?
b. What kind of Global Knowledge and Understanding could help him?
c. What steps could he take to try to build the Global Knowledge and Understanding that he needs?

It is useful to note here that having previously worked in a number of countries, Peter had sufficient self-awareness to be aware of his lack of knowledge for this particular context. He did not assume that because he was moving 'next door' to a country that speaks the same language and is geographically and historically very close to his own, there was little he had to learn or do differently.

For this assignment, Peter's needs for Global Knowledge and Understanding concern two different but interrelated aspects:

- Knowledge and understanding of historical background and its current influence on society and politics.
- Knowledge and understanding of local 'ways of doing things', including communication.

The first is strongly information-based; it can be looked up, read about, queried, and checked. In some respects, it is relatively easy to acquire, because relevant information can be found in books and on the internet. On the other hand, it can also be problematic because it will involve interpretation. This is particularly the case for historical information, as different parties often see things from different perspectives. However, this interpretive element can also apply to other types of information-based knowledge, such as the current political or economic context.

The second aspect of Global Knowledge and Understanding ('ways of doing things') can be even more problematic because some of the influences on practices can be hidden from sight, while others require careful observation and adaptation. This aspect is also very wide-ranging. In the next two chapters (Chapters 4 and 5) we cover elements that are particularly relevant to communication and rapport management. Here we focus on the features that have been widely identified as potentially variable across social groups; in other words, across groups where there are geographic (e.g., country, region), demographic (e.g., age, ethnicity) or identification (e.g., profession, religion) boundaries.

Both types of knowledge and understanding form an important part of Global Fitness and we explore them in turn in this chapter. We label the first type *PESTLE-type Knowledge and Understanding* and we label the second type *3P Cultural Knowledge and Understanding*.

PESTLE-type knowledge and understanding

You may be familiar with the acronym PESTLE, which stands for six societal-level external influences on an organisation. These are briefly outlined in Table 3.1. In fact, we could usefully add History to this table as a potential source of significant external influence, as Case Study 3.1 has demonstrated.

Table 3.1: PESTLE external influences on organisational and individual behaviour

Source of external influence	Examples of indicative influence
Political	Political framework conditions; political stability; foreign policy.
Economic	Interest rates; exchange rates; inflation and wage rates; economic growth (GDP); unemployment rate; taxation; industry regulation; trade restrictions; tariffs; business incentives.
Sociological	Population growth; age distribution; diversity; education; public health and health consciousness; mobility; consumer tastes and fashions; ethnic/religious factors; major events/influences.
Technological	Digital infrastructure; adoption of mobile technologies; disruptive technologies (e.g., artificial intelligence, robotics); rate of technological change.
Legal	Employment law; health and safety laws; environmental legislation.
Environmental	Sustainability; ethical sourcing; pollution and carbon emissions; global warming and carbon capture.

Core information on these external influences is typically needed for most business ventures in unfamiliar contexts, including for risk assessment, business strategy development, and decision-making. This may seem obvious, but sometimes a false assumption is made that these PESTLE-type factors are similar in another region—a danger that Peter successfully avoided.

It is also important to be aware that Global Knowledge and Understanding goes beyond facts and statistics. As mentioned above, the PESTLE-type factors can be affected by subtle interpretive influences, and these are less easy to identify through straightforward enquiries. For example, it is one thing to read a survey about a certain country's political attitudes, but it takes a certain level of experience, following of the news, and participation in conversations in order to understand these attitudes more fully and grasp what they mean in practice. Use Activity 3.1 to reflect on this.

Activity 3.1: Strategies for building PESTLE-type knowledge and understanding

1. Think of a situation where you were lacking some PESTLE-type knowledge and understanding. What did you do to increase your knowledge and understanding of factual aspects?
2. What limitations (if any) in your Global Knowledge and Understanding did you experience after obtaining that factual information?
3. What did you do (or could you have done) to enhance your interpretive insights into the PESTLE-type knowledge and understanding? Note: Peter (Case Study 3.1) mentioned the following: that in addition to reading, he talked to close friends, to people in their different offices, to his predecessor, to his staff, and to people at the Embassy. He commented on the importance of being interested and curious.
4. How far have you used the same strategies as Peter? Have you used any additional ones?

PESTLE-type knowledge and culture

A key challenge associated with building Global Knowledge and Understanding of PESTLE-type information, especially in international contexts, is the impact of what we explain below as 3P Cultural Knowledge and Understanding—Products, Practices and Perspectives.

For instance, in terms of PESTLE-type legal knowledge and understanding, there can be considerable cultural differences over the extent to which business partners expect the right to re-negotiate contracts after signature, despite the relevant contract law making clear the binding character of contracts once signed. Case Study 3.2 illustrates this. It is told by a Chinese manager, Jenny Liu, who works with a department of a Chinese-German joint venture (JV).

She is employed in a major Chinese city by a subsidiary of the JV's German parent.

Case Study 3.2: Re-negotiating contracts

"I am responsible for supporting service contract negotiations between the JV and the German parent. When the contracts run out, they are re-negotiated. The JV always aims to reduce the costs of these contracts. That's OK. The problem is that just a few months after reaching agreement on a reduced price, the JV's team comes back requesting a further cost reduction.

   I feel that trust between my team and the joint venture has gone. I've been trying to understand their perspective and have been told that their finance department is very demanding. However, I would like them to appreciate our position too. That's vital if we are to reach a longer-term agreement and overcome our current unhealthy, untrusting relationship."

Reflect

a. How do you view this request for further cost-reduction negotiations shortly after agreeing on a new contract which already had brought about a cost reduction?
b. Would such behaviour reduce the trust you feel for a client?
c. How do the Chinese partner and the German parent seem to differ in their view of the significance and purpose of a contract?

Of course, there can be many cultural differences in the handling of law-related matters and negotiators need to be aware of these possibilities when working internationally. We return to the possible underlying influences on this kind of behaviour in Case Study 3.7. below, which is a continuation of this incident.

   Case Study 3.2 makes clear that in fact there is no clear boundary between PESTLE-type knowledge and these potential cultural differences. We call the latter 3P Cultural Knowledge and Understanding and we turn to them now.

3P Cultural Knowledge and Understanding

3P Cultural Knowledge and Understanding refers to the knowledge and understanding that is specifically influenced by cultural factors. First of all, therefore, we need to explain briefly what we mean by culture.

What Is culture and what are the 3Ps of culture?

There is no easy definition of culture, but it is sometimes referred to as 'the way we do things around here'[13]. Although this is a very simple statement, it draws out three core features of culture:

---

[13]   Bower, M. (1966). *The will to manage: Corporate success through programmed management.* New York, NY: McGraw-Hill.

- 'We' refers to a particular group of people.
- 'The way we do things' refers to the fact that a particular group of people often develop common patterns of behaviour and tend to expect others to behave likewise.
- 'Around here' refers to a specific situational context in which the behaviour occurs.

The 'we' indicates that culture applies to social groups, such as professional, organisational, religious, ethnic and nationality groups (see Figure 1.1). The groups can vary in size from small to large. We are all members of multiple social groups at one and the same time and socialised into the various ways of doing things within these groups through the influence of family and friends, schooling, the media, workplaces, and so on. This socialisation leads to cultural patterning (i.e., commonly repeated ways of thinking and doing) which affects the objects we traditionally make and use, the way we behave and evaluate other people's behaviour, and the beliefs and values that we hold. We call this patterning the 3Ps of culture:

- Products: the objects (e.g., type of food, style of housing) and institutions (e.g., educational system) that are common in (or apply to) a social group.
- Practices: the conventional ways of doing things within a social group (e.g., use of chopsticks or knife and fork for eating; how a senior manager is addressed by subordinates; whether you can turn left/right on a red traffic light).
- Perspectives: the values and beliefs that underlie many of the practices (e.g., the relative importance of acknowledging hierarchy or seeking harmony).[14]

One way of considering the 3Ps is to think of cultural patterning in terms of trees, where the Products are the leaves, the Practices are the branches, and the Perspectives are the roots (see Figure 3.1). The most noticeable parts of a tree are usually the leaves and the branches, and we can see and appreciate them if we pay attention to them.

The roots are normally hidden under the soil and hence not usually visible. Yet they are the anchor for the tree, providing stability, while also absorbing water and nutrients, nourishing the leaves and the branches. Similarly, Cultural Perspectives have a less visible but significant influence on people's ways of doing things.

Trees are all positioned in a context—they have a physical location, they are rooted in soil, and affected by weather. If a tree is uprooted and transplanted to a new location, it needs time to adjust to the new setting—re-establishing its

---

[14] Moran, K. (2001). *Teaching culture. Perspectives in practice.* Boston, MA: Heinle Cengage Learning.

roots and regaining stability. During that adjustment period, leaves may wilt, and smaller branches may lose strength, but in time they usually recover.

This can be the same for people. If they move to (or are faced with) a culturally unfamiliar context, they need time to adjust and take steps to handle the process. Part 2, and especially Chapter 6, examines how to embrace such change.

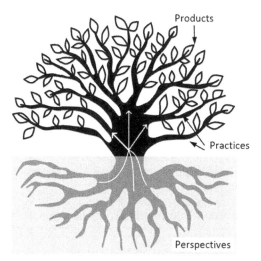

Figure 3.1: The tree as an analogy for culture and its 3Ps

We can also consider the analogy from a different angle—acquiring a new and unfamiliar type of tree. In planning how best to handle it, it is necessary to know a few things, such as how tall it's likely to grow, what types of soil will suit it, and how well it can tolerate exposure to wind. Unless you are an expert in trees, you won't be able to answer these questions simply by looking at the tree. You will need to take steps to find out more. The same is true of intercultural encounters. It should not be assumed that the 3Ps of culture are necessarily given the same meaning or interpreted in the same way across different social groups. To understand this better, let's consider Case Study 3.3.

Case Study 3.3: Business hospitality[15]

A Chinese ministerial delegation visited the USA to meet with staff from their counterpart American ministry. Every evening the Chinese delegation held an internal group meeting to discuss what had happened during the day and to plan for the next day. The visit took place in August and during the first few days, they commented on several unexpected incidents.

---

[15] Wang, J. (2013). *Relational management in professional intercultural interaction: Chinese officials' encounters with American and British professionals.* Unpublished PhD thesis, University of Warwick.

1. At the restaurant lunch on the first day, they were only provided with iced water to drink. Three of the delegates complained that this made them feel 'uncomfortable' and 'desperate'.
2. On the same day, they also remarked that their American hosts had not provided drinks during the meetings; they thought they must have forgotten to do so. In fact, their hosts had provided coffee and tea in an adjacent room and the guests needed to help themselves during the breaks. They were surprised about this.
3. On the second day, they visited a government agency and when going through security at the entrance, they were asked to remove their belts and not take any electronic devices into the building. Many in the delegation were very offended by this and complained.

Reflect
a. Which (if any) of the three incidents did you find surprising and why?
b. For those that you did not find surprising, why were you not surprised?
c. To what extent do you feel able to empathise with, accept or merely tolerate the complaints and the surprise of the Chinese delegation? Or do you reject them as exaggerated?
d. What different expectations around hospitality do these incidents reveal? How do they compare with your own expectations?

When reflecting on these incidents and how surprising they were or were not for you, you would almost certainly have thought about the ways in which you would (or would not) normally handle things or react to things in contexts familiar to you. In other words, you would draw on your cultural expectations in terms of Practices.

These Practices, though, also interrelate with the other Ps of culture.

Incident 1: the serving of iced water at lunch time is a Practice, but, of course, iced water is also a Product that is common in many contexts. Less obviously, for some people (including many Chinese and others) attitudes towards drinking iced water relate to beliefs about the negative effect of a cold liquid on the digestive system; in other words, to an underlying health-related Perspective.

Incident 2: the serving of tea and coffee in an adjacent room is a Practice, and contrasts with an alternative Practice of giving tea to every guest at the meeting room table. Underlying both these Practices is a common Perspective—the importance of warm hospitality, but the challenge is that this Perspective can be expressed through different Practices. For the American hosts, the Practice aligned with a notion of individual initiative and personal choice which was unexpected for the Chinese visitors. It is also related to the notion that work should be separate from socialising.

Incident 3: the set of procedures for going through security is a Practice, but the distinction between who needs to undergo those procedures is a Perspective. The Chinese visitors believed that their importance as ministerial officials should make them exempt, while the American hosts believed all visitors should be treated equally from a security perspective.

Needless to say, there are endless Products, Practices, and Perspectives, so over the years, cross-cultural psychologists and interculturalists have tried to make sense of the 3Ps of culture by identifying key features that can be used to help understand and interpret cultural differences (cf. systems for classifying trees). Traditionally they have focused on Perspectives—values and beliefs that can influence behaviour—and so we consider them first.

Cultural Perspectives

In this section, we briefly explain the Cultural Perspectives that, in our experience, are particularly important to be aware of when working in culturally diverse contexts. Table 3.2 presents a summary of them. It is important to remember, they are continua and not dichotomies, and also that there are many more such variable perspectives.

Table 3.2: Key dimensions of variability in Cultural Perspectives

Dimensions of Variability in Cultural Perspectives	Explanation
1. Hierarchy←→Equality Attitudes	How far status differences are important and accepted.
2. Individual←→Group Prioritisation	How far a person prioritises (or sacrifices) personal / individual needs and desires over group needs and responsibilities.
3. Universalist←→Particularist Standards	How far procedures / regulations apply to everyone equally or need to be adjusted to fit particular situations or particular people.

Becoming familiar with these key dimensions of cultural variability is very useful because they help people understand better why others may behave in unexpected ways that they may find surprising, confusing, or annoying. In subsequent chapters, we illustrate ways in which they can impact on behaviour, decision-making, and evaluative judgements, and hence why developing such understanding forms an important facet of Global Fitness.

Cultural Perspective 1: Attitudes towards Hierarchy–Equality

One important dimension of variability is people's attitudes towards hierarchy: how far power and status differences are important and accepted as desirable and normal or whether the preference is for equality. Some people are happy to accept that power is distributed unequally and believe that acknowledging and displaying differences in power and status are extremely important.

Others have a much stronger preference for equality and want hierarchical differences to be minimised and power shared with more people. Technically, this dimension is known as high–low power distance and, as the label suggests, there is a gradation between the two extremes.

The impact of this dimension can be seen in Incident 3 of Case Study 3.3. The delegation members, as senior government officials in China, were used to not having to undergo such security checks in public buildings on account of their high positions. They assumed that their American hosts would be able to give them a similar exemption and were annoyed when they had to go through the same security checks as 'regular visitors'.

Interestingly, they had not been upset about the security checks at airports en route to the USA, probably because their identity in that context was simply that of 'passenger'. In this particular context, however, their identity was of 'government official' and 'guest' and so they were expecting to be given high status and for the security checks to be dropped.

Power distance can affect many aspects of workplace life, including decision-making, the right to speak in a meeting, and 'freedom' to express disagreement. It can also be reflected in the prevalence of status symbols, such as size of office, designated parking spaces, separate dining rooms. Case Study 3.4 provides some examples of how differences in expectations and attitudes toward power distance in a Korean office can lead to negative reactions.

Case Study 3.4: Power in the Korean workplace[16]

(1) "There are a lot of symbols in Korea. The more senior you are, the more… your office size is big. The way of sitting in your office: Chajang [Senior manager title] sits there, Bubujang [Deputy director title] sits next here. It's all about symbol. Showing people's authority and position all the time. Originally, I just sat anywhere. I realized that is not the Korean way, and now I sit at the end of table. There are so many rules. Ridiculous!"

(Chris, British, Korean finance company in Korea)

---

[16] Spencer-Oatey, H., & Kádár, D. Z. (2021). *Intercultural politeness: Managing relations across cultures.* Cambridge: Cambridge University Press.

(2) "Terms of address are more difficult here. In Japanese, 'Sato-San', San is an honorific, I thought, in Korean, Ssi is also an honorific. One day, I called a female colleague, who is older than me, 'Kim-Ssi'. She got mad. That was difficult. I couldn't understand what was bad about it. She said... 'it is not respectful'. She wanted to be addressed with an even more deferential title and submitted a formal complaint against me."

(Aoi, Japanese, Japanese finance company in Korea)

Reflect

a. How surprised or unsurprised were you by these two examples?

b. What does this indicate about your own attitudes towards hierarchy–equality?

In terms of the Interaction Compass explained in Chapter 2 (see Figure 2.1), the control dimension is particularly important in strongly hierarchical workplaces. Leaders and managers there are typically directive and controlling and subordinates are responsive and obedient. In fact, if leaders are very consultative in high power distance contexts, subordinates may lose confidence in them, assuming they do not have the competence to make decisions or tell them what to do. Conversely, if they are too directive in a low power distance context, and do not consult, it can lead to resentment, as Case Study 3.5 illustrates. It is reported by a Kenyan employee of a Chinese company based in Kenya.

Case Study 3.5: Can my boss decide what we eat?[17]

A small team comprising Chinese and Kenyan employees and a Chinese team leader were on a business trip and the issue of food came up. The Chinese team leader, without any consultation, arranged for everyone to eat Chinese food, but the Kenyan employees were not happy about this decision. One of the Kenyans commented on it afterwards, referring to the directive nature of his Chinese team leader's behaviour: "He will think, oh, I'm the team leader, you must follow everything I tell you. If I tell you to eat this food, you must eat it. You know when I am the boss and I tell you to do something; if you refuse to do it, I feel offended, so I report back to the office that this person refused to follow my instructions."

Reflect

a. Why do you think the Chinese team leader ordered the food?

b. How would you personally have felt in this situation? Why?

Activity 3.2: Your experiences of hierarchy at work

Thinking of your superiors at work:

1. How hierarchical or 'flat' is your interaction with your superiors? How would you rate it on a scale of 1 to 6, where 1 is very flat and 6 is very hierarchical?

---

17 Data collected by Z.H. Tian for her PhD research at the University of Warwick. Used with permission.

2. What aspects lead you to make those judgements?
3. How do you feel about the level of hierarchy you perceive?

Thinking of your subordinates at work:
4. How controlling or consultative are you towards them? Think of some examples to support your judgement.
5. How do you think they feel about the level of hierarchy you display? How could you find out more about their true feelings?

Cultural Perspective 2: Individual–Group Prioritisation

Another area of potential difference that can stem from cultural as well as individual factors is the relative importance people attach to individual needs or wants compared with those of a group they belong to.

This perspective also relates to the connection dimension of the Interaction Compass, which ranges from collaborative (high connection) to self-focused (low connection) and can be revealed in a number of ways. In Case Study 3.3, the Chinese guests were not served refreshment as is normal in China; rather, in a way that prioritised the individual over the group, the guests were expected to go to a different room and exercise their own initiative and choice.

Another example is seen in Case Study 2.5. The British visitor to Oman was very unwilling to change her dress preferences to suit local practices, maintaining that if she feels too hot, she should be allowed to go bare-shouldered. This Perspective difference has also been seen very clearly during the Covid-19 pandemic, such as over issues like mask-wearing, with different individuals making contrasting comments as follows:

> *"I don't see why other people should demand that I wear one, when they don't know anything about my health or my personal situation."* [Individual prioritisation]

> *"I think that it is basic good manners, courtesy, consideration to wear a face mask if you are, for example, in a shop."* [Group/communal prioritisation]

Case Study 3.6 provides a management example, which also illustrates attitudes towards hierarchy–equality.

Case Study 3.6: (Un)Willingness to sacrifice a weekend for the company[18]

Maria was in charge of the Sydney office of a Japanese company. The office manager was a young man called Jason. One week, Maria received a telephone call from the head office in Kyoto. A very senior representative of the company had decided to visit their Sydney office the next Saturday as part of a longer business trip. Most unfortunately, Maria was due in Melbourne that same weekend to represent the company at a business exhibition and to meet with important clients. So she explained the situation to Jason and asked him to meet the Japanese executive and host him for the day. The following conversation ensued:

Jason: Look, Maria, you know I don't work on Saturdays.
Maria: Jason, this is exceptional. You know I can't meet Mr Yamamoto myself and you know how important it is that he be impressed with our operations here.
Jason: Yes, but I have a new girlfriend. She lives in Brisbane and is coming down to visit me that weekend. There's no way I'm going to disappoint her.

Reflect

a. How much sympathy do you have for Jason? If you had been in his situation, would you have responded like this? Why/why not?
b. If you were Maria, how would you feel about Jason's response? What would you do or say next?
c. What do your answers suggest about how you prioritise individual versus group responsibilities?
d. How do you think the power dynamics between Maria and Jason affected his response?

A further nuance on this perspective, which is particularly subject to cultural variation, is the quantity of people's group memberships and the clarity of membership boundaries. We all belong to groups of various kinds and sizes, but our attitudes towards members of those groups can vary noticeably. Some people have loose ties and low perceived levels of responsibility to other members of the group to fulfil any of their needs. They have strong desires to follow their own interests and courses of action. Technically, they are said to have an independent orientation.

Others have strong ties and high perceived levels of responsibility to other members of the group. In fact, it is their group involvement that gives them meaning and pleasure. They are also much more content to be 'one of the group', not to stand out, and to go along with the preferences of others. Technically, they are said to have an interdependent orientation.

---

[18] Christopher, E. (2015). Jason and the jaguar: The case of the unmotivated employee. In E. Christopher (Ed.), *International management and intercultural communication. A collection of case studies, Volume 1* (pp. 69–76). Basingstoke: Palgrave Macmillan.

People's sense of group membership can particularly affect attitudes towards non-group members. We follow up on this in Chapters 5 and 7. The balance between taking a group focus and an individual focus is central to the connection dimension of the Interaction Compass, and we consider that explicitly in Chapter 9 on leadership.

Cultural Perspective 3: Universalist–Particularist beliefs about standards

A third dimension of cultural variability concerns the application of social standards. In some social groups, people believe in *universalist* standards. In this view, ethical standards, rules and procedures—often explicitly prescribed in laws, codes and contracts—should apply to everyone equally. They may regard this as an important ethical principle.

At the other extreme, members of other social groups may uphold *particularist* standards, adjusting rules and regulations to fit the particular relationship, circumstance or need. They, too, may see it from an ethical point of view—that special help should be given to particular individuals who deserve it for a certain reason. To illustrate this, we return to Jenny Liu, who featured in Case Study 3.2 above.

Case Study 3.7: Priorities in re-negotiating contracts

"As this year's negotiations were proving especially difficult, I also talked with the JV's performance manager about why the JV's team has this kind of cost negotiation strategy. I was told that the JV had a very demanding cost-reduction target for the current year. This helps explain the extra pressure applied this time round.

I think the Chinese partner in the JV is treating the German parent's department in the same way they are treating all their suppliers: they are trying to push for a cost reduction even if agreement has already been reached. They are disappointed and maybe angry when the German parent doesn't concede to their demands. They think that they have a special relationship with this particular supplier—it is part-owner of the JV. But personally, I think the Chinese JV partner should treat the German parent as a *partner* and not as a *supplier*.

I have been working for the German parent company long enough to understand that the parent's people see no reason to re-negotiate a contract which has already been agreed. A contract is a contract is what they say.

I have the feeling that if this kind of behaviour continues, the trust between the German and Chinese JV partners will <u>also</u> decrease because of the behaviour of the German parent in not conceding the further price reduction demanded. It is not a healthy approach for a joint venture when the two parties do not consider each other as trusted partners. Sooner or later there will be a more critical issue."

The Chinese partner in the JV has a particularistic view of its relationships with its service providers. It is in a particularly difficult situation this year. So, it expects some concession on the cost of the service contracts charged by the German parent. And in particular, it expects this concession from the German supplier because of the ownership relationship between itself and the supplier.

The German parent has a universalistic approach to behaviour in this business relationship; it behaves in accordance with the agreed contract and is unwilling to change anything. Jenny also understands this. However, Jenny also takes a particularistic view of the matter, which interestingly is different from that of the Chinese JV partner. She feels that because of the close relationship with the parent, the Chinese JV partner is the one who should change its behaviour and make the concession by <u>not</u> insisting on a price reduction.

In all types of cooperation across cultures, the parties to the cooperation need to familiarise themselves with the following issues and build understanding of each of them.

- How do the parties to an agreement regulate their behaviour in the cooperation? Is it more on the basis of a written contract (more universalist) or more on the basis of the perceived nature and quality of the relationship itself (more particularist)? Both approaches create trust in the relationship.
- What does a contractual agreement mean to the other party? Is it more the symbol of a significant relationship or more a description of the rights and obligations of the two parties in a business relationship?
- How far does a contractual agreement mark the end of a negotiation or the first step in an ongoing negotiation?
- To what extent do the length and level of detail in a contractual agreement allow for flexibility?
- To what extent are claims and dispute procedures laid down in the contract?

The universalist as opposed to the particularist perspective can affect many aspects of workplace life, one of which is recruitment practices. In universalist contexts, managers typically feel that employment decisions should be made strictly on merit, with special attention being paid to objectivity and pertinent anti-discrimination legislation. In more particularist contexts, on the other hand, managers often believe that selecting someone they know (or who is recommended by a reliable associate) is likely to be more suitable and less risky. In such contexts, people may regard doing business, signing contracts, and making employment decisions on the basis of existing relationships and personal recommendations as the safer alternative. This is especially true of some particularist country cultures where relevant laws may be lacking and the judiciary not independent. This may make redress in law difficult or impossible.

This Cultural Perspective has major implications for handling ethical issues in culturally diverse contexts. We follow up on this in Chapter 10.

Summary

All of these Cultural Perspectives are typically somewhat hidden. They are the roots of the tree, hidden in the soil. This means that they function as the underlying rationales for people's behaviour, but that this is not necessarily immediately discernible from the behaviour itself.

When people are familiar with the Cultural Perspectives and they experience unexpected or unwanted behaviour from others, they can consider whether one or more of these Perspectives is associated with the issue and thus be in a better position to plan how best to address it. It can warn them against the risk of misinterpreting behaviour. Activity 3.3 provides an opportunity to reflect further on this.

Activity 3.3: Cultural Perspectives & their impact at work

1. How far does your line manager, if you have one, prioritise task over relationship? What evidence do you have for this? How do you feel about it?
2. If a manager spends significant time socialising with his/her team, what are the potential (a) risks and (b) benefits of this? How may such behaviour be influenced by Cultural Perspectives?
3. If a manager gives preferential treatment/contractual terms to clients s/he knows well, how do you feel about this? How may such decision-making be influenced by Cultural Perspectives?

Cultural Practices

We now turn to the second P of the 3Ps of culture, Cultural Practices. Table 3.3 provides a summary overview.

Table 3.3: Key dimensions of variability in Cultural Practices

Dimensions of variability in Cultural Practices	Explanation
1. Task–relationship prioritisation	How far task is prioritised over relationship or relationship over task.
2. Time management	The ways in which people regard and manage time.
3. Rule rigour	The number / complexity of rules / regulations for a given situation and how important it is to adhere to them.
4. Communication style	The ways in which people get their messages across; e.g., how directly or indirectly, with how much deference, and with how much emotion.

The fourth dimension of variability, communication style, is an important Cultural Practice with several different facets. We explore these in Chapters 4 and 5. The other three Cultural Practices are more generic and are particularly widespread and influential. We explain them below.

Cultural Practice 1: Task–relationship prioritisation

This Cultural Practice concerns the relative importance given to task versus relationship. This is particularly important when dealing with clients and/or new members of staff who have (or may have) different priorities.

People who attach great importance to relationships tend to focus on their links and connections and feel more comfortable doing business with people they know. This means that time needs to be devoted to getting to know people and maintaining relationships, often involving eating together, drinking together, or doing other social activities together. It is quite likely that in the early stages of a relationship, no business talk will take place at all during those occasions.

For people who are more task-oriented, this can be extremely unusual and frustrating. They may feel they are wasting their time and want to know from the start whether there is any likelihood of doing business. If not, they don't want to spend any further time on the contact. However, from a relationship-oriented person's perspective, it's not possible to know whether they can form a business relationship until they've got to know each other a little. The *personal* relationship is the driver of the *business* relationship and the platform on which the business cooperation takes place.

The order in which actions related to task and those connected with relationships happen can also influence management situations, as illustrated in Case study 3.8.

Case Study 3.8: Taking up a new role & dealing with a business challenge[19]

Eleanor moved from the USA to Puerto Rico to become manager of a large and complex water infrastructure capital improvement programme. Within days of her arrival, she discovered that the local office team had not been supplying their client with what they had requested and that what they had been supplying was unacceptable. A serious legal case was looming.

Eleanor immediately set about addressing the crisis. Drawing on her extensive previous experience, she assessed the situation and started sending

---

[19] Eurich, T. (2017). *Insight. How to succeed by seeing yourself clearly.* London: Pan Macmillan.

a stream of regular email instructions to her 100-person team. A few weeks went by with her continuing to issue directives like this, but sadly, things still weren't getting done; for example, delivery dates were missed despite her clear instructions. She felt highly frustrated and very alone. She just couldn't understand why she couldn't get the local staff to make the changes needed.

Right at this point, her deputy, Evelio, burst into her room, slammed the door behind him, and in a loud voice said, "You have *got* to stop." Eleanor was totally shocked and stammered "What do you mean?" Evelio continued, "You are driving us crazy! No one is reading your emails!"

Taking a deep breath, Eleanor wisely asked him what she should do instead.

Reflect

a. Why do you think the local team were not implementing Eleanor's instructions?
b. What do you think Eleanor had got wrong?
c. What advice do you think Evelio gave her?

In this example, Eleanor immediately focused on the task because it was so critical. In other words, she prioritised task very significantly over relationship, partly because of the seriousness and urgency of the problem, but probably partly also because she was very task-oriented. What she hadn't realised was that with every task-focused email, she was undermining her staff's morale and building resentment among them.

Evelio pointed out that she first needed to gain the trust of the staff and to do that, she needed to get to know them personally. With his help, she prioritised ways of building relations, including organising socials and regularly having coffee or lunch with individuals. Trust was built up, and within less than six months the team had become the best performing programme on the island.

In terms of the Interaction Compass discussed in Chapter 2, this perspective concerns the connection dimension. Leaders and managers who prioritise task may be aware of the potential importance of this aspect but may not feel very confident about handling it well themselves, especially with people who are culturally very different from them. We explore this further in Chapter 5.

Cultural Practice 2: Time management

A second Cultural Practice that people often notice when working in situations of cultural diversity is the handling of time. There are different aspects to this. Some relate closely to PESTLE-type knowledge, such as being aware of time-zone differences and of different public holidays and festivals.

Others concern people's attitudes towards the sequencing of activities. Some people feel most comfortable doing one thing at a time. They emphasise schedules and promptness and treat activities as separate things that need to be completed one after the other, in an orderly fashion. If this is not done, they can get very annoyed because in the work context they regard it as unprofessional. This preference is known technically as monochronic time or M-time.

Other people, in contrast, are happy to multitask and feel it is more efficient to do many things simultaneously. The emphasis is on involvement with people and completion of things as they come up rather than adherence to pre-set schedules. This preference is known technically as polychronic time or P-time.

The impact of M-time and P-time is particularly noticeable in the service sector. For example, an M-time oriented clerk will serve customers one at a time, making each person wait until the current customer has been fully dealt with. If another customer tries to 'push in', it will easily lead to bad feeling. On the other hand, a P-time oriented clerk may interrupt serving the first person and ask what the next person wants, perhaps proceeding to serve both at the same time, regarding that as a more time efficient procedure to follow. This may be annoying, though, to either or both customers.

Another aspect of time management that can be very influential is punctuality and scheduling. For instance, if you have an appointment with a business client and you arrive after the agreed time, how serious would it be if you arrived 1 minute late, 5 minutes late, or 15 minutes late? Or do you actually arrive before the scheduled time? There can be noticeable differences across cultures in this Case Study 3.8 illustrates.

Case Study 3.9: Start times and arrival times for meetings

Simon is an experienced senior manager from Britain who recently worked in Botswana. He related the following experience:

"The day after I arrived as a new country director, I had to make a speech at an event. I was given the time for the start of this event, and turned up there, but there was absolutely nobody there, so I thought I had got the wrong location. Later I found out that in Botswana everything starts at least two hours after the starting time, and this is something that everybody in the office just knew. But when you get guests coming out from the UK, you have to find ways of dealing with this. We very often told the Batswana in our invitations that an event would start on time. Some of the Batswana were very much against that, saying it was a very cold attitude."

Reflection

a. How important is punctuality to you?
b. How do you think you developed your attitudes towards punctuality?

Cultural Practice 3: Rule rigour

A third Cultural Practice concerns the handling of rules. As discussed above, the Cultural Perspective Universalism–Particularism concerns fundamental beliefs about who rules apply to in given contexts and about how this affects behaviour in relationships. Rule rigour refers to the practical applications of these underlying beliefs: how far rules are specified, how strictly people expect the rules to be upheld, and how people react when they are broken. In Chapter 2 we discussed the significant impact that uncertainty can have in culturally unfamiliar contexts, and one way that both organisations and individuals often try to manage uncertainty is by developing rules, implementing procedures and laying down structures.

Some organisations have very explicit processes for handling certain issues while in other organisations they are fewer, much looser and less clearly specified. Similarly, some social groups have clear and widely held expectations for behaviour in particular settings and dislike any failure to uphold them. Other groups, on the other hand, are much more flexible and casual and accept a considerably wider range of behaviour.

From a behavioural point of view, this Cultural Practice plays out in many different ways; for example, in the degree of specificity of role responsibilities, in the formalisation / lack of formalisation of organisational procedures and management practices, and in the degree of expected / required adherence to any of the Cultural Perspectives discussed in the previous section. Case Study 3.4, on power in the Korean workplace, illustrates the last point. Employees were expected to show respect for the higher status of their superiors in very specific ways and faced criticism when they failed to do so.

Key takeaways

Core insights	Applications for practice

• Common ground and shared understanding are core to Global Fitness.
 • Global Fitness requires two types of Global Knowledge and Understanding:
  o PESTLE-type information
  o 3P type Cultural Knowledge
	• Identify the PESTLE-type knowledge that you need for your current work.
	 • Plan how you could gain that knowledge.

- Culture can be seen as a tree: we see the leaves and branches (Cultural Products and Practices) but not the roots (Cultural Perspectives), yet the roots nurture and influence the tree.

- Build up your awareness of the 3Ps of culture:
  o Look out for evidence of the three Cultural Perspectives we explained (Hierarchy–Equality, Individual–Group prioritisation, Universalist–Particularist standards
  o Look out for evidence of the three Cultural Practices we explained: Task–Relationship prioritisation, Time Management, Rule Rigour

4

Global Communication Skills: Enhancing mutual understanding

Introduction

In numerous studies, experts have highlighted the crucial role that communication plays in contexts of cultural diversity. For example, 97% of team leaders and 98% of team members in one study identified communication as a key competence for leaders of multinational teams.[20] Yet people frequently complain about communication difficulties, especially when they have to interact virtually. Addressing and overcoming these difficulties is fundamental to working successfully together, whatever the level of diversity.

The aims of this chapter are to help you:

- Understand why communication—especially across cultures—can be difficult.
- Learn how the difficulties can be addressed.
- Appreciate the impact that language and communication can have on people's sense of inclusion or exclusion.
- Take account of the impact that communication channels can have, including virtual communication.

We start by considering an introductory case study that raises some global communication issues.

Introductory case study

Case Study 4.1 was experienced by a British young man, Jeremy, not long after he had started working in Germany.

---

[20] Joshi, A., & Lazarova, M. (2005). Do 'global' teams need 'global' leaders? Identifying leadership competencies in multinational teams. In D. Shapiro, M.A. Von Glinow, & J.L.C. Cheng (Eds.), *Managing multinational teams: Global perspectives* (pp. 281–302). Amsterdam: Elsevier.

Case Study 4.1: Confused by laughter

"Shortly after starting to work in Germany, with my knowledge of the traditions and rituals of my newly adopted country still incomplete, I said in English to a group of people I was working with 'OK. Same procedure as last year.' One of the Germans added, 'Same procedure as every year, Miss Sophie', whereupon everybody burst into helpless laughter. I was completely mystified. Why should anybody address me as Miss Sophie? Why were they laughing at me? I was embarrassed and clearly felt I was an outsider."

Reflect

a. Jeremy could understand the meaning of all the words that the German speaker used and yet there was no 'mutual understanding'. What was the source of Jeremy's confusion?
b. Why do you think Jeremy felt an outsider?

In Chapter 3, we noted the important role that Global Knowledge and Understanding plays. In this Case Study, it was crucial for mutual understanding. Jeremy's problem was his lack of knowledge of German popular culture and traditions. This meant, on the one hand, that he was confused by his colleagues' behaviour; it led to him feeling embarrassed (see Chapter 5 on 'face sensitivity') and an outsider. He found out later that the wording was a quotation from an English-language sketch shown every year on German television on New Year's Eve, with many households watching it as one of the year-end's rituals. In other words, Jeremy needed to have the same background knowledge about the programme as his colleagues for mutual understanding to be achieved, and his failure to attain this had a relational impact.

In order to appreciate the potential challenges of understanding each other's messages, including why background knowledge is so important, it is necessary to understand some key features of the communication process.

The communication process: How does it work?

Many people (including many in the international business field) treat communication as though it comprises a set of signals (i.e., sounds or written symbols) that represent exactly the message to be conveyed. In such a view, communication is seen as a straightforward exchange of meaning, involving encoding and decoding language-specific signals, where the only issue of potential concern is the participants' level of familiarity with the signals (e.g., with the words, their meaning, and how they are pronounced).

However, this simple sender-receiver (or encoder-decoder) model of communication doesn't explain accurately enough how communication takes place, and the sources of misunderstanding, especially in communication across cultures. Although communication exploits a language code (such as English, Chinese, German, or sign language) to a large extent, it is not feasible for everything to be conveyed explicitly in the code. Much has to be left for the participants to work out, and they do this by drawing on their background knowledge and understanding of the context. This is why Jeremy in Case Study 4.1 had difficulty—he lacked the relevant background knowledge of German television programmes on New Year's Eve and so could not work out the meaning. In other words, communication always involves some inferring of meaning in addition to simple decoding; that is to say, meaning is not transmitted but 'constructed' jointly by the participants.

This 'meaning construction' takes place dynamically as messages are exchanged. In intercultural interaction, this can be particularly problematic for several reasons:

- Participants may have different—frequently group-specific and culture-specific—background knowledge and hence may simply be confused (as in Case Study 4.1) or may draw different inferences from what is conveyed.
- Participants may focus on different clues when inferring meanings, and/or they may arrive at different meanings from the same clues.
- Participants may have different levels of proficiency in the language / code being used.

As a result, mismatches can occur between what one person thinks they have communicated and what another person has understood them to have said (see Figure 4.1). What, then, can be done about this?

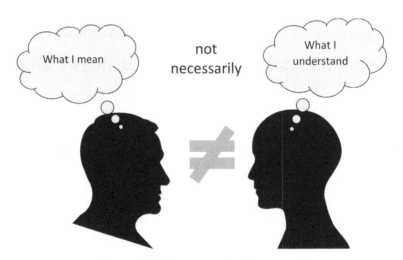

Figure 4.1: The communication process

First, it is important to remember that understanding is not an either-or phenomenon. Rather, there are degrees of understanding, and mutual understanding is built up gradually. Participants need to work on it actively, avoiding common pitfalls. The following sections explain the key issues.

Building mutual understanding: How mindful are you?

As explained above, mutual understanding needs to be built or constructed by all parties. This involves being mindful of each other and attentive to each other's communicative needs, planning thoughtfully our use of language, and listening actively to others. In other words, people need to ask themselves how easily the other person will be able to understand what they say or write and adjust their language accordingly. They also need to pay close attention to the other person(s), looking out for signs—often subtle—as to whether the other person(s) are following them or not. For instance:

- Talking at speed or with a strong, unfamiliar accent can make it very difficult for others to understand.
- Idioms, slang, dialect words, abbreviations, and acronyms may not be known by everybody and need to be avoided. A key problem is that it is often difficult for fluent speakers to have a good sense of the relative frequency of given words or phrases and thus how easy or hard they will be for less fluent speakers. Case Study 4.2 illustrates the unmindful use of an abbreviation.

Case Study 4.2: Interpreting company-internal abbreviations and procedures

A UK-based company manager, Angela, submitted a proposal to the UK offices of an international company, regarding a piece of work the company had requested. When checking whether or not the proposal had been accepted, Angela received the following email message from Jack, her contact at the other company: "I've been informed that the OTV has been sent through and I have the reference if needed." Angela did not know what 'OTV' stood for, nor what having a reference indicated. She did an internet search for OTV and also asked colleagues but did not find the answer. She was therefore left confused and unsure over the status of her proposal.

Reflect

a. What abbreviations and / or acronyms are commonly used in your organisation?
b. How widely do you think they are used / understood outside your organisation?
c. How can you best be mindful in relation to the use of abbreviations and/or acronyms?

Words—Are you assuming shared meaning?

Sometimes an unfamiliar word may lead to understanding problems, but very often a different kind of word-meaning challenge may arise. Case Studies 4.3 and 4.4 illustrate this.

Case Study 4.3: Interpreting 'teacher training'

A British third sector organisation had negotiated a teacher training project with the Chinese Ministry of Education (MoE), in which Chinese teachers of English were to be re-trained after the disruption of the Cultural Revolution. British staff were recruited to set up and run 6-month teacher-training courses in several centres in China and all seemed to go smoothly for the first few months. However, towards the end of the first year, the MoE complained to the British party about the design of the teacher training syllabus, maintaining that instead of aiming at English language improvement, the British teachers were focusing on improving teaching methods.

Case Study 4.4: Interpreting 'affiliate'[21]

"We once worked with a distributed group of 32 stakeholders who were discussing the requirements for a large online bookstore. Progress broke down over the term 'affiliate'. Stakeholders could not agree on what rights and privileges affiliates should have."

Reflect

a. What do these two case studies have in common?
b. How could the issue have been avoided / resolved?

In both these cases, the problem arose from different interpretations of the meaning given to a word or phrase that all parties were familiar with. For Case Study 4.3, the two organisations had different interpretations of the meaning of 'teacher training' in this context. To the British, 'teacher training' meant training teachers in the pedagogy of teaching—in other words, in <u>methods</u> of teaching English as a foreign language. To the Chinese (in this context), it meant improving the teachers' English language proficiency. Neither party was aware of their different respective interpretations and a year of time was lost before the difference emerged. Both parties overlooked one simple factor: the need to check how others were using and interpreting a crucial term.

For Case Study 4.4, the breakdown in progress led the participants to explore what they each understood by the term "affiliate". It emerged that among the 32 stakeholders there were five different meanings for the term, "affiliate". The team then decided to use a different term for each of those five

---

[21] Nunamaker, J.F., Reinig, B.A., & Briggs, R.O. (2009). Principles for effective virtual team-work. *Communication of the ACM, 52* (4), 113–117.

meanings, and agreed that nobody would use the term, "affiliate" for the rest of the project, to minimize confusion.

Directness–indirectness: Is your wording too blunt or too vague for others?

In addition to the potentially different interpretations of familiar words, care also needs to be taken over the clarity with which messages are communicated. One particularly important aspect is the level of directness or indirectness with which messages are worded. This can lead not only to interpretation problems but also offence or annoyance. Consider Case Study 4.5.

Case Study 4.5: Interpreting a request

A British university lecturer, Shirley, needed a second opinion on some students' work, and she asked a colleague, Anke, if she would mind helping. Anke was very happy to do so, and the following conversation took place:

Anke: When do you need my comments?
Shirley: Oh no hurry. Perhaps the middle of next week.

The following Wednesday, Shirley asked Anke how she was getting on preparing her feedback:

Anke: Oh why? Do you need it this week?
Shirley: Well yes, I mentioned the middle of this week.
Anke: I didn't realise that, Shirley. You really need to speak more clearly.

Reflect

a. Why do you think Shirley said "Oh no hurry"? What did she mean by it?
b. Why did Anke regard Shirley as unclear?
c. How do you think they each felt about the incident?

In this example, Anke did not understand the timeframe that Shirley thought she had made clear. Shirley was aware that she was imposing on Anke's time and so used what some speakers of English consider 'polite language' ('Oh no hurry. Perhaps ...) to try to compensate for this. Shirley did not intend for such phrases to be taken literally and assumed Anke would be aware of this. However, for Anke (originally from Germany), this was not at all obvious. She took the words at face value and thus did not complete the work when Shirley wanted her to. Here we see not only that the level of directness—indirectness can affect the clarity of a message for the recipient, but also that it can impact on rapport (see Chapter 5 for a detailed examination of Global Rapport Skills). In this case, both parties ended up feeling annoyed and upset with each other.

So how else could Shirley have responded? Activity 4.1 suggests some alternatives.

Activity 4.1: Levels of directness

Look at the following responses that Shirley could have given to Anke's question about when the feedback was needed. Then consider the reflection questions.
1. Would you be able to manage next Wednesday?
2. Next Wednesday.
3. Next Wednesday would be best.
4. Well, I need to submit my feedback report next Friday.
5. Maybe around the middle of next week.

Reflect

a. Which is the most direct and which the most indirect of the responses above? How would you rank order them for directness—indirectness?
b. If you were in this situation, how would you respond and why?
c. Ask some colleagues how they would respond. How similar or different are their views to yours?
d. Do you generally appreciate indirectness as a kind of politeness?

Numerous factors affect the suitability of different levels of directness or indirectness; key ones are the relationship between the participants, including:

- whether there is a hierarchical difference between them,
- how well they know each other, and
- how far the task falls within the rights and obligations to communicate in a certain way because of the nature of their role in the interaction.

There can also be significant cultural differences in overall preferred levels of directness, as well as the ways in which meaning is indirectly signalled.

As a result, this aspect of language use is extremely difficult to handle well. If we consider it from an Interaction Compass (see Chapter 2, Figure 2.1) perspective, there is no one-to-one correspondence between high control and directness. Often the two correspond, but this is not always the case. Sometimes high control can be conveyed directly and explicitly, but sometimes it can be conveyed much more indirectly, for example by saying 'You may like to try ...' when what is meant is 'you should try ...'.

The acceptability of directly or indirectly expressed control can vary. For example, in settings where directness is more usual, indirect control can be perceived as being manipulative or dishonest. In other words, Global Communication Skills entail being able to vary flexibly the level of directness or indirectness.

In communication situations characterised by diversity, this can be particularly challenging and can lead not only to message interpretation problems but also to potentially 'unfair' interpersonal evaluations. Those who have a preference for more indirect and implicit communication often evaluate a more direct person as unfriendly and rude, and they may also struggle to convey their meaning successfully since their subtle signals are often overlooked by direct speakers.

Conversely, those who have a preference for more direct and explicit communication may perceive indirect communicators to be evasive and potentially dishonest. In addition, they may find it difficult to be very indirect themselves; if they do express themselves indirectly, they may worry whether or not their message has really got across and may feel uncomfortable at not being straightforward. They typically find it hard to interpret the other person's 'real meaning'. For example, if a potential client says, 'We'll look into the possibility', can this be interpreted literally or is it an indirect 'No'? The key here is to learn to pick up on subtle signals in the context (i.e., to be mindful) and to tolerate any remaining ambiguity. Case Study 4.6 illustrates one such case.

Case Study 4.6: Reluctance to say 'no'

Tony, a UK clothing business manager discusses his experiences with Asian suppliers.

"I would go on buying trips to India, Sri Lanka and Bangladesh. One of the big issues was always around late deliveries. My personal relationship was always with the factory manager, but he would often be quite removed from what was actually happening in the factory. So when I wanted to know what was going on, I would speak to the manager on the factory floor. When I started, I wanted to give the factories a target date for the delivery and asked, 'Can you deliver by this date?'. The manager would look uneasy and hesitate very slightly before always saying 'yes sir, no problem'. However, the delivery would then be late."

Reflect
a. What clues should Tony have paid attention to?
b. How could he have worded his question to obtain a more accurate answer?

Clues as to the manager's 'real meaning' could be picked up from his facial expressions and brief hesitation before replying. In time, Tony learned to re-phrase his wording, asking "When will the delivery be ready?" and this was much more effective. As we'll see in the next chapter, 'face' is another crucial factor, and it played an important role here. The manager felt embarrassed to say 'no' to Tony's question; it was much easier for him simply to state when the order would be ready.

On other occasions, the comprehension difficulties are related to an inadequate explanation. For example, when Angela received Jack's email saying, 'I've been informed that the OTV has been sent through and I have the reference if needed,' she not only did not know what OTV stood for but was also unclear where it was being 'sent through' to and for what purpose. In other words, Jack was not explicit enough for Angela to be able to interpret his message.

Mindfulness—How attentive are you?

Successful Global Communication requires careful, ongoing attention; in other words, it involves active listening and mindful attention towards the other person and the context, as well as to our own use of language. As explained, this means we need to consider:

- Our speed of delivery, our choice of words and phrases.
- How similarly we are using certain key words or concepts.
- How directly or indirectly it is best to communicate.
- How much background knowledge we probably share or need to share explicitly with the other person.

Such mindfulness involves both other-attentiveness and self-attentiveness, in particular external self-awareness (cf. Chapter 2). The greater the gaps in PESTLE-type knowledge and 3P cultural knowledge, the more there is to pay attention to, and the more challenging mindfulness becomes. Case Study 4.7 illustrates the difficulty of achieving it, even when someone very much wishes to do so.

The example comes from the start of a meeting between several British and Chinese professionals (about 10 people altogether) who were just beginning a joint project. The participants had not met previously, except for a social dinner the previous evening, and the purpose of the meeting was to explore possibilities for collaborative research. Two of the Chinese spoke fluent English, one spoke basic English, and one spoke no English at all and needed one of his colleagues to interpret for him. The Chair, Marilyn, who is Scottish and a senior manager, introduced the meeting as shown in Case Study 4.7.

Case Study 4.7: The challenge of mindfulness

Marilyn:	"Right, I think we'll make a start now. It's a very warm afternoon for getting down to business, but we have some exciting discussions to have this afternoon. We're going to focus on research. I'm going to ask everybody to speak very clearly and without heavy accents if possible.
Everyone:	[*Laughter, as the Chair speaks with a pronounced Scottish accent*]
Marilyn:	And we may take some pauses just to make sure everybody is keeping up with the conversation, 'cos we can sometimes, each of us, speak very quickly when we get excited. This afternoon is a chance for us really to explore the research issues. I think it would be very helpful for one of our colleagues to volunteer to—[*speeds up speech and starts using a more pronounced*

> *Scottish accent*] as we say in Scotland—start the ball rolling 'cos we really love football. I think I think it would be fair to ask one of our colleagues to start the ball rolling and [name of British colleague] if you would like to kick off for us."
>
> **Reflect**
> a. In what ways does Marilyn show mindfulness in her introduction?
> b. In what ways does Marilyn show a lack of mindfulness in her introduction?
> c. What do you think might be the reason(s) for the mixed levels of mindfulness?

We can see that at the start of the introduction, Marilyn was very conscious of the need for mindfulness, referring explicitly to the need for clarity, 'standard' accent, and pausing. Initially, she put this into practice herself, speaking quite slowly and with quite a number of pauses. However, later she suddenly spoke more quickly, used a stronger Scottish accent, and used two idioms ('start the ball rolling' and 'kick off'). This change left all but one of the Chinese participants with blank faces, indicating that mutual understanding had been undermined.

There can be a number of reasons why people fail to interact with mindfulness. For Marilyn in Case Study 4.7, it was probably her nervousness or enthusiasm over starting the discussions. Table 4.1 shows a fuller list of possible reasons why people may go onto autopilot and thereby fail to show mindfulness.

In Part 2 of the book, we consider ways in which you can enhance your own mindfulness by applying the E4A tool (see Chapter 1 and Introduction to Part 2).

Table 4.1: Possible reasons for mindlessness

Possible reasons for mindlessness
1. Strong desire to convey your own message; this could be through nervousness, excitement, or involvement.
2. Planning what you want to say next, perhaps through nervousness about how to word your contribution.
3. Assuming things will proceed as expected, often because you are thinking about something else.
4. Listening to confirm your pre-existing ideas and viewpoints, especially when you are convinced your argument and position are correct.
5. Listening to confirm your pre-existing opinion of the other person, such as when you dislike that person.

Involving and respecting each other

In Chapter 2, in our consideration of the Interaction Compass, we introduced the connection dimension. One aspect of this is the extent to which people work collaboratively or independently. For collaborative working, people need to be treated as co-members and feel able to participate. This is not only to maximise creative ideas but also to help provide a sense of belonging, and well-being (see Chapter 11). Involvement—the opportunity to participate in a joint activity— has a very strong communication aspect to it, and so we explore it next.

Managing language choice: Do people feel included or excluded?

A very fundamental way in which people may be included or excluded is through the language we choose to use. This applies not only to major deci- sions as to which language to select for official purposes, but also to everyday choices in the workplace. With regard to the former, this can often be a very sensitive issue in mergers and acquisitions, especially when one company's lan- guage is formally imposed on the other. In these situations, people who feel less proficient or less comfortable using this language, may easily feel excluded or at a disadvantage. Even when people are using their first language, some may feel excluded because in their view the language of others is, for example, too technical or too academic for their comfort.

In meetings where some participants are fluent in a language that others are unfamiliar with (e.g., in international negotiations, or after a merger), a change of language during an interaction (known technically as code-switching) can exclude people completely. Case Study 4.8 is an example of this and describes a meeting that took place after a merger between a successful Israeli high-tech company, Isrocom, and an American competitor, Amerotech.

Case Study 4.8: Switching languages deliberately[22]

Two project managers, Tim and Bart, from the New York office travelled to Tel Aviv to train around 30 Israeli project managers on an Amerotech product. In his first presentation, Tim faced many challenging questions. In his second, another difficult question was raised near the beginning. While he was answering it, a senior Israeli manager turned to a subordinate behind him and said loudly in Hebrew, "He simply doesn't understand pricing". His words could be heard across the room. Shortly afterwards, the subordinate started to ask a question, but the manager once again said to him in Hebrew "He just doesn't understand". This was followed by loud whispers across the room in Hebrew. Tim and Bart stared at their audience in puzzlement.

Reflect

a. Why do you think the Israeli manager spoke to his subordinate in Hebrew?
b. What impact do you think it had on Tim and Bart?

---

[22] Ailon, G. (2007). *Global ambitions and local identities. An Israeli-American high-tech merger*. New York, NY: Berghahn Books.

Speaking in another language in this way demonstrates a very clear 'them and us' position. Everybody belongs to multiple social groups simultaneously and these different membership groups can take on varying degrees of significance in different contexts. In this particular example, affiliation to the company as it was before the merger is the most critical group membership factor and the participants' choice of language can play a key role in expressing this affiliation. This is because using a language that not everyone present can understand does not simply reflect different affiliations but can be used actively and strategically to emphasise boundaries and to exclude the 'other'.

This seems to be what happened in this example. The intervention of the senior Israeli manager prevented Tim and Bart from fully answering the question raised. This was disrespectful towards the American partners while simultaneously promoting a sense of superiority among the Israeli team. Although we do not know exactly how Tim and Bart felt, it is likely that they felt a range of negative emotions, including a sense of rejection and alienation from the Israeli partners. But they were spared the loss of face that could have resulted if the Israeli manager had made his comments in English.

Similar issues can occur in multicultural and multilingual workplaces, as Case Study 4.9 illustrates.

Case Study 4.9: Multilingualism at work

Noriko worked for the marketing department of a multinational company based in the UK. The department was divided into several different sections, according to their regional market, including Chinese, French, German, Japanese, Russian, and Spanish. Members of each of the sections regularly spoke among themselves in their respective language, rather than English. Noriko worked in the Japanese section and experienced some problems after a physical re-organisation of the various sections. Someone complained to the Human Resources Department (HR) that members of some of the sections were talking too loudly, so these members did their best to speak as quietly as possible. However, another complaint was later made, and HR asked them to speak only in English. Noriko felt discriminated against by the English staff and also felt that it would make them less efficient and productive in their roles.

Reflect

a. Why do you think complaints were made to HR?
b. If you had worked in HR, would you have asked them to speak only in English? Why/why not?

When people are among others who are speaking a language that they don't understand, they may easily feel annoyed or threatened. They may imagine that they are being talked about; they may think they are just socialising and not working; or they may simply think they are loud and unprofessional, even though their volume of speech isn't particularly high. Perceptions of loudness can be very subjective.

All parties need to pay close attention to this and be sensitive to the position of the other party. In the next chapter, where we consider relationship management, we note how language can also play a significant role in the formation of cliques on the one hand or the overcoming of barriers on the other.

Group discussions: Can everyone contribute?

As we showed in the previous sub-section, people may feel excluded, or actually be excluded, because of the use of a different language. We now turn to another aspect relating to inclusion: that some people feel reluctant to participate, or unable to do so, not because of language per se but because of features of the interactional context.

Case Study 4.10 offers one perspective on this. An Australian Ambassador to Vietnam explained the problems she experienced in getting her local staff to contribute to meeting discussions.

Case Study 4.10: Participation issues in meetings[23]

"We were aware that the Embassy was not working as well as it might. We believe that everybody should be involved in decision processes that affect them in the workplace. We also believe that everyone has something to offer and that you need to draw that out of people if you're going to really make the best use of your staff and get to where you want to go. We found that our usual way of doing this—you sit around, you talk things through, you brainstorm—wasn't working here. We'd have a meeting with staff, we'd put some ideas and there would be silence. Then someone from the local staff would get up and say something and there would be more silence. Then perhaps someone else would say something. We'd ask everybody what they thought about those ideas and there would be no response. The meeting would then break up, not having got very far."

Reflect
a. Why do you think the local Vietnamese staff didn't openly share their ideas?
b. How do you think they could be encouraged to contribute their ideas?

One of the reasons why the local Vietnamese staff felt uncomfortable sharing their ideas openly relates to one of the Cultural Perspectives explained in Chapter 3: Attitude to Hierarchy. The Ambassador's key cultural informants

---

23 Byrne, M., Twitchin, J., & Viswalingan, P. (1996). *What makes you say that: Cultural diversity at work*. VHS recording. SBS-TV.

(see Chapter 12) told her that the staff were reluctant to share their views in case they were different from those of their superiors. If that happened, the staff would feel they had been disrespectful to their superiors and so didn't want to speak up. They also worried that they themselves would be embarrassed and would lose face if their ideas were not well received by others. (We explore the issue of face in the next chapter.) They thus preferred to keep silent.

Another important reason why some people may feel unable to join in a discussion is that they cannot find the 'space' in the discussion to join. There are significant differences across cultural groups (as well as between individuals) in their preferred pattern of turn-taking, in other words, in how the change from one speaker to another is handled.

Some people like the turn-taking to be fast and precise, so that as soon as one person has finished speaking the other starts within milliseconds. Others engage in an overlapping style in which one person starts speaking before another has finished; they feel that this shows enthusiasm and interest. Yet other people like to have quite long pauses between turns (e.g., 2 or 3 seconds or more) to ensure the other person has finished, to show respect, and / or so they have time to think carefully about what the other speakers have said.

These pattern differences are extremely important when working across cultures, and managers and team members need to pay great attention to them. If individuals are used to a style that has pauses between turns, they will have real difficulties in sharing their ideas when there is overlapping or fast change-over. This will be especially the case if they are less confident in the language. As soon as they are ready to say something, the conversation is likely to have already moved on. They can then feel excluded and, equally importantly, others will have lost the benefit of their ideas. Case Study 4.11 illustrates this. An Australian immigrant from Southeast Asia, Bernie, describes his challenging turn-taking experiences when he first started working in Australia.

Case Study 4.11: No 'space' to come in[4]

"When I first came to Australia and was working for [name of company], personally I found it very, very hard to express something, even to come into a discussion when I was with my other marketing colleagues. There just wasn't any gap for you to come in, so I felt very, very threatened and very uncomfortable to express my point of view because I couldn't find any space. I cannot seem to find the opportunity to do that. The situation does not allow most of the time."

Reflect

a. Have you ever noticed someone having difficulties contributing to a meeting?
b. What did you do, if anything?
c. Have you ever personally found it difficult to contribute to a meeting? Why/why not?

Almost inevitably, people make judgements of those whose turn-taking style is different from their own. 'Overlappers' may be evaluated as enthusiastic by those who like overlapping, or as inconsiderate by those who do not. Those with no overlap and no pause may be regarded as objective and professional by some or as too 'forensic' by others. For those with gaps in their turn-taking, some may feel uncomfortable in the pauses and regard the speaker as 'slow' or with 'no ideas'; while others may feel it to be considerate and allows for deeper thinking. We consider ways of addressing these issues in Chapter 8.

People's suggestions: How much do you value them?

Contributing to an ongoing discussion is only the first step in the process of being included and respected. An important complementary aspect is paying careful attention to what others say and valuing it appropriately. Unfortunately, this does not always happen. This could be for a range of reasons. For example, it could be that others are so pre-occupied with their own thoughts and goals that they do not listen carefully enough (i.e., they are not mindful—see the section above on mindfulness).

However, prejudiced attitudes can be another source of problems. Sadly, there is a strong tendency for people to link fluency in the official language of use with intellectual capacity and usefulness of ideas. In other words, fluent speakers all too easily tend to dismiss very valuable suggestions made by others because they are not expressed in linguistically fluent or persuasive ways and are thus regarded as less convincing. This means that potentially creative and innovative ideas may be lost to the team because none of the fluent speakers recognises them.

In fact, any kind of prejudice, including attitudes to out-group members—members of other social groups (e.g., different ethnic groups, age groups, gender groups)—can lead to the same issue: suggestions that are made by a group member who is judged by the majority to be 'peripheral' may simply be ignored. This can contribute to issues such as institutional racism and glass ceilings. Case Study 4.11 presents a sobering case.

Case Study 4.12: Dismissal of novel approaches[24]

Katalin Kariko is a Hungarian scientist who used to work at the University of Pennsylvania. Her research focused on manipulating messenger ribonucleic acid (mRNA) with the hope and belief that it could be used as the basis of cures for cancer and other diseases. For years she experienced rejections from funders,

---

[24] Basken, P. (2021) How the academy shunned the science behind Covid vaccine. *Times Higher Education magazine,* No.2476, 18 February–3 March 2021. Retrieved from https://www.timeshighereducation.com/news/how-academia-shunned-science-behind-covid-vaccine

journals, and her own university, including sarcastic ridicule from the latter, all of which she acknowledges was extremely frustrating. She left the university and joined BioNTech where her work subsequently fed directly into the development of a leading Covid-19 vaccine. In 2021 she won (along with her research partner) the Rosenstiel Award for Distinguished Work in Basic Medical Research.

A former colleague at the University of Pennsylvania reflected on why the university and the academic world had treated her with disdain. He pointed to the need for good networks of professional contacts, high levels of proficiency in English, and the need to be able to promote work convincingly to others—all aspects that were challenging for this particular scientist.

Reflect

a. Have you personally experienced disregard of your ideas from those around you at work?
b. What do you think might be the reasons for this?
c. What innovations might you be overlooking because the person suggesting them is not very skilled in 'selling them'?

Managing communication channels: Does it matter?

Nowadays, there is a wealth of communication channels to choose from, including: face-to-face spoken, video-conferencing, mobile messaging, telephone, email, texting, and written document.

Selecting the most suitable communication channel(s): How do you choose?

An important communication issue that needs attention is how to choose which channel to use and whether there are cultural issues that affect the choice. Look at Activity 4.2.

Activity 4.2: Choosing a communication channel

Consider the following possible reasons for choosing one communication channel over another:
1. The amount of information to be conveyed
2. The complexity of the information to be conveyed, sought, and / or understood
3. The extent to which different viewpoints or ideas need to be understood and discussed
4. The amount of shared background knowledge and information
5. The sensitivity of the topic and how likely it is to cause disagreement
6. The need for speed/quick response
7. The need for a traceable record

Reflect

a. To what extent do you consciously choose which communication channel you want to use on any particular occasion?
b. Which of the above criteria have you used?
c. To what extent have you found the communication channel to be important?

On the whole, the more complex, the more debatable, and the more sensitive the subject, the wiser it is not to restrict communication to a written channel. This is because the usually asynchronous written communication channel lacks or reduces the opportunity for immediate or rapid response which enables you to react sensitively to disagreement or emotional reactions which may damage relationships.

Writing also lacks the paralinguistic features of the spoken language such as tone of voice, volume, and speed, which are crucial in the expression and management of emotion. However, as we have noted above, interpreting emotion accurately is difficult whatever the channel, especially across cultures. SMS and instant messaging use emoticons as a kind of compensation for the lack of signals in written language yet can only do this very partially and are also highly subject to cultural variation.

On the other hand, when the topic is controversial, it may be wise to choose the written channel because it allows time for a more considered response. In summary, selecting the most suitable channels requires mindful attention to the possible benefits and limitations of the different options, and awareness that a combination of channels may be the most effective.

To return to Case Study 4.2, Angela asked Jack to telephone her as she was unable to interpret the brief email messages. Jack declined and continued using email, seemingly unaware of the source of Angela's confusion. He also did not give her a telephone number that she could use and was therefore inflexible in his choice of communication channels. As a result, the two never reached mutual understanding.

Communicating online: What are the potential pitfalls?

Developments in technology have meant that more and more communication is digital, with much of it utilising the internet for transmission. Concerns for the environment mean that many people are reducing their international travel and the Covid-19 pandemic has also led many people to reconsider their travel plans, even nationally. As a result, there may well be a sustained reduction in the amount of face-to-face interactions for work.

Nevertheless, communicating online in real time is often difficult and exhausting. A fundamental reason for this is that all the important yet challenging facets of communication explained in the previous sections of this chapter are often multiplied in online contexts. These include:

- Checking that you are all using key terminology with the same or similar interpretation.
- Regularly checking that you are speaking at a speed that suits everyone.
- Regularly checking that you are using words and phrases in a way that others will understand.
- Asking for clarification when anything is unclear.
- Taking steps to ensure that everyone feels able to participate.

In an online context, when connections may be unstable, when low bandwidth may require video cameras to be turned off, and/or when the number of people present makes seeing everyone difficult, the challenge of handling all of these facets is magnified. If language proficiency issues and cultural differences (e.g., different beliefs around hierarchy) are added to this mix, it can become even more daunting and tiring.

These numerous challenges make clear that ideally, in situations where the same group of people repeatedly meet for video calls, it can be wise to agree explicitly on how best to contribute to the meeting to ensure maximum comprehension and participation.

Even email communication can be problematic when there are different protocols of interaction and when contextual factors are interpreted differently. Case Study 4.13 illustrates this. It reports on an experience that a British project manager experienced when she was managing a set of teams in Britain and China.

Case Study 4.13: Email etiquette

Marie was the British manager of a Chinese-British intergovernmental programme in which about 50 British and Chinese professionals were working together in teams on a range of collaborative projects. Marie needed to communicate with the teams by email and when she did so, she copied in all those for whom the content of the email was relevant. However, after a month or so, she received the following email from one of the partners in China.

Sending mass emails is a good way. But when we send such emails, it will infringe Chinese principles. If I send such an email to a person in a higher position, s/he will feel offended. Nowadays we send various materials by email, but Chinese are special, superiors will feel particularly insulted. Sending emails to superiors is not a good way, because it shows no regard for status differences between people. Some superiors dislike equality, so the best way to communicate with them is to submit a report, either in written or oral form.

> **Reflect**
> a. What Cultural Perspective (see Chapter 3) was underlying the feedback to Marie?
> b. What do you think Marie did in response?
> c. If you had been in Marie's situation, what would you have done in response?

In fact, Marie continued to send emails to the senior Chinese participants; she did not replace emails with reports. However, she changed the people she copied in to her emails. Even if the content of the emails was identical, she sent separate emails to those in senior positions and those in less senior positions. This raises another fundamental issue when working across cultural boundaries: the extent to which one makes behavioural adjustments. We consider this further in Part 2 of the book.

Key takeaways

Core insights	Applications for practice
• Communication is not simply a matter of sending and receiving, encoding and decoding; rather it entails an active process of constructing meaning in which participants draw on relevant background and contextual knowledge.	• Take conscious and careful steps to build mutual understanding.
• Choice of words and levels of directness / indirectness can all lead to misunderstandings and need mindful attention.	• Be mindful of turn-taking preferences and work with others to help everyone participate comfortably.
• People can be included or excluded by the ways in which communication takes place.	• Pay attention to choice of language as it impacts on many things, for example, goal achievement, task efficiency, and inclusion / exclusion of others.
• Communication success is greatly affected by the communication channel used.	• Choose the communication channel carefully as it can have a significant impact on communication success.

5

Global Rapport Management Skills: Developing strong relationships

Introduction

Relationships are central to success in every walk of life, helping us achieve our goals and providing us with a wide variety of positive emotions. They are vital to our professional lives as well as our personal lives. Importantly, they can never be taken for granted. They need to be managed and nourished carefully and this is never easy, particularly in contexts of cultural diversity. It requires Global Rapport Management skills.

Rapport refers to the quality or nature of the links among people. It exists in both the links between specific individuals (i.e., their relationships) as well as in the feelings and behaviour among people more generally (e.g., social or professional relations). Rapport is dynamic—it can increase, decrease or change as a result of interaction. So, by rapport management, we mean the handling of these dynamics. From a Global Fitness perspective, rapport management involves the building and maintaining of fruitful connections with others (see further below for more details on this).

The aim of this chapter is to explore these people-focused matters, including the following:

- Rapport and the process of judging others.
- Managing disagreement and learning from each other.
- Building rapport and managing impressions.
- Managing the influence of identities and groups.

As usual, we start by considering an introductory case study and reflecting on the rapport management issues it raises.

Introductory case study

Case Study 5.1 took place in an English language class in the UK.

Case Study 5.1: A rejected offer of help[25]

When a French student couldn't understand the grammar point and the teacher moved on, a Chinese student, Xiao Li, tried to help the French student. Afterwards Xiao Li commented as follows:

> "As I was sitting next to her [the French student] and I understood the expression, I wanted to give her a hand, so I said, 'I know it's meaning'. But she simply turned her book to the other page. I was very angry with her at that moment because I thought she was looking down upon me, or us Chinese. Wasn't I capable of sorting out such a minor grammar problem? I was really angry."

Reflect

a. Why do you think the French student declined Xiao Li's offer of help? Think of several possible reasons.
b. Why was Xiao Li angry?
c. How justified do you think he was in feeling angry? Give reasons for your answer.

In this example, Xiao Li was angry with the French student, and he interpreted her behaviour as condescension towards him or towards Chinese people as a whole. His relationship with her was damaged. Sadly, such seemingly minor incidents that have consequences for rapport can occur relatively frequently, often arising from differing interpretations of each other's behaviour. To build Global Rapport Management skills, it is important to understand how people make judgements of others, so the first main section of this chapter examines this.

Rapport and the process of judging others

An important element of rapport concerns the judgements (e.g., rude, friendly, arrogant) that we make of other people and the judgements they make of us. This can be particularly difficult in situations of diversity as the factors and criteria that people draw on in their evaluations may be different. This in turn can lead to very different judgements and interpretations. It is important, therefore, to understand how people make their judgements, as this can help to reduce misinterpretations and misunderstandings and keep relations positive. There are three key elements: expectations, evaluation criteria, and judgements (see Figure 5.1).

---

[25] Spencer-Oatey, H. (2002). Managing rapport in talk: using rapport sensitive incidents to explore the motivational concerns underlying the management of relations. *Journal of Pragmatics, 34*, 529–545.

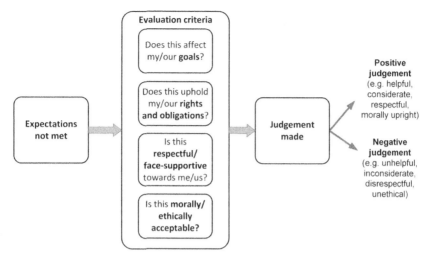

Figure 5.1: Key elements of the judgement process

Attending to expectations

The starting point of any evaluative judgement is located in the expectations a person has. People need to pay attention to these and try to take them into account when responding or reacting.

Whatever people do or say always takes place in a context, such as in a team meeting or during a working lunch, and they have all kinds of expectations as to what will happen in that context. This includes things like what happens at what point, who has the right to say and do what, and so on. It is when the expectations are not met in some way that the evaluation process is triggered. In fact, in many business meetings, one of the parties may very well ask about the aims and expectations of those present. Let us consider Case Study 5.2, where this did not happen.

Case Study 5.2: Expectations of an initial business meeting[26]

An Australian businessman, Jim, wanted to sell his cream cheese products to Japan and arranged a meeting with Mr Iguchi, a representative of a Japanese company based in Melbourne. At the meeting, Jim made it clear right from the start that he wanted either to export the cheese to Japan or manufacture it there. He brought samples with him and wanted Mr Iguchi to taste them. If Mr Iguchi was interested in the product, he would continue the discussions and provide more samples to be sent to Japan. On the other hand, if he wasn't interested,

---

[26] Marriott, H.E. (1990). Intercultural business negotiations: the problem of norm discrepancy. *ARAL Series S, 7*, 33–65.

no more time need be wasted on the matter. By the end of the meeting, though, Jim wasn't sure whether Mr Iguchi was interested or not, and concluded that this probably meant he was not. He felt frustrated by this, maintaining that Mr Iguchi should have made his intentions clearer.

For Mr Iguchi, on the other hand, the purpose of this first meeting was to learn more about Jim's company and its plans. He asked quite a lot of questions on this, since Jim was not forthcoming on them, and he negatively evaluated Jim afterwards for not pro-actively providing this kind of information. He declined to taste the samples but asked to visit Jim's cheese factory so he could gather more information. His plan was to send as much information as possible back to his head office in Japan and for them to decide whether to continue discussions. He regarded it as not part of his role to make an initial decision.

In separate meetings afterwards with a researcher, they both expressed dissatisfaction with the meeting and each other's behaviour.

Reflect

a. What was Jim expecting from the meeting and from Mr Iguchi?
b. What was Mr Iguchi expecting from the meeting and from Jim?
c. What Cultural Practices or Perspectives might underlie each of their expectations? (Refer back to Chapter 3 if you need to)

In this example, Jim wanted to know whether Mr Iguchi was interested in purchasing his cheese product, and he was expecting Mr Iguchi to make an initial decision at the end of the meeting. Mr Iguchi, on the other hand, was expecting to obtain information about Jim's company as well as his product, so that he could pass this on to his head office for them to make the decision in due course.

Expectations were not met in that Jim did not provide Mr Iguchi with the amount and type of information he was expecting and needed, while Jim did not receive the feedback on his product that he was expecting. Both gave negative evaluations of the other in follow-up interviews by the researcher. In other words, the expectations of both men were not met and this triggered their negative evaluations of the meeting and of each other.

In Case Study 5.1, expectations may also have played a role. The teacher would be expecting all students to pay attention to her in class. The French student may have been very conscious of this and may have ignored the Chinese student's offer for that reason.

So, the first key question to consider when meeting with people from different backgrounds is:

- What are your expectations for the event / interaction and how similar or different might they be from others' expectations? [Our 3R Review tool, explained in Part 2 of the book, offers support in handling this question.]

If they are noticeably different in some way, people will usually start making judgements. This entails drawing on several evaluation criteria.

Applying evaluation criteria

People usually apply four main interconnected criteria when making evaluative judgements of events and behaviour:

- The impact on their personal and/or professional goals.
- The extent to which others have fulfilled their obligations towards them.
- The level of respect they feel they have been treated with (i.e., how much face they have been given).
- The moral or ethical acceptability of the behaviour.

These four criteria act as fundamental principles against which behaviour is judged. To put it another way, if any of the principles is undermined in some way—for instance, by a goal not being fulfilled or some kind of disrespect being conveyed—a negative evaluative judgement is likely to result. From a Global Fitness perspective, the challenge is that there can be significant differences—not only individual but also cultural—in the interpretations resulting from people's application of each of these criteria. The following discussion will help to explain and illustrate this.

In Case Study 5.2, the primary evaluation criterion that Jim and Mr Iguchi applied was the achievement of their respective goals. As explained, they each had different goals for the initial meeting and the failure to achieve them was the main source of their dissatisfaction and disappointment with their meeting. However, Jim also assumed that Mr Iguchi had decision-making rights and was disappointed when he failed to indicate what he thought of Jim's cheese product. Yet, it emerged later that Mr Iguchi did not have that right; his role was information-gathering. Here we see a mismatch between Jim and Mr Iguchi in their understandings of each other's roles, and the associated rights and obligations.

In fact, beliefs and assumptions around the rights and obligations associated with people's roles (e.g., what a manager 'should' do and what an employee has the 'right' to expect from the manager) can vary extremely widely across cultural groups. It is thus a particularly common source of negative evaluative judgements. Case Study 5.3 illustrates this further.

Case Study 5.3: Interpreting roles

A delegation of Chinese businesspeople visited a British company from whom they had bought a large engineering product. During the first few days, a number of issues arose that they very much wanted to talk over with Tim, the British sales manager, whom they had met and hosted in China. Unfortunately, however, Tim was away on a six-week East Asian trip and was not returning until the Thursday evening prior to their departure the following Tuesday.

The delegates expected him to come and meet them immediately after his return, and when he did not do so on the Friday, they started asking to see him. This continued all over the weekend (when other British staff were accompanying them on excursions), with comments such as the following: *"His old friends from China are here, in fact his major market. This morning he should have taken us out sightseeing."*

Tim, on the other hand, had been away on a long trip. He commented that he was tired and that his wife and son were expecting to see him over the weekend, so he prioritised that. He knew that it was important for him to meet them but felt that waiting till Monday was perfectly reasonable.

Reflect

a. In your view, how obligated was Tim to meet the delegation at the office on the Friday morning? Give reasons for your answer.
b. In your view, how obligated was Tim to take the delegation sightseeing at the weekend? Give reasons for your answer.
c. In your view, what kind of person counts as an 'old friend'?

In this example, the delegates maintained that they were 'old friends' with Tim and that this meant he had an obligation to meet with them as soon as possible. Tim, on the other hand, did not regard his single prior meeting with them in China as constituting an 'old friendship' and felt under no obligation to prioritise them over his immediate family (also see Case Study 3.7). So, we can say that there were two discrepancies in this example:

- Interpretations of the nature of a relationship (in this case, 'old friend'), and
- The rights and obligations associated with that relationship, and how they compare with those of other relationships, such as family.

The incident further illustrates the interconnected nature of the evaluation criteria, as it also included a goals element. The delegates wanted to meet with Tim so they could talk over some issues with him; Tim was also aware that meeting with them was important for future business. Thus 'addressing business needs' was an important goal for both parties; however, it was their different interpretations of obligation priorities that was primarily responsible for the delegates' disappointment.

Case Study 5.1 illustrates further interconnections. The Chinese student wanted to help the French student achieve her goal of understanding the grammar point. However, he overlooked the likely desire of the French student to meet the teacher's expectations that she would pay attention in class and her likely ongoing goal of wanting to understand the teacher's next point. Instead, he interpreted her behaviour as a lack of respect and felt face-threatened because her rejection of help seemed like a rejection of him personally and of Chinese people more generally.

Face can be a powerful factor affecting rapport and interaction in many different ways. The term 'face' is not always easy to define, but it is associated in some way with people's sense of worth and their need for dignity and respect. When someone's competence, dignity or worth is challenged, they may 'lose face' or feel 'face-threatened', and thereby experience hurt, discomfort and/or embarrassment. Alternatively, they may feel they've 'gained face' or been 'given face' if others praise, congratulate or compliment them.

Concerns about face can lead people to be unwilling to suggest ideas, in case they are rejected by others, and they appear in a bad light (see Case Study 4.10). It can also lead to a reluctance to convey unwanted news, such as an inability to meet a delivery deadline as we saw in Case Study 4.6. See Activity 5.1 for a follow-up reflection.

Activity 5.1: Experiences of face threat/face enhancement

Face can be linked with different elements, including (a) people's sense of personal competence / skill, (b) others' acknowledgement of their social status, and (c) others' respect for the social group they belong to.

1. Look back at the following Case Studies: 3.4, 4.6, 4.10 and 5.1. How do face sensitivities affect relations among the participants?
2. Think of an occasion when you have felt a face threat. What happened, why did you feel as you did, and what judgements (of the behaviour and/or the person) did you make?
3. Now think of an occasion when you felt your face was enhanced. What happened, why did you feel as you did, and what judgements (of the behaviour and/or the person) did you make?

A fourth evaluation criterion that we sometimes apply is the moral or ethical acceptability of the behaviour. We discuss this in detail in Chapter 10.

Making judgements

The second key question to ask yourself when building your Global Rapport Management skills is:

- How similarly to or differently from the other person(s) are you interpreting and applying your evaluation criteria?

The answer to that question affects the degree of similarity of the judgements that each party makes.

When people make judgements, they may evaluate both the person and what they did or said. Very often, the two are merged, such that they are barely distinguished from each other; in reality, the judgement is frequently made only of the other person(s) on the basis of what they did or did not do or say.

For example, with regard to Case Study 5.3, the Chinese delegates were very critical of their hosts, saying "right from the start they were commanding, in control, contemptuous". This negative judgement of their hosts was based on their own expectations and norms; they did not consider the possibility of different interpretations. The same was true of their British hosts, who had a similarly negative interpretation. At the end of the visit, and after a number of other problems had arisen, one of the British hosts commented: "they haven't any ethics, they had no due respect for their hosts, were arrogant, and demanded this and demanded that".[27]

The third key question when building your Global Rapport Management skills—which in a sense should be both your starting point as well as your re-consideration point—is:

- How fair or valid are your judgements of others and their behaviour, given the possible differences in expectations and evaluation criteria?

Recognising differences in judgement

In our discussions of the various case studies in the book, it has become increasingly clear that participants often see things from different perspectives, especially when their backgrounds, expectations and patterns of behaviour are different. This also applies to assessing whether offence has been given or taken, that is, whether or not you have unintentionally offended somebody or hurt their feelings.

Sometimes it may not be obvious that a person feels offended. This can be particularly the case when:

- others do not feel it appropriate to display their emotional reactions, so that there is only a subtle indication, and/or when
- people's expectations are very different, and they are not paying attention to any possible signs of offence.

---

[27] Spencer-Oatey, H., & Xing, J. (2004). Rapport management problems in Chinese–British business interactions: a case study. In J. House & J. Rehbein (Eds.), *Multilingual communication* (pp. 197–221). Amsterdam: Benjamins.

In Part 2 of the book, especially Chapter 7, we consider ways of handling this 'judgement' aspect of rapport management.

Managing disagreement and learning from each other

We turn now to another aspect of rapport management: disagreement. It is often assumed that disagreement is a bad thing, and yet that is not always the case. This is particularly true for teamwork because research has shown that diverse viewpoints can stimulate interest and curiosity if handled well and can thereby lead to innovative and creative ideas (see Chapter 8).

Unfortunately, this does not always happen. Sometimes, people do their best to avoid disagreement, ignoring potentially controversial issues, with the result that although superficially things may seem to be going well, the quality of the work turns out to be below the standard expected or desired. On the other hand, at other times, the disagreement can be so intense and bitter that the project fails. In both cases, such situations need to be avoided because different ideas and viewpoints need to be addressed constructively if new thinking is to emerge.

An important way of helping prevent such problems—and to overcome them when disagreements occur—is to build strong relationships. This links with the Task–Relationship Cultural Practice that we introduced in Chapter 3. It also links with the high end of the connection dimension of the Interaction Compass, which emphasises the value of collaborative connections.

A key aspect of this concerns the way that people talk and listen to each other. Very often, when disagreements arise, people talk at each other, simply asserting their own viewpoint and not actually listening to and taking in the other person's arguments. Case Study 5.4 illustrates this. It reports on discussions at a small conference on the challenges of globalisation, in which some delegates criticised the USA and thereby offended some of the American participants. Their reaction is completely natural and understandable, but unfortunately the discomfort that followed meant there was little attention or mutual appreciation of everyone's viewpoints on the topic being discussed.

Case Study 5.4: Unproductive discussion[28]

"The hot issue of the meeting was the behavior of the United States. Many participants sharply criticized the country, and some of the Americans, including one of the meeting's main corporate sponsors, were defensive. The chairman was frightened that the Americans would feel uncomfortable and walk out,

---

28   Kahane, A. (2004). *Solving tough problems: An open way of talking, listening, and creating new realities.* San Francisco, CA: Berrett-Koehler.

and so he asked the critics to tone down their remarks. Then he invited the American sponsor to make the final speech of the meeting. The sponsor presented a confident, sweeping survey of the state of the world, complete with 100 PowerPoint slides.

This meeting failed to achieve its objective of creating forward movement towards a new system of global governance. In a series of orchestrated monologues, all the main points of view were re-presented, with preference given to the famous. The panelists did not listen to each other but merely waited to give their prepared remarks. Everybody could talk, as long as they did not discomfort the powerful. The American sponsor had the final say—and it was a lecture.

The meeting was organised entirely around talking. No attention was paid to listening—to the process of taking in something new and being unsettled and changed by it. The chairman discouraged impoliteness and discomfort. We ended up with a dialogue of the deaf, and the enormous potential of this marvellous group was therefore unrealized."

Reflection

a. Think back over your own experiences and identify a time when you found yourself acting in any of the ways described in this mini case, or when you experienced others doing so.
b. How did you feel?
c. Why did you act as you did?
d. Why do people often find it difficult to truly listen to other people's ideas?

As Case Study 5.4 illustrates very clearly, no progress can be made in overcoming different viewpoints if, while one person is talking, others are not paying attention and are simply rehearsing their own counterarguments. It completely undermines collaborative innovation. What needs to happen instead is to engage in reflective talk, with people genuinely listening to each other, taking in and reflecting on other people's ideas and then building on them as a group so that the discussion can lead to the emergence of creative and synergistic ideas.

This can be illustrated using the Interaction Compass we introduced in Chapter 2. As Figure 5.2 illustrates, innovative ideas emerge where individuals do not simply focus on their own viewpoints and on persuading others to agree with them, but rather are willing to listen to others' ideas, to reflect on them and to find points of synergy. If they do not do this, the result will be either dominating talk where individuals' personal ideas are promoted, or else superficial engagement.

Positive rapport in which people value and support each other can help provide the foundation for such synergistic, creative and innovative talk. In this way, new practice can emerge. This then brings us to the next issue: how can we promote 'good' relationships, especially in culturally diverse contexts?

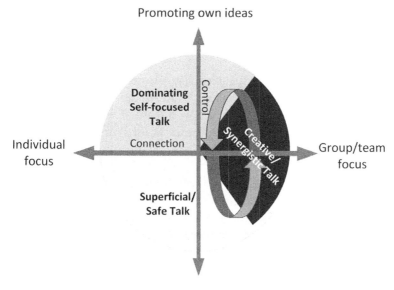

Figure 5.2: Creative and uncreative ways of talking

Building rapport

It is widely argued that "successful business is built on good relationships"[29] and yet we reported in Chapter 3 that there can be cultural differences in the relative importance attached to a focus on the task in hand as opposed to a prioritising of the relationship amongst those involved. In this section, we look more closely at rapport and consider what it can involve and how cultural factors can affect interpretations of it. In Chapter 7 we consider the issue from a more practical, developmental perspective.

Rapport as fruitful connections

Rapport can be seen as a fruitful connection between people. The nature of that fruitfulness can be varied and can include the following:

- Collaborative
- Stimulating
- Trusting

---

[29] E.g., see Hovsepian, T. (2018). Business and people: Why relationships are essential for a successful business. Forbes Los Angeles Business Council. Retrieved from https://www.forbes.com/sites/forbeslacouncil/2018/07/20/business-and-people-why-relationships-are-essential-for-a-successful-business/?sh=f36ebdf74f23

- Supportive
- Inclusive
- Respectful

Such fruitful connections help people collaborate well with others, trust them, feel supported and respected by them, and can lead to a sense of inclusion and belonging. This in turn can promote a sense of well-being and psychological safety for all concerned. (See Chapter 11 for a further consideration of well-being.)

The exact details of what this means in practice will depend on the type of relationship in question. For example, what it means to have a trusting relationship between a supervisor and a staff member, between an employee and external client, and between two members of a team is likely to differ in its precise details. Moreover, country cultural differences are likely to add to this variation. One particularly widespread difference is the nature and distinctiveness of the personal–professional divide with respect to discussion and argument. Case Study 5.5 illustrates this.

Case Study 5.5: Arguing in meetings[30]

"I [Emily] was in Germany for my first management meeting with my new colleagues from the German parent company. (...) There was a very heated discussion amongst the German colleagues about the best way to go ahead, which I felt was a real row. So, I was rather insecure and nervous about putting my view across. But in the end, I said my piece and I think people understood. But I didn't join in the shouting. As it was our first international meeting, the German colleagues took us all out for a meal and a drink. I was extremely surprised by the fact that they all seemed to get on so well together and have so much fun."

a. Why do you think the German colleagues could argue so strongly and yet have a good relationship?
b. How likely is this to happen in your own workplace?
c. What dangers could it have for 'good' relations in culturally diverse workplaces? How could that be handled?

In this case, Emily was taken aback by the level of disagreement expressed in discussions and how that was kept very separate from personal feelings—something that can be very difficult for those who experience the personal and professional as being closely intertwined.

---

[30] Franklin, P. (2006). *Communicating and cooperating with German business people: A Guide for the British.* CD-ROM. Konstanz: KIeM.

There can also be other ways in which the interconnection between the personal and the professional is important. For instance, consider the comments made by an experienced British senior manager working internationally for a third sector organisation with offices throughout the world. She reported in an interview with us that in Sri Lanka, if a relative of somebody in the office dies, not necessarily a close relative, everybody who is working in the office should go quickly and pay their respects to the body. The local expectation is that staff can do that in their work time and that the organisation would even provide a vehicle to take them there. The British manager commented that being a 'good' boss had a much wider remit than she was expecting. This brings out an important issue that deserves careful attention: there can be significant cultural differences in the obligations that are seen to be associated with given roles.

Managing impressions

Another perspective on rapport—both the building of fruitful connections and the judgements that people make—is the issue of impression management. Everybody tries to control the impressions that people form of them, especially in critical situations such as in job interviews or important client meetings. Unfortunately, however, this is not always easy and is particularly problematic in situations of diversity where people may draw on different criteria in forming their impressions. Case Study 5.6 illustrates the subtle way in which the use of a different and unexpected style of language can convey an unintended impression, in this case of arrogance.

Case Study 5.6: Unintentionally conveying an impression of arrogance[31]

An American businessman, James, was working in Paris and he invited two local professionals to join him for lunch at a local restaurant popular with businesspeople. On arrival the following conversation took place:

James: (to the waiter who was greeting them) *Table pour trois.* [Table for three]

Waiter: *Bonjour... Suivez-moi, s'il vous plaît.* [Good day... Follow me please] (The waiter took them to a table at the back of the restaurant, handed them the menu, and returned a few minutes later to take their order.)

James: C'est quoi ton spécial pour audjourd'hui? Est-ce que tu as toujours ce truc au porc que tu avais l'année derniére? [What's your special for today? Do you still have that pork thing you had last year?]

---

[31] Lutz, N. (2010) *French and American perceptions of arrogance in the other.* Saarbrücken: VDM Verlag Dr. Müller.

After an uncomfortable silence, the waiter responded and took their orders. One of the local professionals commented afterwards that James had come across as arrogant for the following reasons:

- He failed to greet the waiter appropriately, not responding to 'Bonjour'.
- His brief 'table for three', which is normal in English, sounded too informal and directive.
- He repeatedly used the familiar form 'tu' for 'you', instead of the more respectful form 'vous'.
- His whole style of interaction was unexpectedly informal.

The local professional further commented that these breaches of expected patterns of behaviour caused the waiter discomfort, making him feel disrespected.

Reflect

a. In contexts you are familiar with, would James' way of greeting the restaurant staff be appropriate or inappropriate?
b. How would you normally greet staff in a restaurant?
c. How similar or different is the rest of the conversation to what you would expect?

Here we show the very close interconnection between language and impression management, and how this is also closely rooted in cultural patterns and expectations. James was fluent in French, but the problem was that he paid insufficient attention to his style of use, especially his level of directness and formality, and he wasn't aware of the impressions his choices of style were making on others.

Moreover, when the local professional talked to him about his use of the informal 'you' rather than the more respectful pronoun, instead of taking it as an opportunity to learn about local people's expectations and adjust to them, he dismissed the distinction between 'tu' and 'vous' as an inappropriate relic from a previously hierarchical society. In terms of the Interaction Compass, he was functioning only at the low end of the connection dimension, ignoring other people's reactions and preferences, and continuing to follow his personal beliefs.

Managing the influence of identities and groups

Identity and group belonging

As mentioned in Chapter 4, everybody belongs to many different social groups, based on characteristics such as geographical region, age, profession, religious belief, and club. Our membership of such groups forms an important part of our identities, particularly because our sense of belonging and sense of worth is closely associated with them. This has several consequences, as illustrated in Figure 5.3. (See Chapter 11 for a more detailed discussion of identity and discrimination.)

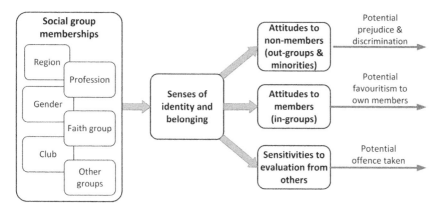

Figure 5.3: The potential impact of social group memberships and identities

One of the potential impacts of group memberships and associated senses of identity and belonging is that people can easily feel offended, not just when they personally are evaluated negatively (as discussed above), but also when their social group is criticised, even when no offence or criticism are intended.

For instance, in Case Study 5.4, when a number of the participants criticised the USA, this led some of the Americans to go onto the defensive and the chairman asked the critics to tone down their remarks. The purpose of the meeting, which was attended by a very diverse group from around the world, was actually to discuss the role of the USA in an impending war with Iraq. It would therefore be highly likely that some negative sentiments could be expressed about the USA. Yet despite this, the American participants found the criticism hard to receive.

This illustrates how important it is to be very careful when making negative comments about a social group that someone else belongs to. We may think we are having an objective discussion, but members of that group may easily feel hurt or offended (i.e., face-threatened) by any indications of disapproval.

The risk of upsetting members of another group by being open in our evaluative comments is made even greater by a psychological tendency to regard our own social group (known as the in-group) more positively than a comparable group that we don't belong to (known as the out-group). In line with this, people easily attribute anything negative that an out-group member does, to a negative characteristic of the group as a whole, rather than as something specific to the individual. This can give rise to negative stereotyping and possible discrimination against people who are different from ourselves, including those who are different in terms of gender, race, age, or other personal characteristics.

This tendency has the further danger that people may show favouritism towards members of their own groups and exclude others. Such favouritism can be shown in a number of ways, such as in recruitment and promotion. In Case Study 5.7 a senior female business leader in Kenya, Dawn, comments that it affected the power relations in the institution where she started to work.

Case Study 5.7: Favouritism and exclusion[32]

"I was thrust into a leadership role in an institution where staff members were loyal to other people or had godfathers.[33] It was an institution that, because of whom you knew or were related to, a staff member could be more powerful than a director, even a messenger. It was the most difficult time of my professional life."

Reflect

a. What experiences have you had of feeling excluded from a group or by a group?
b. What do you think were the reasons for your sense of exclusion?

Reducing sub-group divisions

People have a natural tendency to build closer relations with those who are similar in some way to themselves. For this reason, there is a particular risk of unhelpful sub-group divisions forming when several group members have a number of characteristics in common, but which are different from others.

For instance, suppose a project team has members who have different first languages, professional backgrounds, and length of time in the company. Half of the team speak English as their main language, have a marketing background, and are all relatively new recruits to the company, while the other half speak French as their main language, have an engineering background, and have all worked for the company for ten years of more. It is quite likely that, because of the alignment of their similarities, they will tend to form two sub-groups and side with or socialise more with the members who are similar to them. Then, if some kind of critical issue arises, it is quite possible that the group will split into factions, with tensions emerging between them. Case Study 5.8 illustrates this.

---

[32] Mutooni, K. Ng'weno, B., & Jordans, E. (2020) Changing leadership perceptions: Leaders in the private sector in Kenya. In E. Jordans, B. Ng'weno, & H. Spencer-Oatey, H. (Eds.). *Developing global leaders. Insights from African case studies* (pp. 211–257). London: Palgrave Macmillan.

[33] By 'godfathers', Dawn is referring to the word's meaning as 'any influential leader or powerful figure'.

Case Study 5.8: Splits among staff

Djamila, an experienced international leader working for a third-sector organisation, experienced a problem with a split team when she took up her role in their Omani office. She found that there was a 'war' between two sets of staff who had different roles, with no one speaking to those in the 'other' team. She arranged a training day, where everyone would participate in a planning meeting, but the tensions and communication issues remained, and the outcomes were unproductive.

Djamila realised that she needed to understand the underlying problems and found that the staff were split along the following lines: nationality (local versus expatriate), professional role, working hours, holiday dates, and religious belief. In other words, for each of these elements, members of one group shared exactly the same characteristics, all of which were different from members of the other group, who also all shared another set of identical characteristics. Since members of the two sub-groups rarely overlapped in the office, mainly because of their work roles and different religious observances, resentments started to build up, with neither 'side' understanding the true nature of the other's position.

Reflect

a. What experience do you have of team splits?
b. In your experience, what identity factors have played a critical role in dividing teams?
c. How do you think such splits can best be prevented or overcome?

In this case, the lack of diversity within each group of staff, combined with the differences that existed between the two groups, meant that a fault-line split occurred among the staff. It is important, therefore, to pay attention to the nature and distribution of personal characteristics when establishing any kind of working group so that the risk of this kind of division can be avoided as far as possible.

Key takeaways

Core insights	Applications for practice

• Rapport can be seen as fruitful connections among people.
• Rapport is affected by the judgements people make of each other.
• Three key elements are involved in the judgement process:
  o unmet expectations
  o application of evaluation criteria
  o the judgement that is made
	• Be mindful of what judgements you are making of others and why.
	• Seek to clarify mutual expectations.
	• Expect disagreements—they are inevitable.
	• Be open to others' ideas and perspectives and be willing to learn from them.
	• Foster fruitful connections actively and manage impressions carefully.

- Culture affects all three of these elements.
- Disagreement can be productive when people value each other's contributions and build on them.
- People's management of rapport can affect the impressions others make of them.
- A person's sense of identity and belonging is closely linked with the social groups they are members of.

- Be careful not to undermine rapport by criticising someone else's social group.
- Be mindful of shared identity subgroups and put in place opportunities to bridge gaps.

Part 2

Mastering your development toolkit: Global Fitness Engagement

Introduction to Part 2

Mastering your development toolkit: Global Fitness Engagement

In Part 1 we introduced you to the four key goals of Global Fitness: Global Personal Qualities, Global Knowledge and Understanding, Global Communication Skills, and Global Rapport Management Skills. We showed how the lack of these competencies can create problems and misunderstandings in culturally diverse settings and how their mastery can help navigate such misunderstandings and avoid confusion and potential conflict.

In this part, Part 2, we explore how you can develop each of these fitness 'muscles' and how you can learn to flex them when working and interacting with culturally diverse others to achieve better results. As always, we use real-life case studies to illustrate how to do this in context and to highlight the missteps to avoid.

As we briefly explained in Chapter 1, we take a transformational learning approach to development, which for Global Fitness we label E4A transformational learning, shown again here as Figure P2.1.

The key starting point is for people to move out of their comfort zones and Engage with the Unfamiliar. Sometimes this comes from their own choice and sometimes the unfamiliar is thrust upon them. Either way, if they are to learn and grow from the experiences, they need to pay attention to them and deal with any issues they bring to light (i.e., Attend). This requires curiosity—the desire to seek insights into the issues, ask questions as they read or consult others (i.e., Ask). They need to think over and reflect on their experiences (i.e., Analyse), and then to try and put their learning and insights into practice, in their thinking, feeling, and behaviour (i.e., Apply).

As you progress through Part 2, we'll illustrate how this can work in practice and we'll also introduce you to some specific tools to help you with particular elements of the learning process.

E4A Transformational Learning

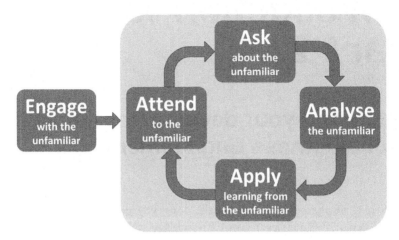

Figure P2.1: Transformational learning steps for developing Global Fitness

There are five chapters in Part 2. Chapter 6 focuses on ways of handling unfamiliar situations. Chapter 7 explores how to build global relations and enhance rapport. Chapter 8 looks at how to collaborate and succeed in global teams, while Chapter 9 turns to global leadership and ways of handling global contexts. The final chapter of Part 2, Chapter 10, considers the ethical challenges that global working can bring and how to maintain integrity.

6

How to embrace the unfamiliar, reflect and adapt

Introduction

This chapter focuses on a fundamental topic associated with cultural diversity—the issue of adaptation. It is common to hear people making assertions like 'When in Rome, do as the Romans do', but actually it is not always easy to know who should adjust to whom or to what, and in what contexts. Moreover, changing our behaviour (as well as our judgements and feelings) is often more challenging than the saying might imply. It's part of a process—the E4A transformational learning process that we introduced in Chapter 1 and in the introduction to Part 2.

The aims of this chapter are:

- To illustrate the adaptation process with the help of case studies.
- To introduce you to two tools:
  - the 3R Review tool for reflecting on unexpected experiences
  - the SOS Adapt tool for adjusting to different ways of behaving

Introductory case study

Consider the following case study.

Case Study 6.1: A disastrous first encounter

Dan, a British project manager, was very excited as he walked into the office of the Global VP of Marketing of a large multinational in Paris. He was here to discuss a new project his company had just won to develop a pan-European marketing campaign for the firm, and Dan was to lead the project. The VP of Marketing was very late for the meeting, but Dan was relaxed. In preparation for this project, he had read a book about French culture which suggested that 'the French have a tendency to be polychronic'. This meant that 'French people were often late for meetings'. Dan was fine with this—for the project to succeed, he understood that he had to play by his client's rules.

When the VP turned up 40 minutes late and apologised, Dan breezily said that it was not a problem because he was well aware that the French culture allowed this. *"I myself am quite partial to more relaxed time-keeping,"* he said, *"I am fully prepared to work with your cultural preferences".* What happened next was not what Dan expected. The VP looked at him with incredulity. He was clearly angry. He turned to his secretary and started talking about other issues, ignoring Dan for a while. In fact, the rest of the meeting was held in a frosty atmosphere.

Although Dan tried very hard to appear enthusiastic, his client remained formal and remote. He made very little effort to engage with the details of the project and raised several questions and doubts that did not previously seem to be an issue. Dan was frustrated. Clearly the French VP was having a difficult day, and Dan was getting the brunt of it! Or was it something he should have done differently at the start?

Reflect

a. Why do you think the French VP reacted the way he did?
b. What do you think Dan did wrong?
c. What should he have done after the VP reacted as he did?

In this case study example, we see that Dan was willing to 'do in Rome what the Romans do', but things went wrong. His company gave him a project which involved Engaging with the unfamiliar (the E of E4A) and he was excited about doing so. He was aware that there might be some cultural issues that he needed to take into account, and so he Attended to that by doing some preliminary reading (the first two As—Attend + Ask—of E4A). What then went wrong?

The process of Analysing

Dan knew that acquiring cultural knowledge about the French working environment would be a good idea. This is in line with our explanation in Chapter 3 of the importance of Global Knowledge and Understanding. However, while knowing about other cultures—both prevalent Practices and Perspectives as well as what we called PESTLE knowledge—can prove useful, no book or training programme alone can prepare anyone for responding appropriately to a real-life situation. In fact, there is quite a danger that armed only with a theoretical knowledge of another culture, any person may fall into the same trap as Dan did, misjudging and misusing what they think they know.

Reading about French culture was a good first step and being prepared to be flexible was certainly good advice. However, Dan then made a number of mistakes, particularly relating to reflecting on what he had read and what he experienced. First, he assumed that general traits of the French culture were the only reason that could explain the behaviour of his client that day. He also assumed that it was acceptable to talk explicitly about this—effectively referring to a hidden Cultural Perspective, as if it was an accepted and talked about Practice.

He also failed to consider the nature of the relationship between him and his client, wrongly assuming greater hierarchical equality than the French client did. Finally, observing his client responding in an unexpected way to what Dan considered a 'light-hearted' attempt to establish rapport, Dan assumed that it was his client who did not understand or was too preoccupied to appreciate his efforts and took no further steps to 'repair' the situation.

In other words, Dan failed to Analyse (the third A of E4A) what he had learned from his reading, not reflecting on it critically or considering how it might apply in concrete situations. Years later, thinking back on this experience, Dan said:

> *"To this day I cringe about how arrogant I was. I realise now that I effectively told my client he had no regard for business conventions that day—and this coming from a junior upstart! It was awful. No wonder he felt insulted and froze me out after that. It was very traumatic, but the experience taught me a lot. For one thing that understanding culture is as much about understanding your own cultural assumptions and that you have to be very careful how you apply what you think you know about someone's culture to a specific situation and context. In retrospect, I would have done much better to have asked my colleagues to tell me about the company and the specific VP and their experience of working with them. Finally, I learned that being flexible does not just mean being prepared to adapt to others' work patterns and preferences. It also means being able to read a real-life situation and being mindful and responsive to it."*

In these reflections, Dan identifies several key points:

- He asked the wrong questions of the wrong sources.
- He was lacking self-awareness.
- He interpreted adaptation too narrowly.

What happens in a particular situation is not just a matter of the 'other culture'. Being aware of our own cultural assumptions and preferences is equally important, as well as being able to understand and manage the specific dynamics of the situation in which we find ourselves.

This is complex because it is influenced not only by cultural conditioning and assumptions, but also by the purpose of the interaction, the overall context, as well as the relationship between the individuals. Global Fitness in these situations therefore involves:

- Being prepared by understanding the potential differences and how they may affect the interaction.
- Having the awareness, sensitivity, and flexibility to 'read' what is happening.

- Checking potentially faulty assumptions and misunderstandings.
- Adapting your response accordingly.

Below we describe two tools and practices you can use to develop your skills in these areas. The first, the 3R Review tool, will help you interpret unexpected incidents; the second, the SOS Adapt tool will help you adapt, if needed.

The 3R Review tool: Reflecting on unexpected incidents

The 3R Review tool—Report, Reflect, Re-evaluate—provides a valuable framework that can help you analyse your reactions to unexpected or unwanted experiences. It helps you to develop your cognitive flexibility and self-awareness 'muscles'; it enhances your self-knowledge, gets you used to questioning your assumptions and interpretations and makes you more open to multiple perspectives. In other words, it plays an important role in supporting your transformational learning and thereby helping you on your journey towards Global Fitness.

This tool is extremely valuable when you have experienced something upsetting, annoying or confusing and when you want or need to understand why it happened and manage your reactions. We start by considering Case Study 6.2 and then explain the tool.

Case Study 6.2: Criticism at work

Clara was devastated. She was working really hard in her new role as a communications manager for a complex global change project in a multinational corporation. She thought she was doing a good job; however, she was finding it hard to produce speedy press releases, as it was not one of the things she had done before, and English was not her native language. She knew she was taking longer than ideal, but thought she was making progress and that given time she would get there. So, she was taken aback when her boss called her into the office and said to her: "You are clearly struggling with this. Give it to Peter to do and concentrate on your other jobs".

Clara tried to argue for a little more time, but Angela, her boss said, "We are running out of time. It's better this way, just do it". Clara felt upset and demotivated, particularly because she thought she was getting on well with Angela and overall, she was doing a good job. She tried to work on her other projects but found it difficult to concentrate. So she rang her mentor, Julie, for advice. "Only yesterday Angela told me she thought you were doing a very good job", Julie said. "Are you sure you did not misunderstand? Tell me again what happened."

Julie took Clara through a process of analytic reflection using the 3R Review tool (see Figure 6.1). This simple tool is particularly useful when you experience disagreement, misunderstanding or conflict and need to understand, reflect on, and manage your reactions. Analysing a critical incident, like the episodes Clara or Dan related, in a systematic way helps you to understand and re-evaluate your own and others' assumptions and responses in context and to reflect on how you might approach the same situation differently in the future.

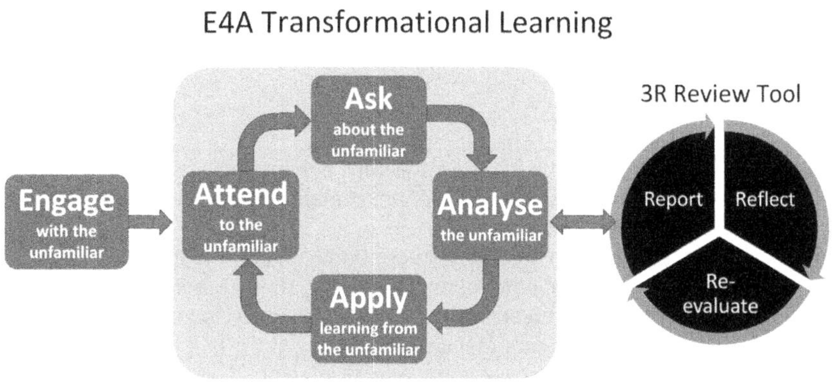

E4A Transformational Learning

Figure 6.1: The 3R Review tool and its links with E4A transformational learning

Although you could use the 3Rs on your own, it is helpful to have someone who can ask you questions, challenge your thinking and gradually work out alternative interpretations of what you describe. So, we would recommend you do this with a friend or colleague where possible, particularly someone who has had their own experience of intercultural interaction.

Once you identify the situation you want to analyse, there are 3 steps to the process, as shown in Figure 6.1 and explained below.

STEP 1

Report	Describe what happened in as much detail as possible: • Describe the setting. • Identify who was involved. • Explain step by step what happened (i.e., who said or did what). • Describe your and other people's reactions, including what your thoughts were, how you felt and what you did.

This should be about the facts: what happened, how you felt, and how others reacted. You should try to remain as objective as possible and avoid interpretations or judgements. For example: "He raised his voice and started speaking fast" is ok, but "he got angry and started shouting at me like a madman" is not. The first describes what happened. The second gives that event a particular emotive meaning, which reflects your first automatic interpretation, but may not be what was intended by the other person.

When Clara was describing what happened, she said "Angela was very dismissive of my work. She clearly doesn't think I can do the job. She thinks Peter is better than me. She does not appreciate how hard I have been trying....". Julie interrupted her: "Try not to jump to conclusions; take a deep breath and just describe what happened; what did she actually say?"

STEP 2

Reflect	Question what happened and why, trying to take alternative viewpoints and seek different explanations, with the help of a colleague or coach: • Explore the reasons for your behaviour and your reactions—what typical patterns of behaviour (i.e., your behavioural expectations) and / or underlying cultural assumptions might be influencing your reactions? • Explore the possible underlying influences on the other person's behaviour—why do you think the other person did what they did? • Ask for or seek alternative explanations—could there be a different meaning/reasons for what happened?

This part of the process may not be easy. People are often unaware of and/or misinterpret the reasons for their behaviours and those of others, especially if these are based on deeply held, 'hidden' cultural assumptions (i.e. Cultural Perspectives), which are not usually questioned on a day-to-day basis.

In our example, Clara, although she wasn't a native speaker of English, was used to a British work environment where a manager's critical feedback and request for an action would normally be 'cushioned' by carefully chosen, indirect language. She therefore interpreted Angela's directness as total rejection. Furthermore, she did not see that her own approach to time management—believing that it was possible to take the time to keep working on something until it was good enough—was in conflict with Angela's more experienced judgement of the urgency of the situation and of the need to keep within the project budget.

To help Clara reflect on these different practices and perspectives Julie asked: "What if Angela had said 'since we are pressed for time would you mind focusing on your other work; we could always ask Peter to give you a hand with the press release as that's his main thing'. Would you have reacted the same way?"

STEP 3

Re-evaluate	• Revisit your understanding of what happened and why. • What have you learned about yourself and your cultural preferences and assumptions? • Reflect on what you could have done differently and how you may approach a similar episode in the future.

Clearly, the quality and depth of this step will depend on the support you get from your colleague and your own knowledge and expertise. The more you engage in doing this kind of reflection, the better and more nuanced your re-evaluations will be and the richer your personal insights and learning. Do not be afraid to revisit and question early evaluations with the hindsight of new experience and to test your conclusions with others, particularly those who might have shared in the same interaction.

With Julie's help, Clara reflected on her own assumptions about feedback and deadlines and came to see that what she thought was a disastrous rejection by her new boss was simply a very direct piece of feedback in a context of increased time pressure. She was able to focus on her other work and later that week she was complimented by her boss and others on her strategic action plan. Clara went on to work very effectively with Angela and learned to recognise and handle direct feedback and even give direct feedback much more effectively herself.

Trying out the 3R Review tool for yourself

To help you gain confidence and familiarity with the 3R Review tool, we offer two follow-up activities below.

Activity 6.1: Reflecting on a critical incident

First read the following incident:

Karin, a German student in a British university, was increasingly exasperated by the way her tutors gave feedback in class. At the end of one of her lectures she stayed behind, walked up to the tutor and said "I'm afraid I do not understand all of you British tutors. Whenever one of us says something in response to one of your questions, even when the answer is clearly wrong, you do not correct us. You always say something positive like 'that's a very good point' or something annoying like that. But you never tell us that we are actually making a mistake. I want to be clearly told when I am wrong and when I am not. How else am I supposed to learn?"

The tutor, who was not British, was taken aback by Karin's 'blunt outburst', but promised to think about how to address it. She felt that Karin did not appreciate the pedagogic importance of encouraging people to speak up. She also later reflected that even though many of the staff at the university were also German, they had adopted the same approach to giving feedback to students. She shared the feedback with her colleagues but found it difficult to make any changes to accommodate Karin's request.

Reflect

a. If you were supporting Karin and her tutor in a 3R exercise, what questions would you ask them to help them consider each other's perspective?

	Questions to Karin	**Questions to Karin's tutor**
Report		
Reflect		
Re-evaluate		

Activity 6.2: Reflecting on a personal critical incident

Think back to a situation in which you experienced a misunderstanding or conflict or felt uncomfortable in an intercultural encounter. Use the 3R Review tool to describe it to a partner, reflect on what happened and evaluate your and others' responses.

Report	
Reflect	
Re-evaluate	
What have you learned about yourself?	

The SOS Adapt tool: A tool for effective adaptation behaviour

Introduction

People do not need to travel to a different country to experience intercultural conflict. It can often happen when they simply change jobs or join a new group or organisation for social or other reasons. In situations like these, Global Fitness can make the difference between success and failure in the new environment. Whereas someone lacking this kind of fitness would automatically reach for their familiar frames of reference to interpret what they see people doing around them, a person with more Global Fitness would be able to use their observation, questioning and slower judgement 'muscles' to consider whether that automatic first impression is indeed correct or needs adjusting. They would then be able to better calibrate their personal response, as a result. Consider Case Study 6.3.

Case Study 6.3: An 'unacceptable' work culture

Jasper accepted the position of managing director of a small business consultancy with excitement. A high-flyer, with an impressive track record in senior roles in large service companies, he was certain that he had what it takes to succeed. His first days in the job were challenging; he observed his new team turn up for work late, take long lunches, go out mid-work, and 'being too familiar with clients'. When he asked for plans and key performance indicators, he was told there were none. Yes, the little company was profitable, but imagine what they would be able to do 'when he whipped them into shape'. Jasper started by introducing some of the products and practices he was used to from his work in larger companies, for example early Monday morning meetings which everyone had to attend. He was surprised when his team resisted this, and people refused to turn up. "How dare they," he thought, "after all I am the boss!"

Reflect

a. Why do you think Jasper's approach was met with resistance?
b. What did Jasper fail to understand about the culture of the organisation he joined?
c. What would you have done if you had been in Jasper's shoes?

Having worked in large, formal business service conglomerates, with very well-defined practices and rules all his professional life, Jasper assumed that people in his new company were lazy, unprofessional, and undisciplined, simply because they did not behave in ways he recognised as 'normal'. Had he taken a step back to observe and understand how the local culture worked, he would have also seen people working hard through nights and weekends to deliver projects, and that much of the creative work happened over lunch, informal walks, and even at off-site meetings, which were important rituals in this highly relationship-oriented organisation. He would also have noticed that seniority did not mean much in this very egalitarian workplace and that the way to get people to do things was not through hierarchy, but through trust and relationships. Jasper did not, however, consider any of this. Convinced that he was in the right, he kept pushing harder. A few months later, unable to do any of the things he set out to, he left the company.

Selecting your focus

When you find yourself in a new cultural environment it is important to pay close attention to the Products and Practices around you, even if they look familiar. Using a diary or other similar tool (something along the lines of Table 6.1 below) and focusing on particular contexts (for example business meetings, social events etc), note down the unexpected behavioural patterns you see in these settings. Then consider your reactions and make a note of these too. Then use your notes to help you select a behavioural pattern to work on.

Table 6.1: Template to help notice unexpected patterns of behaviour

	Work life	**Social life**
Event/setting	e.g., Departmental meeting	e.g., Meal at friend's home
Behaviour • What happens? • What do people do? • What are the outcomes?		
Personal reaction • How similar/different is this to your experience? • How do you personally respond to this product or practice? How does it make you feel? Why? • What do you think it means?		

Introducing the SOS Adapt tool

Once you have selected a behavioural pattern to focus on, the SOS Adapt tool will help you take the necessary steps to adjust (if need be). As Figure 6.2 shows, it entails three recurring elements: Study, Observe, and Stretch.

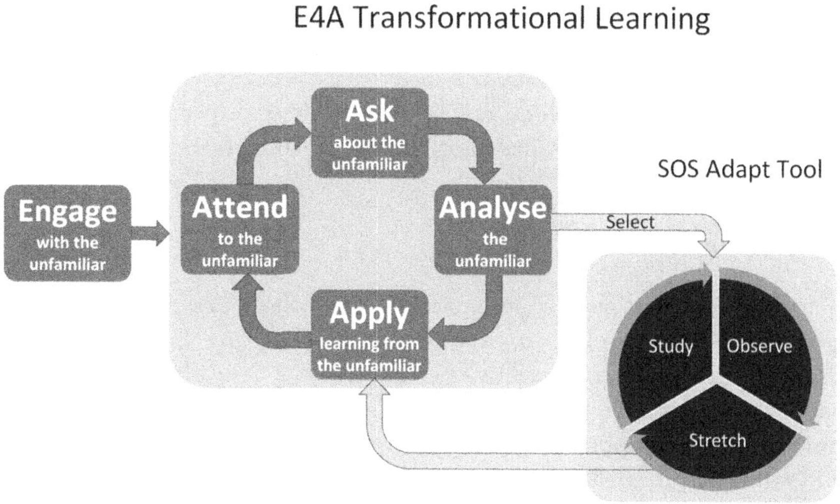

E4A Transformational Learning

Figure 6.2: The SOS Adapt tool and its links with E4A transformational learning

Study

Thinking first of 'Study', it is often good to talk to people who can function as cultural informants—people who know, for example, the country culture or organisational culture well—about the behavioural pattern you want to focus on, asking questions like: Why does this happen? What are they actually doing? It is possible that you may get many different answers and that often people may not be clear about the underlying reason something happens. After all, to paraphrase Edward Hall, 'culture is very effective at hiding itself from its own participants'.[34]

What the questioning will help you do, however, is to test your own initial assumptions about the meaning you have given to the behaviours you observe and to consider alternative potential meanings and perspectives. If Jasper had asked his team about their long lunch breaks for example, while they may not have said "because relationships are very important here", they may have said "because that's when we do some of our best thinking, and you should join us some time".

Once you have some insights from culture insiders, you should consider what you know about the culture—what, for example, you have read in textbooks—and/or use expert advice (e.g., see the example of John in Case Study 9.6) to dig deeper into your cultural analysis. What might these different Products and Practices indicate about important underlying

---

[34] Hall, E.T. (1973). *The silent language*. New York, NY: Anchor Books. (Originally published in 1959 by DoubleDay.)

Cultural Perspectives, for example attitudes to hierarchy, rules, or time? And what does any difference between your initial interpretation and the local meanings suggest about the differences between your Perspectives and preferences and the local culture? In all these respects, draw on the Global Knowledge and Understanding you've gained from the chapters in Part 1 of this book.

Observe and stretch

Having gained insights from studying the behavioural pattern you've selected, the next step is to move into the recurring SOS sequence—Study→Observe→Stretch as illustrated in Figure 6.2. It involves careful observation, behavioural stretching, and more questioning and reflecting (including on your own assumptions and actions), and all of this requires an open mind and willingness to challenge your own mindset.

Intercultural competence scholar and consultant Andy Molinsky[35] suggests that in situations like these, successful adaptation depends on identifying the 'optimum zone of performance'. This does not mean completely adopting behaviours that are strange to you, particularly if they make you feel uncomfortable. Rather it involves finding a way to stretch your own behavioural range (your personal comfort zone) just enough to get close to local expectations. Not 'When in Rome do as the Romans' but go as far down the road to Rome as you feel comfortable with. Table 6.2 explains how the recurrent SOS steps could unfold.

Table 6.2: The recurring SOS (Study, Observe, Stretch) moves to aid in effective adaptation

SOS recurring steps	Guidance
Identify a good reason to change	Why does this matter? (link to your specific purpose and/or your inner values) What will be the benefits to you and others if you do this? What would be the implications if you do not?
Find a small change to make which feels more manageable	What can you do which brings you closer to the local expected behaviour without feeling too uncomfortable?

(Continued)

---

[35]   Molinsky, A. (2013). *Global dexterity*. Boston, MA: Harvard Business Review Press.

Table 6.2: Continued

SOS recurring steps	Guidance
Try it in a safe space	Is there an individual group or situation where there is some trust / where it will be ok to 'get it wrong' and you can get some good feedback either way?
Get feedback and adjust	Talk to someone you trust about what happened; how did they see it from their point of view? What would they recommend you do differently next time?
Try again	Try the same behaviour again, using the feedback to help you adjust
Fine-tune (aim to develop 'muscle memory')	Keep reflecting on what happens as you develop the behaviour and use the behaviour in different settings. What appears to work best? Why? What makes you feel more comfortable? Why?

As can be seen from Table 6.2, any adaptation comes at the end of an SOS development process—it doesn't happen overnight. Bit by bit, you will be able to apply your learning to the unfamiliar behaviour and fine-tune how you perform it (see Figure 6.2 for the links between the SOS Adapt tool and E4A transformational learning steps).

To help bring this alive, consider Case Study 6.4.

Case Study 6.4: The challenge of small talk

Aleksy, a Polish engineer, loved his new job. After a very successful period in Switzerland, where the headquarters of his firm were based, he was sent for a short assignment to Britain. There he was expected to train the local engineering team on the new product that the company was about to introduce. Aleksy was very proud that he had been selected to do that and was determined to make a success of his assignment. He prepared very well for every meeting, setting clear objectives and agendas, making detailed slides and even setting preparation work for his co-workers.

However, he was frustrated to find that they didn't seem to take the training seriously. They would turn up to the meetings, pick up a cup of coffee and then spend as much as 15 minutes talking about irrelevant things, like what they did at the weekend, the rugby, or the weather! In fact, every meeting which Aleksy attended seemed to start with this 'irrelevant talk' ritual. Discussing it with his mentor, a German senior manager, was helpful as she pointed out that there was a function to this 'small talk'. "Most people here feel uncomfortable getting straight to work without establishing some kind of rapport first. That's what this small talk does—it establishes connection, trust. It says, now we have something in common, we can work together better. I know you may not be used to this, but you will get on much better with your teammates if you do learn to participate in the small talk."

Aleksy, half-heartedly tried to imitate his colleagues and participate in the small talk but he felt very uncomfortable: "Why do I have to pretend to be interested in the weather and what people did at the weekend when I am not! This is not who I am!" he complained.

Reflect

a. Why do you think Aleksy found it difficult to change his behaviour?
b. Should someone like Aleksy have to change the way they do things in order to fit in, if it makes them feel uncomfortable?
c. What could Aleksy do to adjust his behaviour successfully?

Aleksy knew that, however uncomfortable 'small talk' made him feel, he somehow had to master it as he needed to build rapport with the local engineers for the training to succeed. He noticed that it was much easier to talk to one of his teammates, because they both had an interest in the same kind of music; 'small talk' with Jack became about the bands they liked and the music gigs they had been to. Aleksy reflected that this was easy to do and felt natural. In other words, he found the common ground that we noted in Chapter 5 is so important.

He commented afterwards as follows:

Case Study 6.5: Overcoming the challenge of small talk	
"I realised that while I could not pretend to care about the weather or the rugby, there were several topics that my team mates and I had in common, from young children, to politics, to travel that I would very happily talk about… These may not have been the traditional small talk topics, but I felt that for me to do this well, I would have to talk about things that meant something to me. I made a point of finding out about each of my teammates and made sure I used the right topic with the right person or group. I did think about it a lot at the beginning and did do a couple of 'dry-runs' with a smaller group, asking Jack for feedback. I must admit I did not always get it right, but my teammates were forgiving; I learned from both my successes and my failures (I learned that laughing at your own gaffes worked really well with this group for example) and it has become easier. I now don't really think much about it; I just do it. The other day I even caught myself enjoying it! I would never have believed it!"	Identifying topics of common interest Aleksy's 'study' moves Aleksy's fine-tuning through 'study-observe—stretch' moves Aleksy's successful application and adaptation

Trying out the SOS Adapt tool for yourself

Activity 6.3 provides an opportunity to try using the SOS Adapt tool for yourself.

Activity 6.3: Practising adapting	
Think about a behaviour outside your comfort zone that you need to learn to adjust to when in a particular context. Use the steps below to plan and try altering that behaviour a little.	
SOS recurring steps	**Notes**
Identify a good reason to change	
Find a small change to make that feels more manageable	
Try it in a safe space	
Get feedback, reflect, and adjust	
Try again (get feedback, reflect, and adjust)	
Fine-tune	

What have you learned about yourself?

Key takeaways

Key Insights	Applications for practice
• Adaptation is more complex than "When in Rome, do as the Romans do." • The E4A transformational learning framework outlines the developmental steps. • Two particularly important steps in the adaptation process are (a) asking questions and (b) analysing the information you receive or obtain.	• Use the 3R Review tool (Report, Reflect, Re-evaluate) to understand an event that was unexpected in some way and that annoyed you, upset you and/or made you feel uncomfortable. • Use the SOS Adapt tool (Study, Observe, Stretch) to consider and plan how to adapt your behaviour to suit the context.

7

How to build global relationships and enhance rapport

Introduction

Talking about the development of the Covid vaccine[36], Pfizer's Kathrin Jansen recalled how early in the pandemic she was asked by her long-term collaborator in Germany, BioNTech's Uğur Şahin, if she was interested in helping to develop a vaccine against Covid. She agreed immediately and they started collaborating straight away. In fact, they began working together on the project before any official contracts were signed. Jansen went on to explain that this would not have been possible without the strength of the relationship that existed between her and the German team. In an industry where the focus on safety and fear of litigation make people very cautious and risk-averse, and processes are deliberately slow and rigid, it was the trusting relationship between Jansen and Şahin that made it possible to cut through all this and almost literally save the world.

In Chapter 5, we emphasised the importance of building and maintaining rapport for Global Fitness and explained the significance of finding common ground. Jansen and Şahin had a lot in common—both scientists working in the same field, both having grown up and been educated in Germany, both having left their home country early in their lives (in Jansen's case fleeing from East to West Germany, in Şahin's emigrating to Germany from Turkey). They spoke the same language in more than one sense. A history of long-term collaboration gave them the opportunity to discover and build on those similarities and work on their differences too.

However, what do you do when you have a difficult relationship, and this is creating problems and misunderstandings? Our aim in this chapter is to explore the practical steps that can be taken to build rapport by:

- Attending to judgements that affect rapport
- Understanding and addressing the different types of challenge people face in rapport management

---

[36] *BBC Horizon Special: The Vaccine*. June 2021, BBC2. Retrieved from https://www.bbc.co.uk/programmes/m000x2tf

- 'Stretching' your comfort zone
- Identifying blind spots and overcoming them
- Becoming conscious of your group identities and life story
- Finding ways to build bridges and global connections

Introductory case study

Case Study 7.1 concerns a young project manager, working in the UK, who experienced a relationship clash.

Case Study 7.1: A relationship clash

Miranda increasingly dreaded going into the office. Since Mike had joined the team that she was managing, the easy, collegiate atmosphere had disappeared. There was more and more friction, Mike refused to do what she asked of him, and she now even found Mike turning all the engineers in the team against her! Yesterday she discovered she had been excluded from the after-work pub invite, even though she had worked as hard as everyone else to address the problems identified in an earlier meeting.

Miranda had to admit she did not like Mike and knew he did not like her. Despite her attempts to be friendly, he remained detached and frequently complained that she came too close to him when they were talking. He also said that she was too loud and 'pointed at him in an accusatory way'. Miranda thought that Mike was being ridiculous—that he was being oversensitive to what after all was simply her natural style of communication. As far as she knew, none of the others in the team had a problem with that.

She spoke to her boss hoping to get some understanding, but her boss suggested she should look at things she could do to fix it. 'But it is not me, it's him! He was antagonistic right from the start,' Miranda complained. 'Are you sure? He seems to have good relationships with the rest of us…." her boss said.

Reflect

a. Why do you think Miranda's boss thought this was Miranda's problem to solve?
b. How would you have reacted if you had been in Miranda's and in Mike's shoes?
c. What do you think Miranda could have done to address the issue?

In Chapter 5 we talked about the importance of initial expectations and judgements in helping to establish and manage rapport with others. It is clear in this case that both Mike and Miranda's initial expectations of how they should work together were not met. As a result, they both ended up making negative judgements of each other. These judgements were further reinforced by their respective ongoing behaviour, such as excluding Miranda from social activities.

How did this happen? It would be worth analysing the encounter using the judgement process we discussed in Chapter 5 (see Figure 5.1). Although we do not have Mike's direct testimony, we can see from Miranda's account that he was uncomfortable with her style of communication and management. His expectations of being accepted and welcomed as a new member of the team were compromised since he found Miranda's behaviour unwelcoming.

For her part, Miranda's expectations that Mike would fit in and accept her were also not met. Her evaluative judgements of Mike were that he was too detached, not doing what she asked him to do, 'turning others against her' and so on, and thus endangering her personal goals (e.g., furthering her career) and the goals of the project.

For his part, Mike clearly felt that his rights (for example for his personal space not to be 'invaded' by Miranda) were not being met and that Miranda was not being respectful towards him. As we saw in Chapters 3 and 4, communication Practices, including those that deal with paralinguistic aspects of communication such as tone of voice, body language and proximity may be very different in different cultures and these differences when not understood or attended to can be face-threatening and create misunderstanding. This happened in this case: whereas Miranda thought she was simply being herself, Mike saw disrespect and aggression. The stage was set for negativity and loss of rapport on both sides.

Sadly, this kind of situation at work is not uncommon and, once created, it can be difficult to overcome. We consider possible reasons why and suggest some ways of addressing the challenges.

Attending to rapport feedback—overcoming relationship challenges

One of the key skills in building and maintaining rapport is the ability to be mindful of and responsive to feedback from others on your interaction behaviour. Interestingly, Miranda was aware of what aspects of her behaviour Mike objected to:

- Her non-verbal behaviour: being physically too close to him when talking, and pointing at him.
- Her manner of communication: 'too loud'.

Yet she dismissed his concerns as 'ridiculous', maintaining that he was being over-sensitive towards her 'natural style' of interaction. She also wasn't sure what she could do to overcome the problem. Later she commented:

> *"Mike's negativity towards me really took me by surprise. I could see that he was well liked by the others and worked well with them, so that puzzled me. Even when I reflected that I may have contributed to the problem, I found it difficult to know how to bridge the gap between us."*

If we apply the E4A transformational learning tool (see Introduction to Part 2 and Chapter 6) to this situation, we can note that Miranda appears to be stuck at the Attend point. Although she paid attention to the issues in the sense that she was consciously aware of them, and she reflected a little, she did not make any great effort to address them. Rather, she dismissed Mike's concerns and blamed their relationship problems mostly on him. In other words, she did not seriously move to the Ask, Analyse, and Apply steps of the E4A sequence, but stopped at Attend. What then might be the reasons for that?

Types of challenge that may hinder adaptation

Scholar and consultant Andy Molinsky[37] maintains that there are three main reasons why people may find it difficult to adapt their behaviour:

- An authenticity challenge: the feeling that their current behaviour is a reflection of their core identity and that to behave in a different way would seem inauthentic or false in some way.
- A resentment challenge: the feeling that it is annoying and burdensome to have to change behaviour to suit others.
- A competence challenge: the feeling that they don't know how to overcome the problem and behave in a way that others want.

It seems that for Miranda there were elements of all three challenges. She felt her current behaviour was her 'natural style' and so probably felt it was part of her identity; in other words, changing it would likely be an authenticity challenge for her. She also regarded the issue as Mike's fault and hence it was his responsibility to change, not hers, saying *"It's not me, it's him"*, perhaps suggesting a resentment challenge. She also acknowledged that she didn't know how to bridge the gap—a competence challenge.

In Case Study 6.4, a similar set of challenges for Aleksy can be noted. He felt uncomfortable trying to engage in small talk—a key tool of relationship building in some cultures—and protested *"This is not who I am"*, thus reflecting an authenticity challenge. He also complained *"Why do I have to pretend to be interested in the weather and what people did at the weekend when I'm not"*, indicating a resentment challenge. In contrast to Miranda, Aleksy found ways to overcome these problems, using reflection and planning.

Had Miranda followed similar steps to reflect on her situation and challenges, she could have resolved her dilemma. Table 7.1 below shows how she could have used the 3R Review tool to reflect on the three adaptation challenges she faced.

---

[37]   Molinsky, A. (2013). *Global dexterity*. Boston, MA: Harvard Business Review Press.

Table 7.1: Using the 3R Review tool to help address adaptation challenges

Report (to yourself)	Authenticity challenge	Why is this communication behaviour important to me? How does changing this behaviour (as Mike demands) challenge my sense of who I am? How genuine does it feel for me to change?
	Resentment challenge	How necessary do I feel it is to engage in this behaviour change?
	Competence challenge	How easy or difficult is it to do so?
Reflect	Authenticity challenge	How could changing/adapting my communication behaviour towards Mike help me to achieve my goals for this team/project?
	Resentment challenge	How could changing my behaviour link with one or more of my values?
	Competence challenge	Given I am finding it difficult, what or who could help me change?
Re-evaluate	Authenticity challenge	Re-assess the link between this behaviour and identity: e.g., Although I am comfortable with this style, toning it down to achieve better rapport with Mike does not mean I am losing my sense of who I am. On the contrary, I am gaining by being included in the group and being a more effective project manager
	Resentment challenge	Re-assess link between the behaviour and the need for you to change: e.g., If I change, it will help the project and the team succeed; it will make work fun again
	Competence challenge	Plan one concrete step you can take to work on the behaviour: e.g., I will ask others about my communication and ask for advice. At the next meeting with Mike I will .....

Having identified and worked through the issues, the next step is to reduce the gap between the behaviour that each person is expecting, bringing them closer together. A helpful way of doing this is by stretching their comfort zones—that is, the range of behaviour that each feels comfortable with. The SOS Adapt tool that we introduced in Chapter 6 can help with this, and we noted there how Aleksy used it successfully.

Since everyone tolerates a certain range of 'acceptable' behaviour, there is no need to change your behaviour completely to match the other person's wishes exactly. That could be too challenging in terms of authenticity, resentment and/or competence. Rather the aim is gradually to 'stretch' your comfort zone so that part of it can just overlap with what you think the other person will feel comfortable with. This means changing your behaviour bit by bit, thereby stretching and strengthening your 'comfort zone muscles'.

Figure 7.1 illustrates this with regard to Miranda and Mike and physical distance / closeness. For Miranda it would mean gradually increasing the physical distance between her and Mike, so that she remains comfortable with the progressive amount of distance, until eventually she has stretched her comfort zone sufficiently not to make Mike feel uncomfortable. In the figure it is only Miranda who stretches her comfort zone, and this may be necessary when adjusting to a group of others. If it is just between two individuals, ideally both should stretch their comfort zones, although that may not always be possible.

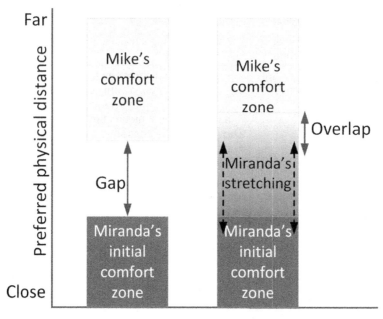

Figure 7.1: Stretching to adapt and achieve overlap in comfort zones

Now try this out for yourself by working on Activity 7.1.

Activity 7.1: Learning to stretch

1. Reflecting on your interactions with others (e.g., colleagues), select a behaviour or style that you feel uncomfortable with but that you think others expect from you.
2. Reflect on it in the manner shown in Table 7.1.
3. Plan how you could gradually adapt your behaviour to bring it closer to what others are expecting, using the SOS Adapt tool (see Activity 6.2)

Recognising blind spots and overcoming them

As well as paying attention to your preferred interaction style and how that may affect the judgements that you and others make, it is also important to seek to identify any potential blind spots and sub-conscious assumptions, which might influence the judgements you make of others.

Some years after the events discussed in Case Study 7.1, Miranda took part in a professional development exercise which encouraged her to plot her trust network—those people she was close to and trusted at work and socially—in order to identify her connection weak points or blind spots. Unexpectedly, this helped her gain further insights into her difficulties with Mike. She reflected: *"One of the things that became very obvious to me was, that although my network of friends and trusted colleagues was very diverse, I knew no-one remotely like Mike. He was very different from me in many cultural categories (ethnicity, age, education, professional background, socio-economic background), and, as a result, I lacked the background knowledge to understand him. I suspect this was the case for him too. And because the communication style differences got in the way, neither of us tried to get to know the other better—something that we could and should have done. What we did instead was to reach for the ready-made stereotypes that were already in our heads. I dismissed Mike as uncooperative, unfriendly, ridiculous, and small-minded and I dread to think what he thought of me!"*

In-group—out-group judgements

In Chapter 5, we noted that one of the key issues when building relationships with culturally diverse others results from our group memberships and the judgements we make about those we consider members of the in-group. These judgements may be different in nature from the judgements we form about those perceived as outsiders. People tend to attribute positive characteristics to the former and are prepared to see them in more complex terms. This makes it easier to explore what people have in common beyond the obvious categories (for example, shared interests and passions or common experiences in the past). In contrast, we often see the latter in more simplistic terms. As Miranda discovered, this can be a significant barrier in finding common ground and building bridges.

So, take a few moments to reflect on your own relationship networks and potential blind spots (Activity 7.2). What do you see that's interesting?

Activity 7.2: Exploring potential relationship blind spots

a. Think of a context in which you have recently found yourself—it could be your work environment or a specific social setting—and try to plot your most trusting relationships.
b. Consider if there are any social group members missing from your list.
c. Reflect on what this might indicate about your potential relationship blind spots

Who	In common	Main differences

Social group members missing from my trusted list

My potential relationship blind spots

Personal partially conscious biases

Actually, people's blind spots are not always so hidden. Sometimes people may have personal biases that they are conscious (or partially conscious) of. This can become apparent if they just pay attention to their reactions and the lightning quick judgements they may make. Becoming more aware of our spontaneous judgements is important for rapport purposes in order to avoid unfairness and potential discrimination.

Consider Activity 7.3. Try to be completely honest with yourself—after all, everyone has biases of some sort and being aware of them is an important first step in managing them. Only you yourself will know how you grade yourself—unless of course you choose to share with someone else—so there's no personal risk.

Activity 7.3: Exploring partially conscious biases						
When you meet another person for the first time in a work context, what spontaneous reaction do you usually have if they …						
	Negative spontaneous reaction		**No particular reaction**		**Positive spontaneous reaction**	
Have a strong accent that to you sounds uneducated	1	2	3	4	5	
Are much taller or shorter than you	1	2	3	4	5	
Are significantly overweight or underweight	1	2	3	4	5	
Have difficulty communicating in the working language	1	2	3	4	5	
Are from a different ethnic group	1	2	3	4	5	
Have a physical disability	1	2	3	4	5	
Are dressed in a way that you regard as sexually provocative	1	2	3	4	5	
Are clearly from a different country than you	1	2	3	4	5	
Show their religious belief through their dress or jewellery	1	2	3	4	5	
[Add other noticeable characteristics, if you wish…]	1	2	3	4	5	

Reflect

Now consider your responses. If you had a negative spontaneous reaction to any characteristic (i.e., rated it 1 or 2) or a positive spontaneous reaction (i.e., rated it 4 or 5), consider:

1. Does your initial reaction stay with you, or does it quickly become less or disappear? Consider why this happens.

Now move on to Activity 7.4.

Activity 7.4: Considering your spontaneous reactions in relation to your own key group identities and values

Often people's spontaneous judgements are related to their social group memberships and personal values.

Look back at your responses to Activity 7.3 and consider the following questions:

1. What do your reactions indicate about your personal values and preferences?
2. How do they map against your group identities (i.e., the social groups you belong to)?

In answering these two questions, we recommend the following:

a. Draw up a list of your own key social group identities, e.g., nationality, ethnicity, profession, position / role, education, age, gender, religion, language(s), wealth, physical appearance. There may be other group identity features that are important to you, so think about those too
b. Then look back at Activity 2.3 and the top values that you selected there. Add them here and any others you now feel are important for you

My key social group identities	**My important values**
....	....
....	....
....	....
....	....
....	....
....	....
....	....

Overcoming personal biases

Consider Case Study 7.2, reported by a Turkish professional woman, Elif, who works for a Dutch company in Ankara. Educated in an international school in Turkey and having studied abroad, she has already forged a successful managerial career working in several European multinationals in Turkey and elsewhere in Europe. In the case study, she reflects on her experience of working in diverse cultural environments.

Case Study 7.2: Learning to appreciate the 'other'

"I have always found it easy to work with other Europeans. I love working with Dutch people in my current job. Because of my background and training, I actually find that we have a lot in common.

To be honest, in my new job 'the other' are not the Dutch, but the other Turks. Not the Europeanised professionals like me, who speak several languages and have worked abroad etc., but the people who come from the countryside and wear the head scarf and are religious. This is a difficult thing to admit. They are my fellow countrymen, but like other secular Turks I was brought up with some very negative stereotypes about this other Turkey. Similarly about the Arabs. I had to confront this when I met my fiancé, who is an Arab. We have been fed these very negative ideas growing up. 'They are not like you etc…' These are very deep prejudices—they live in our stomach, not our brain.

But I learned interacting with [my fiancé's] family how much we really have in common, how much I was not able to see. I had to confront my own bias and in the process my sense of who I am has changed too. I can now see I am also Middle Eastern. In fact, I now feel like a bridge between the two cultures."

Reflect

a. How did Elif start to appreciate the 'other'?
b. How might you be able to apply this to your situation?

We see in Elif's story many of the Global Fitness qualities we mentioned in Chapter 2—she is supremely aware of her own background, preferences and biases and shows positive curiosity towards learning about others who are different from her. She shows flexibility and is prepared to connect with others more effectively and, in doing so, she both changes and enriches her own life story and personal and group identity.

In Elif's case she initially perceived Arabs as an out-group but her fundamental openness enabled her to get to know an Arab who later became her fiancé. Her relationship with him then made it easier for her to begin building a bridge with his family and other Arabs and start getting to know them.

Becoming conscious of your developing life story

When considering who you are and what is important to you, it's useful to go a step further and think about personal life stories rather than just labels. We are never just 'German' or 'from the North' or 'musician' or 'parent'. The experiences associated with these labels—experiences of personal growth, loss, strife, achievement, celebration, togetherness, isolation, migration, and so on—become personal stories we tell others and which help us understand, explain, and live out our identities and values.

Think, for example, about Jansen or Şahin, whom we mentioned at the beginning of this chapter. Their families would have heard many times their stories of leaving their countries and all would have had the opportunity to share them with others. Their stories and how others reacted to them over the years will have become part of the kind of Germans they may or may not perceive themselves to be. Similarly, their story of collaborating to produce the BioNTech—Pfizer Covid vaccine will now inevitably become part of their 'scientist / researcher' identity.

To return to Case Study 7.1, Miranda reflected that her 'European / citizen of the world' identity grew out of a story of her growing up in a provincial, small town and being inspired by her parents, who encouraged her to learn languages, read widely and travel, and to look outside to the world for more open attitudes and broader horizons. This helped her to connect effectively with many people who had similar experiences and identities, irrespective of which country they came from. Interacting and building relationships with such people was easier and more meaningful as the many points of connection made potential differences less important and/or easier to navigate. At the same time, Miranda recognised that when it came to people who did not belong in this in-group, like Mike, she lacked any shared background to use as a basis for building the relationship. The common ground had to be built from zero and in Mike's case the initial misjudgements got in the way of making it a positive one.

As you think about your own story, look at Case Study 7.3 and reflect on the questions it raises.

Case Study 7.3: Shifting identities

Helmut, a German manager interviewed in Asia, said: "I have Arabic heritage, so I always felt different growing up in Germany. I intentionally looked for international work that took me to other countries because I was always interested in different people and people who were different like me. But I have discovered that the more I work abroad, the more German I feel. This means that aspects of my identity that are Germanic (at least in my mind), like being direct, believing in taking personal responsibility, have become more important to me and almost less negotiable than when I was in Germany. Having that clarity about who I am and what matters is very important to me as a leader, and it is also important that people understand this when they work with me."

Reflect
a. Have you had similar experiences or realisations to Helmut's?
b. Has an international experience or a new context strengthened or weakened any aspects of your identity?
c. What have been the implications for the way you build relationships/work with others?

Strategies for building relationships

Gaining insights into your own identities, values and stories can not only help you understand your personal reactions to other people but can also be used pro-actively to learn how to build specific relationships. However, what can be done when people don't have any specific context to help them build links? For example, how do you develop a fruitful conversation with a stranger or a colleague who seems to have little in common with you?

Finding and building common ground

One important feature of successful social conversations is finding and building common ground. This can include the following:

- Finding points of common interest.
- Finding shared contacts.
- Finding shared experiences.

For instance, it can include discovering hobbies that you both enjoy, realising that you have mutual friends or colleagues, or discovering that you've both been on holiday to the same place.

Finding such points of shared interest or experience can be extremely useful professionally as well as personally, as Case Study 7.4 illustrates. It reports how Wing-Sin, a Hong Kong manager, uses different aspects of his cultural identity and associated stories to build meaningful relations with different groups of employees in his organisation.

Case Study 7.4: Using common ground to connect

"I am very aware that I am a middle-aged, middle-class Hong Konger, and at work I have a very senior position. But I am also a Christian and my faith is very important to me—this provides sometimes a very strong link to others. I am also someone who was educated in the United States and lived and worked in several countries across Asia, including Australia and Japan. In addition, I am a father of teenage children who are now students. I intentionally use different aspects of who I am to reach out to different people depending on who they are. I tell stories and I ask for their own stories.

For example, I was recently asked to speak to young bankers in our Korean operation. These are colleagues who are university-educated, mostly overseas, many female, similar in age to my own children and early in their career with the Bank. So, I kicked off the session by talking about my university experience in the States and my early personal work experience, how I handled unreasonable requests from seniors and they found it very interesting; with a male senior manager group I would have looked at our points of connection and picked a completely different story."

Reflect

Think of an occasion when you could usefully have used common ground to connect with unfamiliar others:

a. Did you have any difficulty finding common ground to build a connection? Why/why not?
b. What common ground did you refer to or could you have referred to?
c. How did the other person or people react?

Holding social conversations and building common ground is often not as easy as Case Study 7.4 might imply. So, Activity 7.5 identifies a number of ways of engaging in social conversation with those you know little about. Look at the various possibilities and note how often you use each of them.

Activity 7.5: Finding ways of making social conversation					
Consider how often you do the following ...	Rarely				Often
... listen for personal information that the other person mentions and then refer back to it?	1	2	3	4	5
... offer personal information in passing which the other person can build on in the same way?	1	2	3	4	5
... seek common ground—experiences, interests, views you share—with the other person	1	2	3	4	5
... integrate and connect the experiences and views of the other person with your own, rather than seeking contrasts?	1	2	3	4	5
... ask friendly, productive *open* questions rather than less productive *closed* questions?	1	2	3	4	5
... look and sound genuinely interested in the other person and what they have to say?	1	2	3	4	5

Now look at your ratings. Are there some strategies that you could use with someone you don't know well and/or you would like or need to find more common ground with? If so, practise using those strategies and, with the help of the SOS Adapt tool, pay attention to how well they work, fine-tuning your use of them accordingly. Practise them in a mindful manner. If there are strategies that you find uncomfortable, reflect on why this may be using Table 7.1 on the challenges that we introduced earlier in the chapter.

Self-disclosure—sharing 'personal' information

In order to identify aspects of common ground, each party needs to be willing to open up and share something of themselves with the other person (see also above on life stories and Chapter 8 on personal stories). This raises the question as to how appropriate it is to 'self-disclose' in this way, on what kind of issues and in what contexts (see Activity 7.6). Different people are likely to make different evaluations.

Activity 7.6: Sharing 'personal' information

Suppose you were meeting a new potential client for the first time and want to build common ground with them.

1. What type of 'personal' information would you be willing to share?
2. What type of 'personal' information would you be reluctant to share on first meeting?
3. If possible, compare your preferences with a colleague, including someone whom you regard as different from you.

Note: By 'personal' information, we mean things such as family situation, e.g. marital status, children; hobbies; age; salary; holidays.

One of the benefits of building common ground is the sense of affinity or personal closeness and understanding that can emerge. During a Chinese delegation visit to America (the same trip as reported Case Study 3.4), an American speaker used some Chinese characters in his presentation; the delegates were hugely impressed and commented privately afterwards that this had brought them closer.

　　Other strategies for building affinity include:

- Doing things together
- Joking and moaning together
- Helping others
- Appreciating others (e.g., through compliments or expressions of gratitude)
- Gift-giving

Gift-giving

An issue that can be particularly problematic in intercultural contexts is gift-giving. In many cultures, giving gifts—including in professional contexts—is an extremely important way of signalling positive attitudes towards the other and thus may need to be planned extremely thoroughly and carefully.

　　For instance, for the visit referred to in Case Study 3.4, the delegates spent large amounts of time every evening planning in detail exactly what gifts they would give to each organisation and individual they were to meet the next day. Then, in the evening of the following day, they discussed how well their gifts were received. They linked the 'success' of their gift-giving with relational strength and found it hard to understand why the Americans only gave them small gifts in return.[38] Clearly, in many countries, gift giving and receiving raises ethical and indeed legal issues and so can be challenging to handle from a relational point of view. (See Chapter 10 for further discussion.)

Key takeaways

Core insights	Applications for practice
• Many relationship difficulties are due to people blaming others and rejecting any negative feedback on their own behaviour.	• Be sensitive to and respond to feedback on your interaction style when building rapport.
• There is often an unwillingness to change, and this can be due to one of more of the following challenges: authenticity challenge, resentment challenge, competence challenge.	• Be mindful of the judgements and assumptions you may be making when a relationship breaks down.
• People may also have blind spots that hinder them from forming positive relationships with people from certain backgrounds.	• Use the 3R Review tool (Report, Reflect, Re-evaluate) to help you think through any reluctance you may have to change because of authenticity, resentment and/or competence challenges.
• These blind spots may lead people to make assumptions about others on the basis of their group memberships or other characteristics.	• Practise stretching your comfort zone by first choosing any behaviour you want or need to adjust. Then make gradual changes until there is a little bit of overlap between your comfort zone and that of others.
• Finding points of common ground are key to building relationships with strangers and those from unfamiliar backgrounds.	• Explore your personal and professional life stories and consider how they have helped form your identities, values, and blind spots.
• This requires disclosure of 'personal' information and there can be significant individual and cultural differences in what people feel comfortable talking about.	• Pay conscious attention to and practise different ways of engaging in small talk / social conversation.
• Other strategies that are widely used in different contexts include paying compliments and gift giving. Again, there are individual cultural differences over their perceived acceptability.	• Seek out common ground when talking with unfamiliar people and build on it.

[38] For more details, see Wang, J., & Spencer-Oatey, H. (2015). The gains and losses of face in ongoing intercultural interaction: A case study of Chinese participant perspectives. *Journal of Pragmatics, 89*, 50–65; Spencer-Oatey, H., & Wang, J. (2020). Establishing professional intercultural relations: Chinese perceptions of behavioural success in a Sino-American exchange visit. *Journal of Intercultural Communication Research, 49*(6), 499–519.

8

How to collaborate and succeed in global teams

Introduction

Many organisations now seriously embrace the power of diversity, aiming to recruit talent from as wide a pool of cultural groups as possible and creating inclusive environments where diversity is encouraged and celebrated (see Chapter 11). But diversity by itself is not enough to guarantee effective and creative collaboration. Diverse teams can certainly outperform homogenous teams when they are able to properly leverage their diversity. However, different Cultural Perspectives and Practices, including communication styles, among members can seriously undermine team effectiveness, by creating misunderstanding, conflict and exclusion. This chapter thus focuses on ways of overcoming the differences, of enhancing collaboration and maximising success.

Our aims in this chapter are to explain:

- How to build team relations and why this is important.
- The importance of clarifying goals and ways of doing this.
- How to promote effective team communication.
- How to manage conflict and enhance trust.

Introductory case study

Case Study 8.1 reports the experience of a manager, Ivan, who is working in a project team with people whom he has known professionally for some time.

Case Study 8.1: A mediocre team

"We got together to review the year's activities and discuss our plan for the next phase of the project. I had several ideas of things that I wanted to improve, but in the event, I did not even bother to raise most of them. In the past, I would argue quite forcefully, to the point where it would feel uncomfortable and would mostly be met with a passive aggressive response from the leader: 'it cannot be done; this is how we always did it; x y or z won't like it'. This has made it very

---

difficult to bring my full self to this team. On the face of it, I am very supportive and have good relationships and all that. We all sit there and each of us has their say and we politely listen to each other and then we agree we will do what the majority thinks. But I am convinced that as a team we remain mediocre, and our output is only just good enough and I know I am partly to blame for this."

Reflect

a. Why didn't Ivan put forward his ideas?

b. He says 'on the face of it' he has good relationships with others. What do you think he really means by this? What kind of relationships does he really have?

c. How do you think the project leader might have been affected by Ivan's previous behaviour in the team?

d. How can Ivan's and his manager's behaviour be related to the Interaction Compass?

Sadly, the kind of situation described in Case Study 8.1 is surprisingly frequent: superficial harmony, but at the expense of creativity and innovation. From Ivan's perspective at least, this team did not engage in enough constructive discussion by carefully listening to each other's viewpoints (see Chapter 5, Figure 5.3). Instead, they suppressed any kind of disagreement that made people feel uncomfortable or threatened in some way. There was polite talk, where each person put across their own ideas (although as Ivan says some were clearly self-censoring their most controversial thoughts), but there was no serious consideration or challenge of each other's ideas. We could say that they listened to confirm or agree (or in some cases to close down / disagree) rather than to understand, question and possibly change their mind. This led Ivan to withdraw, moving to the low control and low connection ends of the Interaction Compass dimensions. As a result, team performance became mediocre and the opportunity for new ideas emerging was lost.

Management scholars DiStefano and Maznevski[39] found that diverse teams could be broadly divided into three types, which they labelled and explained as follows:

- The destroyers: members mistrust each other, do not share important information, and attack other members. As a result, they destroy value rather than create it.

- The equalisers: members report getting on very well together, but senior management rate their performance as mediocre. Members suppress differences of opinion, seemingly in order to maintain smooth relations. As a result, they are unable to leverage innovation.

---

[39] DiStefano, J., & Maznevski, M. (2000). Creating value with diverse teams in global management. *Organizational Dynamics, 29*(1), 45–63.

- The creators: members explicitly recognise, accept and even nurture differences; they appreciate the expertise of others and the potential for synergy from their varied contributions. The team's interaction processes—how they understand, incorporate, and leverage their differences—are key.

Interestingly, it may be the 'equalisers'—as seen in Case Study 8.1 and labelled there as mediocre—that are the most problematic. When a team is having a major conflict (i.e., 'destroyers'), everyone concerned is aware of it and the need to address the problems is usually clear. With 'equalisers', on the other hand, team members often take up a denial stance—differences of various kinds are ignored or minimised, and on the surface, all seems to be well. However, this prevents the leveraging of difference and the achievement of innovation.

In this chapter we explore how to avoid becoming 'destroyer' or 'equaliser' teams and how instead to become 'creators'.

Team relations: Getting to know each other

The starting point for collaborative success is good team relations. For task-oriented individuals and groups (see Chapter 3), there is often a strong desire to get on with the project task as quickly as possible. However, Canney Davison[40] offers international teams some excellent advice on this: "Start slowly and end fast; start fast and maybe not end at all." This draws attention to the importance of taking time at the very beginning of a newly assembled team project for members to get to know each other.

Case Study 8.2 illustrates the value of this and hints at ways of achieving it. It reports the experiences of a student team who were set a research project to work on collaboratively and who achieved a highly professional, creative result. The comments come from Susan, one of the tutors.

Case Study 8.2: Building strong relationships

"I noticed that team meetings were always very lively and sometimes chaotic; team members frequently interrupted and corrected each other when they were discussing topics or talking to the tutors. Opposing ideas were vigorously debated, but always with good humour. I wasn't sure how much progress they were making, but in the end, they presented a fantastic, highly creative project in a very professional, highly connected way.

---

[40] Canney Davison, S. (1996). Leading and facilitating international teams. In M. Berger (Ed.), *Cross-cultural team building. Guidelines for more effective communication and negotiation* (pp. 158–179). London: McGraw Hill.

When asked what made their project so successful, the team highlighted the importance of the following:

- Getting to know each other very well at the beginning, including identifying key individual strengths and how these related to what they had to deliver.
- Working to build strong relationships and trust with each other with regular meetings, having fun together, and showing concern for each other.
- Having a clear shared goal.

They felt this allowed them to identify and allocate roles and responsibilities well, support each other properly, test and challenge ideas vigorously and continue to push each other to perform."

Reflect

Think of a team that worked well for you.

a. To what extent did you take time to build strong relationships and trust with each other and how did you do it?
b. How did you handle differences of opinion?
c. What benefits did you experience as a result?

Next, we consider some practical ways of building strong team relations. Handled well, they can build a sense of team identity and belonging, which stems from understanding and acceptance of each other.

Learning about each other—personal stories

It is a well-accepted practice when putting a new team together to engage in activities that help the team to 'bond'.

In the previous chapter, we noted that people can have blind spots about themselves and that this can lead to sub-conscious biases which can influence their judgements of others. We recommended drawing up a list of key group identities and personal values (see Activity 7.4) and reflecting on them. We also talked in that chapter about becoming conscious of personal life stories.

Both of these reflection activities can be very useful for teamwork and for learning about each other. However, many people—depending on their personality and cultural background—may find it intimidating to talk about personal matters. So, the key is to find culturally-sensitive ways of encouraging people to get to know each other better.

For some this may mean participating in social events, for others it may mean the opportunity for casual chat before or after a meeting (perhaps over tea / coffee or lunch), and for yet others it may mean participating in ice-breaker activities or games. In all cases, the aim is gradually to build up mutual understanding through talking more with each other, and thereby gradually becoming more confident and trusting of other team members. Activity 8.1 encourages you to reflect on preferred ways of learning about each other.

Activity 8.1: Learning about each other and comfort zones

1. How comfortable do you feel sharing with other team members something about your personal background?
2. What topics are 'shareable' for you and what topics are too intimate?
3. In what sort of contexts do you feel most comfortable getting to know other team members?

Some people, though, may welcome the opportunity to share their personal background and stories with members of their team. So, if team members are comfortable and if you're the team leader or coach, you could arrange an activity as described in Activity 8.2.

Activity 8.2: Sharing personal stories

1. Ask members of the team to draw up a list of personal identities and values as we explained in Activity 7.4 in the previous chapter. You may have to explain briefly the importance of these in building relationships and managing rapport.
2. Once each person has created their list, invite them to share their lists and tell a personal story that explains why these identities / values are important to them right now and how they link to their goals for the project.
3. At the end of the conversation, encourage the team to create a shared map that shows their commonalities and differences. They can continue to build on this as they grow together.

Although this exercise can work really well for many groups, you should not try to impose it on individuals and groups who feel uncomfortable in sharing personal information of this kind. Those, in particular, who believe that there is a clear distinction between the professional and the personal sphere, will struggle with the need to reveal themselves to others so early on in the relationship (or even at any point). In such situations you can still ask those individuals to personally reflect on their identities and values, but only share what they are comfortable with; for example, to find similarities with other team members.

Examples of alternative ways of helping team members start opening up to others are as follows:

- A team of software engineers we recently worked with, who were initially unwilling to engage in what they felt was 'unnecessary talk', found themselves successfully sharing a lot of personal information in the course of playing online games during 'downtime'.

- The very reserved Japanese are known for the practice of 'nomination'[41], where colleagues go out drinking together after work, a ritual that allows opening up, sharing and building relationships outside the office constraints.

Being accepting of each other

An important aspect of building trust is accepting others. Sharing stories that reflect identity characteristics and values can help with this and understanding each other's personalities is an additional way. In developing Global Fitness, it can be very helpful to understand both our own personalities and those of our colleagues.

One of the most robust frameworks for understanding personality, widely used by psychologists, is known as the Big 5 or the OCEAN model. This model identifies five personality domains, in which everybody displays a certain characteristic to a higher or lower degree. Each of the main domains has several component facets, which again range from low to high. This means that a wide range of subtle differences can be captured, and people are not classified as one particular type, with the risk of associated stereotyping. Rather, they are located on dimensions from low to high for both the main domains and each of the component facets.

Table 8.1 below shows the 5 main personality domains of the Big 5 framework, their component facets, and the characteristics of low and high scorers.

As can be seen from Table 8.1, both low and high scores on each of the domains have strengths and weaknesses, meaning that there is no ideal personality. In fact, in a team, a range of personality qualities can be highly beneficial; for instance, some may be naturally good at attending to detail while others have vision and focus on the big picture. Both are needed.

It is vital to remember, however, that any insights into each other's personalities should be used for mutual understanding and mutual acceptance, not for stereotyping others.

Many websites offer the opportunity to take a Big 5 personality test free of charge[42], providing you with useful feedback for personal reflection, raising self-awareness (see Chapter 2) and for sharing with team members when appropriate. If all members participate, it increases the likelihood that each will be more willing to acknowledge their respective strengths and weaknesses for given tasks and contexts, and it also provides a common vocabulary for talking together about themselves and each other.

---

[41] 'Nomination' is a combination of two words which are 飲み (nomi) and communication.

[42] For example, see https://projects.fivethirtyeight.com/personality-quiz/

Table 8.1: An overview of the Big-5 (OCEAN) personality framework

Main personality domains	Component facets	Characteristics of low scorers	Characteristics of high scorers
Open-mindedness	Intellectual Curiosity Aesthetic Sensitivity Creative Imagination	Prefer the familiar over the new, the concrete over the abstract. Tend to be traditional and to stick with tried and tested ways.	Open to new activities and ideas, tend to be creative, intellectually curious, and sensitive to art and beauty.
Conscientiousness	Organisation Productiveness Responsibility	Tend to act spontaneously rather than make plans, prefer to jump between tasks, find it easier to look at the big picture than pay attention to detail.	Organised and responsible, work hard to achieve their goals, see tasks through to completion.
Extraversion	Sociability Assertiveness Energy Level	Socially and emotionally reserved, keep opinions to themselves, prefer to work independently.	Energetic, comfortable asserting themselves in a group, often experience positive emotions.
Agreeableness	Compassion Respectfulness Trust	Enjoy competition, don't hesitate to start an argument, take risks, tend to be sceptical of others' intentions.	Considerate, polite, enjoy cooperating, find it easy to trust people, feel compassion for others.
Negative emotionality	Anxiety Depression Emotional Volatility	Emotionally stable and resilient, usually stay calm in stressful situations, bounce back quickly from negative events.	Emotionally sensitive, have up-and-down mood swings, tend to react more strongly to negative events.

Clarifying goals and agreeing methods

Once a team has gone through a number of 'getting to know you' activities and discussions—beginning to develop mutual understanding—it may be important to spend some time discussing goals and methods. As we noted in Chapter 5, goals can affect interpersonal rapport and so it is an important factor to manage well.

Often a team will have been given a set of project goals by a line or more likely a functional manager. However, usually these goals will need clarifying to create a common understanding in the team. This requires everyone to feel able to put forward their own questions and ideas freely. Yet as we noted in Chapter 4, some people find it difficult to do this in a group. This is particularly the case in a multi-cultural team, where people may have different levels of proficiency in the working language and/or may have different turn-taking preferences (see also below). It can be helpful, therefore, for a team leader (or facilitator) to manage this explicitly, encouraging everyone to listen to each other so that everyone's point can emerge. This will involve bringing hidden assumptions into the open and helping the team explore and negotiate a common goal and method that everyone is clear about and can commit to. Activity 8.3 suggests one way of doing this.

Activity 8.3: Agreeing explicit goals and methods

The team leader or facilitator asks three questions:

- What are we aiming to achieve?
- How are we going to do it?
- Who is best suited to do what?

Teams then take each question in turn starting with the overall goal: 'What are we aiming to achieve?'

a. Each person writes down what they think the overall goal is
b. Each person calls out their interpretation of the goal and they are all put on a board or flipchart
c. The team then goes through the list, consolidating common elements, discussing any differences and then chooses from a final list to agree a common understanding of a goal or method
d. The team then tackles the next level of objectives, in other words 'how we are going to do this', in the same way

Reflect

1. How does this process compare with your own experience of clarifying goals and agreeing methods?
2. How might cultural factors affect the dynamics of discussing and negotiating these issues?

Although this process may appear cumbersome and time consuming to some, in our experience it is worth undertaking because it can significantly reduce uncertainty and the potential for misunderstanding and deteriorating relations. Taking the time to create clarity around shared goals and methods early on in the project can help minimise such problems at a later date.

Promoting effective team communication

Throughout the book we have pointed to the importance of 'good' communication, not just in terms of what is talked about or conveyed, but equally—or more—importantly how this is done. This is particularly true for teamwork when the members are from diverse cultural backgrounds.

Promoting mutual understanding

In Chapter 4 we explored the importance of achieving mutual understanding and the factors that can affect it. Case Study 8.3, which was reported by Edward, an HR manager working in a global virtual team, illustrates the kind of communication problems that can arise in teamwork.

Case Study 8.3: Lost in translation

"I have just been reading a set of minutes from the last time the team met, to make sure that I have completed the tasks I had committed to. But the minutes that were written by my colleague were not what I had in my notes! It turns out I promised to do something different than I had noted down—so yesterday I frantically spent the time calling him and then trying to do what I was supposed to have done! This does happen. You go away from a team meeting thinking everyone heard the same thing and often it is a question of emphasis. I wouldn't be surprised if someone said, 'We need a development plan for remote managers and it needs to be different for each country' and I just heard 'we need a development plan', but my colleague heard 'different for each country' and to him that had much more weight than it did for me."

Reflect
a. Why do you think this particular misunderstanding occurred?
b. How could it have been avoided? [See Chapter 4!]
c. What similar examples of misunderstandings have you experienced in teamwork?

Case Study 8.3 clearly illustrates how meaning is constructed rather than decoded (see Chapter 4); in other words, what we 'take' from an exchange is influenced not just by our level of shared familiarity with the communication code (the words and grammar), but also by our own interests and what we pay attention to. That is why the mindfulness steps which promote mutual under-standing—explained in Chapter 4—are so important.

Helping all team members feel able to contribute

In Chapter 4 we also pointed out the difficulties that some people can expe-rience in contributing to group discussions. These difficulties can arise from various sources, and it is essential that they are handled well. It is the responsi-bility of all team members to ensure that everyone can contribute—both for equal opportunities reasons and to maximise the creativity and innovation that comes from leveraging diversity in ideas.

The cost of team members feeling unable to contribute

One recent study[43] looked at the participation of different team members in group discussions over eight months of teamwork. Initially two members, Bruno and Alden, had more difficulties speaking in English than the others did, and both were identified—even in their presence—as too silent and hence problematic. Bruno would challenge this by immediately taking the floor and putting forward his viewpoints. As the weeks and months unfolded, he was gradually able to overcome his language difficulties. Alden, however, contin-ued to be regarded by the other team members as silent and incompetent, someone the team had to 'carry', and they continued to speak publicly about this in his presence. Yet whenever he tried to contribute to discussions, he was ignored, treated with token interest, or simply contradicted—even though later, others proposed the very same ideas as he had put forward earlier. As a result, he became more and more silent and disengaged as the months pro-gressed. Everyone lost out as a result and the impact of failed mutual responsi-bility was clear to see.

Some practical steps can be taken to help overcome such problems and maximise the active participation and contribution of all team members. It usually requires specific facilitated activities to challenge and help improve team communication practices. Activity 8.3 illustrates such an exercise.[44] Each step follows the basic principles of the SOS (Study Observe Stretch) Adapt tool (see Chapter 6), but with a facilitator structuring what team members need to observe and how they need to stretch.

---

[43] Debray, C., & Spencer-Oatey, H. (2019). 'On the same page?' Marginalisation and posi-tioning practices in intercultural teams. *Journal of Pragmatics, 144*, 15–28.

[44] Byrne, M., Twitchin, J., & Viswalingan, P. (1996). *What makes you say that: Cultural diver-sity at work.* VHS recording: SBS-TV.

Activity 8.4: Turn-taking and active listening

Give the team a topic to discuss or let them choose one.

Step 1: Allow the team to discuss the topic freely for about 5 minutes. Observe what happens—who talks and who doesn't, who interrupts whom etc. Stop the action and get the team to share feedback on their experience so far, adding your own observations. How aware are individuals of their behaviour when talking?

Step 2: Resume the discussion but ask the team to speak in the order they are seated (or if the session is online, agree a different order). The next person cannot start until the previous person has finished talking. Everyone must speak. As before, stop the action after five minutes of observation and share feedback. What are the challenges and advantages of this approach?

Step 3: Resume the discussion, but this time introduce a three-second silence gap between turns. Make sure this silence is actually observed. Watch carefully how people are responding to the enforced silence. After five minutes or so stop the action again and encourage people to share their experience. One of the things that becomes obvious during this part of the exercise is how useful silence is for those people who need time to reflect and also those who need more space to come into the conversation.

Step 4: Resume the discussion for one final time. The rule this time is that before they can say what they want to say, individuals first must reflect back on what the previous person said. Ideally, they should link their point to the previous point. Inevitably, this makes people put much more effort into actively listening to others.

　　Conclude the exercise by a final round of feedback on what they observed and how they felt about being stretched in the different ways.

Reflect

a. Which pattern of turn-taking, described in the four steps above, happens most frequently in your team?
b. How well does it work from the point of view of including everyone?
c. What steps do you think you could take to maximise contributions from all members?

The feedback and discussion around this activity is as important as the exercise itself. During this, facilitators can help individuals to:

- Acknowledge their own behavioural patterns and preferences and the impact they have on others (this should also include the use of language by native speakers).
- Recognise that others may have very different turn-taking patterns or language fluency but are no less worth listening to because of that.
- Appreciate the difference it makes to the quality of the discussion if you ensure everyone has space to speak (e.g., a brief gap between turns when someone can feel able to say something) and is properly listened to.

During the discussion it is worth linking what is happening during the exercise with different communication styles (see Chapter 4). It is likely that, as you go through the different stages of the exercise and particularly when you introduce opportunities for reflection and active listening, the synergistic, creative talk intensifies. The facilitator should point this out and ask the team to consider how they would use what they learned from this exercise to change the way they run their discussions in the future.

Collaborating online

In recent years, as a result of most teams being forced to work virtually because of the Covid-19 pandemic, holding team discussions and sharing ideas have become even more challenging. Issues such as power differentials, language differences and concerns for face are being amplified in environments like Zoom and MS Teams, as well as in a range of other online sharing tools. (See also Chapters 4 and 9, where we also consider issues connected with online communication and cooperation.)

Case Study 8.4 describes the experience of a British project manager, Andrew, who needed to work online with unfamiliar colleagues.

Case Study 8.4: Difficulty of challenging as an outsider

"I joined a team during the Covid pandemic; we are working on a complex project and our timelines are tight; collaboration in the team to achieve our objective is essential, but I have found it quite tough working only online. For one thing, the rest of the team—who have known each other for some time and have similar professional backgrounds—have developed this common language, like a shorthand and I really feel I am missing something when we have meetings. Sometimes I am not sure I have understood, and it is not easy to ask. At other times I can't get through to them, for example when I raise an important problem which they can't see. It really worries me. I think this would not happen if we were in the same room."

Reflect

a. What is your experience of team collaboration while working remotely?
b. How would you ensure that new members of remote teams did not experience the sense of exclusion this manager describes?

Case Study 8.4 underlines several of the points we have made already:

- The challenge of really understanding each other.
- The importance of truly listening to each other and making an effort to understand the other person's points.
- The impact of rapport on interaction.

The explanations and activities given in previous chapters (see especially Chapter 4), along with those in this chapter and other chapters in Part 2, will help with each of these issues.

Managing conflict, promoting trust

At the beginning of this chapter, we referred to three types of teams: destroyers, equalisers, and creators. We pointed out that destroyers—as the name indicates—destroy value rather than create it. Case Study 8.5 illustrates one such team that Wilfred, a British marketing manager, experienced.

Case Study 8.5: The team as a fighting ground

"The team worked, but with a lot of tensions. There were a lot of politics and a lot of differences of opinion, and it would become a game. It would be almost 'if he says this, I'll say that'. Everyone was fighting their corner, but once you start fighting your corner it becomes a boxing match really. I found it frustrating and counterproductive. After I had been doing it for a long time, I learned to listen to what I thought was important and ignore things that were not important. But I know from the experience of other people in the meetings that they found it frustrating."

Reflect

a. How would you evaluate Wilfred's way of handling the situation?
b. Why do you think others also found the team discussions frustrating?
c. Why do you think they didn't do anything about it?

It is very unlikely that the team described in Case Study 8.5 were able to leverage any of their various expertise and viewpoints to achieve innovative solutions. In terms of the Interaction Compass discussed in Chapter 5 (see Figure 5.2), they were engaged in self-focused talk, each just wanting to get their own points across, instead of taking part in creative, synergistic talk by listening carefully to each other and building on each other's ideas. They used differences of opinion and diverse interests to drive conflict ('a boxing match') rather than as an opportunity for synergistic breakthroughs. As a result, the team was not performing to its maximum.

So, this raises the question: since none of them were satisfied with the status quo, why didn't they do something about it? Breaking an established pattern and building a new one is always more difficult than preventing a problem from arising in the first place. That is why it is so important to build good relations from the start, as prevention is easier than cure. Nevertheless, in terms of addressing the problem (as well as preventing it), the steps outlined in Activity 8.4 above can be extremely helpful in getting a team that is not communicating effectively to examine and improve their turn-taking and active listening practice. Another essential element, particularly in dealing with disagreements, is team trust and we turn to this next.

Team trust

It is important to remember that maintaining team rapport is an ongoing process. It should never be confined to the initial meetings and then forgotten. In fact, as the team members gain more experience of working with each other, new issues are likely to emerge as they become aware of differences in preferred ways of working. This can be in a range of things, including communication style (e.g., level of directness / indirectness—see Chapter 4), attitude to time and deadlines (see Chapter 3), and so on. All such factors can undermine trust and your ability to collaborate. And, in diverse teams in particular, trust is essential for managing effective collaboration, because without its help members may be reluctant to show any difference of opinion or acknowledge any need for help.

Interestingly, what leads people to trust or distrust others is variable. For instance, some people may attach great importance to reliability—that those who do what they say they will do are trustworthy. Others may attach particular importance, for example, to support—that those who are helpful to other team members and supportive of them are trustworthy. So, a starting point for managing levels of team trust is to explore what factors affect people's trust of others. Activity 8.5 illustrates this.

Activity 8.5: Foundations of collaboration trust

Think of a team member or colleague you can work particularly well with.

a. Look at the list of behaviours below and decide how far you agree with each statement.
b. Then, if you feel comfortable doing so, compare your scores with other members of your team, or simply another person. How similar or different are your scores from theirs?
c. How might this affect rapport within your team?
d. If you wish, try doing the activity again with a different team member and compare the similarities and differences in your responses.

	Strongly disagree					Strongly agree
I can work very well with this team member because they ...	1	2	3	4	5	6
1. ... do as they have promised						
2. ... are hard working						
3. ... complete tasks on time						

4. ... respond quickly to my queries						
5. ... show that they like me and respect me						
6. ... listen carefully to my suggestions and ideas						
7. ... are helpful and supportive towards me						
8. ... acknowledge their own mistakes and shortcomings						
9. ... maintain confidentiality						
10. ... are similar to me						
11. ... have my best interests at heart						
12. ... are a person of integrity						

Another approach to exploring team trust is taken by the *Global Teamworking Profiler (GTP)*. This survey tool explores many aspects of teamwork, one of which is trust (see Chapter 13 for a more detailed explanation). In relation to this factor, team members rate each survey item twice—once for importance to them and then for how often they experience that behaviour. Figure 8.1 shows the results on overall team trust within one project team.

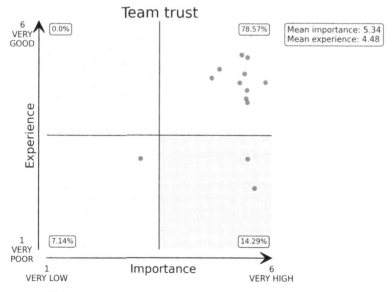

Figure 8.1: Experiences of team trust by one project team

It can be seen from this figure that the majority of the team members trusted each other (see the top right-hand quadrant): they regarded the various trust factors as important, and they were also experiencing them. However, two people regarded them as very important but felt they were not experiencing them (bottom right quadrant), while a third person felt that he or she was not experiencing much team trust but did not rate this as an important issue. This indicates that these three individuals were somewhat separated from the other team members and raises the question of the impact of their viewpoints on the working of the team as a whole. Such diagnostic information, which is provided only to the team leader or facilitator, can be used to generate useful team discussions and reflection, yielding useful insights into reasons for the scores. We elaborate on such professional development matters in Chapters 13 and 14.

Leveraging diversity and enhancing creativity

At the beginning of this chapter, we explained that diversity in itself does not necessarily enhance the creativity of teams or groups. We argued that it can have three effects, only one of which is increased innovation and creativity. For that to happen diverse teams need to work on building deep trusting relationships, agreeing explicit shared goals and methods, and paying attention to the way they manage communication in the team to ensure everyone has the opportunity to join the conversation and everyone's contribution is fully considered. We end with a positive example—an example (Case Study 8.6) of successful leveraging of diversity to yield creative and original results. It is reported by Joanna, a coaching professional.

Case Study 8.6: Leveraging diversity to achieve innovation

"I recently attended a workshop on managing team conflict. Several of my professional colleagues were taking part, together with younger, less experienced professionals and students. We were put together in teams, given a complex scenario of team conflict, and asked to come up with ideas for what we would do to resolve the problem. We first had to think about several ideas on our own and then chose our best idea and offer it to our team. Each team then went through a process of evaluating and building on each other's ideas.

The result was revealing, particularly to us experienced professionals present. Individually, we were all confident that we had come up with some pretty good solutions. However, none of these individual solutions were as good as the solutions the groups arrived at after we had built on each other's ideas. Furthermore, where groups consisting only of experts somewhat struggled to properly evaluate and chose one idea, mixed groups made up of students and less expert professionals ended up producing the most creative and original results."

> **Reflect**
> a. What experiences do you have of successful leveraging of diversity to enhance creativity and innovation?
> b. What do you think helped the process?

Interestingly, despite the 'head knowledge' of the professionals about the value of diversity, their belief in their own experience and expertise misled them into undervaluing the innovation that would emerge from working with others, including with less experienced others.

Key takeaways

Key Insights	Applications for practice
<ul><li>Diversity in teams can lead to different outcomes:<ul><li>misunderstanding and conflict</li><li>mediocre performance</li><li>creativity and high performance</li></ul></li><li>To leverage the diversity and achieve innovation, time investment is needed in building relationships and promoting trust.</li><li>Communication—especially choice of language and turn-taking patterns—significantly affects outcomes.</li></ul>	<ul><li>Create activities and make time to help team members get to know each other.</li><li>Allocate time for building a common understanding of the team's goals and steps for achieving them.</li><li>Pay attention to the ease with which all team members can contribute their ideas in meetings and take steps to address any inequalities.</li><li>Develop some simple 'rules' to promote better communication, including online.</li><li>Explore collaboration trust preferences.</li><li>With the help of the Interaction Compass, Figure 5.2 and Activity 8.3, promote mindful listening and synergistic talking among team members.</li></ul>

9

How to exercise global leadership and handle the context

Introduction

In this chapter we turn to the role of the person with leadership responsibilities (called 'leader' for short in this chapter) and explore what Global Fitness means for exercising global leadership, for example in organisations, projects, and teams. To be effective in such contexts not only do global leaders have to make sure that they personally are able to navigate the complexity and uncertainty they find themselves in. They also need to be able to help their people navigate the same contextual complexity and uncertainty, encouraging and supporting them, and leading them towards the achievement of shared goals.

From a Global Fitness perspective, conflicting advice is given by scholars and consultants about how best to do this. On the one hand, senior managers are told that the way leadership is done in different parts of the world can vary greatly and therefore, if they want to be effective, they must adjust their leadership style depending on where they are and who they are leading. On the other, they are encouraged to be authentic, expressing and using their inner personal values and showing humility and vulnerability in order to connect with followers and build trust and engagement.

This chapter explores these and other challenges. Our aims are to:

- Explain the key elements involved in exercising leadership.
- Consider how to handle leader–follower interaction in global contexts.
- Explain the impact of context and ways of taking it into account.
- Suggest ways of addressing issues of authenticity.
- Link the exercise of global leadership to the Interaction Compass.

Introductory case study

This case study concerns a German manager, Jürgen, who was sent to establish a start-up operation in Turkey. We have divided it into four parts and encourage you to reflect on each part, using (as appropriate) the E4A, 3R Review and

SOS Adapt tools we introduced in Chapters 6 and 7. We'll keep returning to this case study at different points in the chapter.

Case Study 9.1: Establishing a start-up operation in Turkey—Part 1

Jürgen was in his late forties when he was sent to Istanbul to manage a new start-up operation comprising a mainly young local workforce. With a proven track record in senior operational roles in a number of international organisations, Jürgen believed he had the knowledge and skills for the new job. At the same time, he recognised that the cultural environment and market requirements might present him with new challenges, which he welcomed. He wanted an 'opportunity to be learning again', as he said. In preparation, he set out to learn everything he could about his new home, reading avidly about Turkey and the Turkish people and engaging in the local cultural life. Nevertheless, a few months into the job Jürgen appeared stressed and frustrated with the progress he was making.

Reflect

a. How useful do you think Jürgen's preparation was for his new role? What else could Jürgen have done to prepare?
b. Why do you think he became stressed and frustrated?

Jürgen had a very positive attitude towards the new challenge, seeing it as a good opportunity to learn. Take another look at our E4A transformational learning framework in Chapter 1 and the Introduction to Part 2. Jürgen was not only very willing to Engage with the unfamiliar; he also demonstrated that by taking part in the local cultural life (the E of E4A). Moreover, he read a lot about Turkey and Turkish people—the second A (Ask) of E4A. However, we're told that he became stressed and frustrated after a few months. Part 2 of Case Study 9.1 throws more light on this.

Case Study 9.1: Establishing a start-up operation in Turkey—Part 2

Jürgen explained: "I am naturally a very egalitarian leader. I believe in personal responsibility, giving people a task and trusting them to get on with it. But here I have found that I cannot do this. It is different; people are used to this 'father culture' where they expect you to know best. You give someone a task and then you have to follow up and check all the time or it won't get done," he said.

Jürgen went on to describe how he had to adapt his natural style of being 'hands off' because he learned that "things did not get done" unless he constantly checked and directed. He had to do this, he said, although it made him feel uncomfortable and not authentic as a leader. He further confided: "the level of tolerance required is exceeding my limits. I do try to adapt, and I am making progress but it is also painful, uncomfortable—I feel like an actor."

Reflect

c. What do you think Jürgen meant by saying he felt 'not authentic' as a leader? Is it important to you to feel authentic as a leader?
d. How do you think you would have felt in this particular situation, and why?

Part 2 gives one reason why Jürgen felt frustrated and stressed—the work was not getting done and he found that his usual way of leading was not effective. He needed to change but felt uncomfortable doing so. Part 3 identifies another reason.

Case Study 9.1: Establishing a start-up operation in Turkey—Part 3

Jürgen also identified 'inefficiency' as a big issue for him. He knew that spending time to build relationships was an important part of the local culture and he did try to adapt his style to this expectation, but he could not help feeling that much of that was 'a waste of time'. He commented: "And then there is the tea thing—I have to have endless meetings and drink endless teas and coffees and talk about families—this is quite inefficient. I like to be an efficient leader, to keep to the point. When I first came here, we had meetings without agendas. I said we cannot have this; we have to change."

Reflect

e. Jürgen reports that he sees the tea drinking and associated chat as inefficient, even though he knew that relationship building was important. In what way do you think he sees it as inefficient? How would you see it in this context?
f. Why do you think he wanted agendas for meetings?

We see from Parts 2 and 3 that knowing about a cultural difference doesn't necessarily translate into easy adaptation. There are a number of reasons for this, and we considered some of the adaptation challenges in Chapter 7, including the authenticity challenge, the resentment challenge, and the competence challenge. We touch on these issues again later in the chapter. Meanwhile, Part 4 of the Case Study reveals yet further sources of Jürgen's stress and frustration.

Case Study 9.1: Establishing a start-up operation in Turkey—Part 4

Jürgen also struggled with what he saw as a lack of professionalism in the local workforce. He described professionalism in terms of being rational and direct and not bringing personal and emotional issues to the workplace. He commented, "If I try to say to people let's discuss what is going wrong, because it is important to learn from mistakes and get them fixed, people think that you are looking for someone to blame. To me it is important to be direct and to have rational conversations about problems, but they bring in emotions and gossip—it is not professional."

Reflect

g. What did 'professionalism' mean for Jürgen?

h. What does 'professionalism' mean for you? Do you see it in a similar way to Jürgen or do you see it differently?

i. To what extent do you believe there is a universally valid description of professional behaviour?

j. What picture are you building up of Jürgen as a leader? Try to be descriptive rather than evaluative.

The following leadership issues for Jürgen emerge from our analysis of Case Study 9.1:

- How to get people to perform up to his standard.
- How to communicate in an effective manner.
- How to build good relations with staff.
- How to feel comfortable and authentic in doing all the above.

Each of these issues are commonly experienced by those in leadership positions and are particularly acute for those working in situations of cultural diversity. Before we explore further how Global Fitness could help address such challenges however, let us first consider current thinking on leadership and what it means for global leaders who want to develop Global Fitness.

Global leadership as a multifaceted process

Current theories of leadership place the focus of leadership not so much on the leader as an individual but rather on leadership as a process. This process involves the interaction of four main elements: leader, the people whom the leader is influencing (traditionally known as followers), the contexts in which they are working and that they need to take into account, and the goals they are trying to achieve (see Figure 9.1). From a Global Fitness perspective, global leadership comprises the leader's ability to constantly navigate between these elements, taking the diversity of the people, the contexts, and goals into account.

In practice, this means that global leaders cannot simply rely on understanding differences and similarities between them and their followers and changing their leadership style to match these. Leaders need to do much more, particularly in the way they connect, understand, listen, and respond to the people they are leading. They need to remain mindful of what is happening around them (i.e., the organisational and societal contexts they are operating in), which from a Global Fitness perspective means possessing Global Personal Qualities, in particular the qualities of being self-aware and curious (see Chapter 2) and applying Global Knowledge and Understanding (see Chapter 3). They also need to set realistic goals and credible timeframes for achieving those goals in the light of all the influencing factors. Furthermore, leaders need to pay attention to how they themselves are performing and are being perceived by others. Above all—and as we explain more fully later in the chapter—they need to adjust their leadership performance in a dynamic and flexible way.

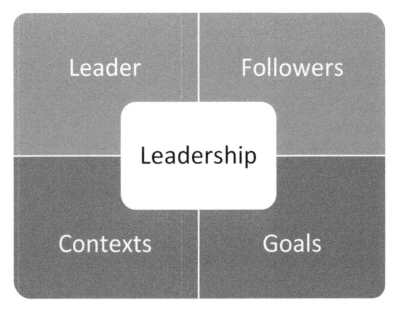

Figure 9.1: Components of leadership

Global leadership: leader–follower interaction

We start by focusing on leader and follower interaction and consider two key challenges we identified in Jurgen's case study: managing performance and handling communication style.

Managing performance

Achieving tasks and completing projects on time, on budget and to a high standard are extremely important in all workplaces. However, the most effective and appropriate ways of achieving this with different groups of employees can vary considerably. In Case Study 9.1, Part 2, Jürgen found that the local workforce did not respond well to his hands-off approach and that he needed to be more directive. So, he started telling people much more explicitly what to do and checking whether they had done it. This realisation that he needed to change was good. However, he himself felt stressed and inauthentic behaving in this way, and, as we explain below, his staff actually did not like the way in which he carried out his directiveness.

Case Study 3.6 (reproduced here as Case Study 9.2 for convenience) also raises the issue of leadership directiveness. In this case, the problem was too much directiveness.

Case Study 9.2: Taking up a new role and dealing with a business challenge[45]

Eleanor moved from the USA to Puerto Rico to become manager of a large and complex water infrastructure capital improvement programme. Within days of her arrival, she discovered that the local office team had not been supplying their client with what they had requested and that what they had been supplying was unacceptable. A serious legal case was looming.

Eleanor immediately set about addressing the crisis. Drawing on her extensive previous experience, she triaged the situation and started sending a stream of regular email instructions to her 100-person team. A few weeks went by with her continuing to issue directives like this, but sadly, things still weren't getting done; for example, delivery dates were missed despite her clear instructions. She felt highly frustrated and very alone. She just couldn't understand why she couldn't get the local staff to make the changes needed.

Right at this point, her deputy, Evelio, burst into her room, slammed the door behind him, and in a loud voice said, "You have *got* to stop." Eleanor was totally shocked and stammered "What do you mean?" Evelio continued, "You are driving us crazy! No one is reading your emails!"

Taking a deep breath, Eleanor wisely asked him what she should do instead.

Reflect

a. Eleanor was being directive and authoritative (what Jürgen felt his people wanted him to be), yet it didn't work well. Why not?

b. How can we explain the difference?

The contrast between Case Studies 9.1 and 9.2 makes it very clear that there is no universal way of getting people to perform to a high standard. Both leaders were directive—Eleanor by personal preference (or excessive focus on the task) and Jürgen in an attempt to adjust to the local context. Actually, both needed to change (further).

In order to understand why this is the case, we return to the Interaction Compass that we have previously discussed in Chapters 2 and 5. In Chapter 5, we applied it to discussions, but it is similarly applicable to leadership (see Figure 9.2).

---

[45] Eurich, T. (2017). *Insight: How to succeed by seeing yourself clearly.* London: Pan Macmillan.

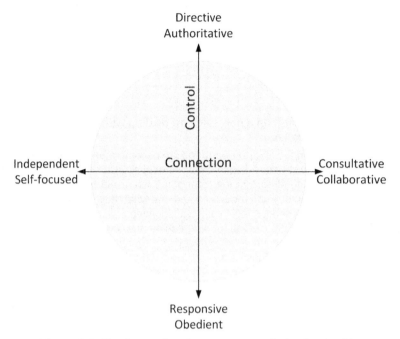

Figure 9.2: The Interaction Compass as applied to leadership

As explained previously, the vertical dimension represents control; in a leadership application, it represents the amount of direction or control that the leader wants or needs to exert. In Eleanor's case, she was highly directive, and she expected her workforce to fulfil her frequent instructions with responsive obedience. In terms of the connection dimension, she was operating with independence rather than collaboratively, and thus didn't involve her workforce in planning.

In Jürgen's case, on the other hand, he was very uncomfortable with being directive and was probably, by preference, midway on the control dimension or even at the lower end. Interestingly, he was similar to Eleanor in preferring the independence end of the connection dimension, with the result that he expected everyone just to fulfil their own roles.

Both needed to work flexibly towards a closer match between their own preferences and those of their workforce. Eleanor had no idea what her employees' preferences were until Evelio confronted her. Then she was wise enough to ask his advice (the second A, Ask, of our E4A transformational learning framework). Jürgen was sensitive enough to realise his staff wanted him to be more directive, yet he felt uncomfortable and inauthentic acting like this. Moreover, the local employees were dissatisfied with the manner in which he carried out his directive behaviour. We turn to that in the next section. First, though, consider Activity 9.1.

Activity 9.1: Personal preferences for managing performance

Now think about your own preferences for getting the best out of people using the concepts from the Interaction Compass above. Think about a particular person or a particular project group or team you are responsible for or involved in.

a. To what extent do you like to be directive to this person or team (or receive a clear directive)? Is there a difference in your preference depending on whether you are addressing the person or the team?
b. To what extent do your direct reports, colleagues or leaders have similar preferences to you? How do you know and/or how do you feel about that?
c. Is your preference to work independently on a project or to work collaboratively with others? Give reasons for your preferences if you can.
d. Do your colleagues (or leaders) encourage collaborative working? How do you feel about that?

Handling communication style

Those with leadership responsibilities not only need to consider the degree of direction that is most suitable for a particular group or person, but also need to pay attention to the communication style in which the message can be delivered most effectively and most appropriately. Consider Case Study 9.3. Melva is a marketing manager with a strong track record in managing international teams in a number of industries. Shortly after taking on a new role during the Covid-19 pandemic which involved leading a diverse team, she commented on her approach as shown in the case study.

Case Study 9.3: Adjusting communication style

"I am aware that some of my natural communication style is too much for people, so I increasingly find as I get more mature, I am happy to work outside my comfort zone and adopt other styles. Sometimes it is exhausting but I feel that as I am the boss, if anyone is going to flex, it's me."

Melva described an episode early in her career as a sales executive when one of her customers told her:

"This is not going to work …you are far too much for me". I discovered that that was an amazing thing to say, and he really taught me that I need to learn to flex my style. I can't just be myself all the time. I really need to be aware of how my personality and style of communication affects other people. I remember that I tried to put myself in his shoes. If I was him, what would annoy me about me? And I thought, probably everything. So, I just tried to mirror him, to reflect his body language back at him, and I do this as a leader.

Reflect

a. What was it that enabled Melva to select the appropriate style for this particular client?
b. What is your opinion of the communication technique of 'mirroring' that Melva mentions in the last two lines of the case?

Melva makes it clear that she is able to use a range of different communication styles. As we explained in Chapter 4, there is no one-to-one correspondence between high control (i.e., a directive leadership style) and directness–indirectness in communication. Often the two may correspond, but this is not always the case. Sometimes high control can be conveyed directly and explicitly, but it can also be conveyed much more indirectly, for example by saying 'You may like to try ...' when what is meant is 'you should try ...'.

This was the issue that Jürgen failed to handle. He often shouted his instructions, had emotional outbursts, and did not deliver the clarity that was needed. This made him come across as insufficiently caring in the eyes of his direct reports. He needed to be more relationship-oriented in his communication and this also applied to his management style. We saw in Case Study 9.1 Part 4 that he wanted to talk over with his team things that had gone wrong, so that everyone could learn from what had happened. However, he found that they often interpreted this from a 'who is to blame' perspective and responded in a negative way. It's quite possible that part of the reason for this was Jurgen's preference for the independent end of the connection dimension. Perhaps if he had established a more collaborative approach in the way he communicated critical feedback, there would have been a more positive reaction. For example, he could have prioritised explorative questions, listened to the responses, and been careful about how he said what he thought was wrong.

Melva, in contrast, was able to adjust her communication style to resemble that of her customer. For her, it was not so much an issue of directness–indirectness as another stylistic difference: her effusive manner (that is, emotional and passionate) as opposed to a more restrained (that is, detached and reserved) manner. This draws attention to the fact that there are actually many different communication styles, including those listed in Activity 9.2.

Leaders need to handle all communication styles with flexibility if they are to be successful, especially across cultures. It is important to remember, though, that for all these different styles, it is not an either-or choice but a more-less choice between two extremes. So, this does not mean that leaders need to alter significantly their communication style every time they change settings or have to influence different followers. As we discussed in other cases of local adaptation (for example Aleksy and small talk—see Chapters 6 and 7), the key to successfully flexing your behaviour, i.e., to adjusting it slightly, is to identify how far you can change in a way that both meets local expectations while also feels comfortable to you.

Choosing the right 'level' for each style is crucial for getting the message across, as both Jürgen in Case Study 9.1, Part 2, and as Melva in Case 9.3 discovered. Activity 9.2 encourages you to think about your own communication style preferences and those of your colleagues in different settings and how far you are prepared to adapt.

Activity 9.2: Reflecting on preferred communication styles

Look at the list below of possible variations in communication style.

Direct	2	1	0	1	2	Indirect
Informal	2	1	0	1	2	Formal
Effusive	2	1	0	1	2	Restrained
Overstated	2	1	0	1	2	Understated
Detailed	2	1	0	1	2	Big picture
Expansive	2	1	0	1	2	Concise

a. How would you rate your preferred communication style when talking with the groups or teams you lead?
b. Now think about those same groups or teams. What do you think their preferences are? What evidence do you have for that?
c. If you think their preferences are different from your own, to what extent would you be willing and able to adjust your communication style as Melva did? Why / why not? (Think here about the challenges we've mentioned: authenticity, resentment, competence.) What level of change would be comfortable for you to make in each case?

Leading and communicating remotely

The flexibility required when it comes to leadership style and communication style is equally necessary when choosing the appropriate communication channel. Since the Covid pandemic, the importance of making the right choice of communication channel has increased. As fewer interactions take place face-to-face, and working from home has become more common, email is now used even more frequently than before and more interactions take place in video calls. We go into aspects of communicating remotely in Chapters 4 and 8 and here we focus briefly on leading remotely.

Deciding how best to lead people under such circumstances and finding the right mix of communication channel for the individuals or people you are leading will be the challenge. Case Study 9.4 illustrates how Melva (the same Melva as in Case Study 9.3) handled this.

Case Study 9.4: Communication and remote leadership

Melva described how working remotely with a new team was a real challenge and one she approached by making time for each person in the team, learning about them, building the relationship, establishing the trust.

"If you are in an office, you stop and talk to people all the time—people talk to each other—I was very aware that I had to replicate these opportunities so that my team got to know me and I got to know them and how they see things, understand each other's perspectives. For me trust is important. [Both pre-pandemic and now] my team know I am always around, and I am accessible. They can book time with me, and it is their time, their agenda, we can talk about anything that is important to them. I listen."

Reflect

a. Given what you know about Melva's preferred communication style, why do you think she found working remotely with her new team so challenging?
b. What advice would you give her?

On the other hand, for others in leadership positions, notably those who are particularly task-oriented, face-to-face leadership has clear disadvantages and remote leadership clear advantages, as Case Study 9.5 illustrates. In the longer-term, though, an ongoing lack of good opportunities for building relationships is likely to have a negative impact on morale and well-being, especially for employees who particularly value social interaction.

Case Study 9.5: A different perspective on remote leadership communication

German former banker and consultant and co-founder currently and managing director of the blockchain company *Immutable Insight,* Katharina Gehra reports on her experience of face-to-face versus online meetings in an interview with the German newspaper Frankfurter Allgemeine:[46]

"Live meetings have disadvantages. There is sometimes a dynamic which doesn't bring the same commitment; people chat and get distracted. Especially in the start-up phase, where it is a matter of how do you set priorities, how do you get your focus right, remote-only has very many advantages: you have a plan, everybody knows what the goal is, when the deadline is. And then there is a great variety of ways of getting there."

Reflect

a. Do you agree or disagree with Gehra's viewpoint on the advantages of remote meetings? Why / why not?
b. Which leadership tasks would you feel comfortable doing under conditions of remote leadership and which not?

Global leadership: Interpreting the context

As we explained above and illustrated in Figure 9.1, leadership always takes place within a context—actually, multiple contexts, ranging from the local, immediate context, to the departmental or organisational context, to the broader

---

[46] https://www.faz.net/aktuell/karriere-hochschule/buero-co/gruenderin-katharina-gehra-ueber-ihr-unternehmen-im-homeoffice-17707919.html?premium

societal context. So far, we have focused on the local interactional context; in this section we consider ways of taking the broader context into account.

Gaining understanding of unfamiliar contexts

For leaders who operate in a new or complex cultural environment, trying to understand the implications of this context for their work is essential. Case Study 9.6 reports how one leader handled this.

Case Study 9.6: Preparing for a global assignment

John is a British manager from the north of England with experience of working in several countries in three continents. When he was interviewed, he was working as a senior leader in an international bank in Asia where he was responsible for teams in a number of different countries across the continent. When he was asked about how he approached his role as a global leader he said:

"When I go to a new country, I pay attention to how things are done; yes, I read books and hire experts, but also I look around me, very conscious to understand what the norms are, not just in the country, but in the particular team and workplace. I watch people around me who are successful in operating in these settings, learning from the mistakes and what goes well. When I first came to China, I hired a culture expert to work with me and my team for us to learn about our different perspectives, but also in my office at the top of my board I had 'Today in China'. I would write what happened and what would be the outcome and the next day the outcome would be exactly the opposite.

So, my experience made me flexible. I learnt to spend time with people to observe and to ask questions and to listen. I would say that I now instinctively understand how to get the best out of my team in India, where people are more adversarial and talk over each other and raise their voice, and out of team in Hong Kong, where you listen with your mouth shut."

Regarding the question of authenticity John said: "I do try to adapt my style to what I know works best, but I also try to be me—I don't try to disguise that I am a Brit and the company I represent is British. My team do not expect me to behave like one of them. They want me to behave like me."

Reflect

a. How does John pay attention to his environment as a global leader and the context of his leadership actions?
b. How does he pay attention to relationships when exercising his leadership?

We can now compare how Jürgen, Melva and John each handled the challenge of context.

Jürgen and John both spent time reading about the unfamiliar countries they found themselves in and engaging in local life. But there was a difference between them as well. Jürgen assumed that his new knowledge about Turkish culture applied to all his workforce and went on to anticipate and interpret their behaviours and reactions through that filter. He tried to adjust his level of directiveness—the control dimension of the Interaction Compass—but did not adjust on the connection dimension in any meaningful way.

John, in contrast, remained open-minded and examined each situation for its meaning as it occurred. He constantly paid close attention to and questioned what he was seeing and what was happening around him; he watched and learned from how others behaved and succeeded in that context. In other words, he adjusted his behaviour in multiple ways, according to the context.

Taking other people's perspective

Significantly, both John and Melva invested time and effort in understanding the context—not just from their perspective, but also from the perspective of their followers, through regular group and one-to-one meetings. In other words, they both engaged fully in the E4A learning approach. This ensured that their understanding of context and how it affected what needed to be achieved was not just a personal goal but also a collective endeavour, leading to shared meaning.

When John brought in a culture expert on China (see also Chapter 12 on the use of informal cultural informants), for example, he did not use her input only to inform himself; he set up a workshop for him and his team. The purpose of the workshop was to help them examine together the possible differences and connections between them and how these might affect what they needed to do and how they could go about it.

Jürgen, in contrast spent very little time outside operational meetings talking to his team. When he was presented with practices he did not approve of, rather than seeking to understand and asking questions, he made his disapproval explicit and simply demanded that things change to fit his expectations. If he had spent more time with his team to understand, for example, their more flexible approach to meetings or projects, he might have come to appreciate their approach and worked with them to use that flexibility to solve some of the problems they were facing as a group.

Seeking cultural change in your existing context

All of the examples we've considered so far have concerned 'newcomers' to an unfamiliar setting and their need to adjust appropriately. Sometimes, however, 'locals' within a setting are dissatisfied with the status quo and want to bring about change through their leadership, either within their organisation or more broadly in their society. This is the case for many young and/or female leaders across many countries in Africa, according to recent research.[47] For instance, Mrs Abby, the CEO of a manufacturing plant, explained the problem as follows:

> Some people do not regard women seriously as leaders; they underestimate you or do not believe what you say. It is a challenge because of culture or religion; especially for younger women it can be tough.

Similarly, Mr Adeniji, a young Nigerian entrepreneur commented:

> In my view, in Nigeria, young people are not afforded the platform to show and demonstrate what they can do. Instead they have to fight the system—so much is stacked against them, there are so many problems [...] But I see some movement—there are more people like me, and together we are raising the next generation of leaders.

In such circumstances it can be particularly difficult to know how to exercise leadership, because of the outright opposition and exclusion that can occur. However, as recent research by leadership consultant Jordans[48] has shown, drawing on the principles behind the Interaction Compass can be extremely helpful. She found that flexibly applying high and low control strategies in combination with high and low connection strategies proved very effective for gradually bringing about change in the beliefs and practices of those who were opposing the change. That is to say, there is no single leadership approach that is always effective, even in the same context, but rather what is needed is the dynamic and flexible use of different types and combinations according to contextual conditions. We consider what this can mean in practice in the next section.

Global leadership: Handling the context through dynamic flexing

We noted earlier in this chapter the problems that can occur if followers' preference for a collaborative (i.e., high connection) leadership style is ignored by a senior manager and a directive (i.e., high control) style is used instead (Case Study 9.2). Problems can similarly occur if the reverse is the case. Here we take this a step further and argue that dynamic flexing between multiple styles is needed, as John demonstrated successfully when he moved from different

---

[47] Jordans, E., Ng'weno, B., & Spencer-Oatey, H. (Eds.). (2020). *Developing global leaders. Insights from African case studies.* London: Palgrave Macmillan.

[48] Jordans, E. (2022). *Transforming cultural norms: The role of women and youth.* Unpublished PhD thesis, University of Warwick.

contexts. By flexing, we mean the repeated changing or adjusting of behaviour to meet the particular requirements of the context and / or leadership goals.

Dynamic flexing within the same context

This need for flexibility does not only apply when there is a significant change of context. Consider the experience of Ian, a Nigerian architect and construction project manager (Case Study 9.7).

Case Study 9.7: Mentoring while taking control[49]

"I recall my days working as an architect. I believed that effective leadership was also about educating or mentoring those that you lead. Every time I came to site, people loved following me around because I constantly gave valuable insight on how to do things better.

I was doing an inspection and had seen a wall that was not particularly straight. I gave my usual guidance on why and how to correct it, but the foreman claimed that it was fine, quoting his many years of experience in the job and his age. Nevertheless, he and his team agreed it would be corrected. At my next visit, nothing had been done yet once again they agreed to put it right. On my return a week or so later the wall had still not been corrected. The foreman began to explain, but I was prepared and had a mallet (a hammer) with me and simply smashed the areas of the wall that needed correcting. I then continued on to other areas for inspection and continued being collaborative and giving guidance and advice as required.

The wall was soon done correctly, and I praised the foreman for a job well done. I noticed that all the workers on the site were now more attentive, quality of work at other areas of the site increased. This way I learned that whilst your style may be highly participative, you must be prepared for low collaboration situations and have that "hammer" firstly visible and ready to smash any hindrances to it. I now carry a hammer with me on all site inspections!"

Reflect

a. Why do you think the foreman did not correct the wall after Ian's first visit? Suggest several reasons.
b. Would you have felt able to use a hammer in these circumstances? Why / why not?
c. What experiences have you had of needing to flex between directive (high control) and collaborative (high connection) leadership styles?

In this situation, Ian flexed between a collaborative (high connection) and a directive (high control) leadership style within the same workplace. In some respects,

---

[49] Jordans, E., Ng'weno, B., & Spencer-Oatey, H. (Eds.). (2020). *Developing global leaders. Insights from African case studies*. London: Palgrave Macmillan. Chapter 7.

his control strategy (destroying the poor-quality work) could be seen as risky, but it achieved his purposes, despite the initial challenge of the foreman.

On other occasions, a leader may need to flex in different ways. For example, Brenda, a young Kenyan female team leader working in the research sector, found that older members of her team tried to undermine and embarrass her by asking difficult questions.[50] She responded with patience, promising to get back to them later if she couldn't answer immediately. If she wasn't sure whether someone's question was genuine or not, she would ask 'Is the reason why you've been having a lot of questions because you didn't understand the training, do you need me to retrain on particular topics?' Brenda handled the challenges from her team in a very different way from Ian. On the one hand, she took steps to build her own personal expertise through researching issues she didn't know the answer to. In this way, she demonstrated low connection through her focus on herself while at the same time she showed high control through her pro-active leadership of the team. Moreover, she liaised closely with the individuals, seeking to understand their attitudes and training needs (high connection, low control).

Both leaders were successful in that they adjusted their styles in accordance with the situation at hand. Ian faced opposition from a single foreman and brought about change in the foreman and his colleagues with a high collaboration / high connection approach. Brenda faced wider opposition and dealt with it with a high collaboration / low connection approach.

The Interaction Compass and multiple leadership strategy options

So far, we have mainly talked of high control and high connection leadership behaviour. The examples of Jürgen and Eleanor, who showed a low connection preference, may have wrongly implied that the low ends of the two dimensions of the Interaction Compass are undesirable. That is not the case, though. As we noted with Brenda, it was useful for her to focus on developing her own expertise and this was a low connection strategy—a focus on self.

Recent research by leadership consultant Jordans[51] has shown that flexibly applied high and low control strategies in combination with high and low connection strategies are highly effective, especially for gradually bringing about societal or organisational change; the latter is often believed to be a key task of leaders. As mentioned above, there is no single leadership approach that is always effective, even in the same context. What is in fact needed is the dynamic

---

[50] Jordans, E., Ng'weno, B., & Spencer-Oatey, H. (Eds.). (2020). *Developing global leaders. Insights from African case studies*. London: Palgrave Macmillan. Chapter 9.

[51] Jordans, E. (2022). *Transforming cultural norms: the role of women and youth*. Unpublished PhD thesis, University of Warwick.

and flexible use of different types and combinations. According to Jordans' research, the deeper and broader the resistance or opposition to organisational or societal change, the greater the need there is to include a low control / high connection approach.

Yet some might ask: how can you be a leader if you act with low control? Doesn't leadership by definition mean influencing and hence some level of control? We would argue not necessarily at all times. Sometimes there is a place for stepping back, listening to others and learning from them (low control / high connection), thereby gaining insights that can feed into future planning.

Sometimes there is also a place for withdrawing and waiting (low control / low connection)—either for circumstances to become more favourable or perhaps for personal stress management purposes.

In other words, we believe that all the 'directions' of the Interaction Compass can play a role in certain circumstances. Figure 9.3 shows schematically the different approaches associated with all these different 'directions' of the Interaction Compass and Table 9.1 gives some examples of possible strategies associated with these different styles.

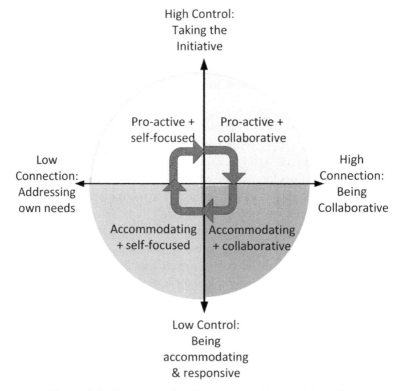

Figure 9.3: The Interaction Compass and leadership styles

Table 9.1: Indicative leadership strategies associated with different locations on the Interaction Compass

High Control [Take initiative, be pro-active]	High Connection [Be collaborative]
• Pursue a vision • Give instructions	• Build connections • Be interested in others
High Control, Low Connection [Take initiative to address own needs]	**High Control, High Connection** [Take initiative to work with others]
• Find a mentor • Build self-confidence (e.g., to get courage to speak out) • Enhance personal expertise / knowledge • Develop skills (e.g., flexing different communication styles)	• Make plans and decisions collaboratively • Initiate team project • Provide mentoring support • Brainstorm ideas
Low Control [Be accommodating and responsive]	**Low Connection** [Address own needs]
• Follow instructions • Accept guidance	• Focus on self • Maintain personal space
Low Control, Low Connection [Be accommodating, manage own needs]	**Low Control, High Connection** [Be accommodating, learn from others]
• Keep calm / manage stress • Wait for things to change • Be patient • Look after own needs • Manage emotions	• Consult with others • Seek others' advice • Understand other people's viewpoints • Participate in focus groups • Model desired behaviour

Succeeding as a global leader

As we near the end of the chapter, we consider some further perspectives on succeeding as a leader.

Managing authenticity as a leader

As mentioned at the beginning of this chapter, leaders are often encouraged to be authentic in order to build trust and engage their followers. Given that flexible behaviour is a key competence of the global leader, what conclusions can we draw about authenticity, adaptation and global leadership from these stories? On the face of it, Jürgen tried to adapt by adopting a more directive style of management but that made him feel totally inauthentic and uncomfortable and it did not work with his followers either. John and Melva seemed to strike the right balance of knowing how far to adapt in different settings, while still remaining within their personal comfort zones. Ian and Brenda demonstrated flexibility within a single setting.

Learning to be flexible in these multiple ways is not easy—there will often be competence challenges. Yet coming to the realisation that successful leadership involves ongoing flexing in multiple directions and that there is no single 'right' way of exercising leadership may help to address the challenges of authenticity and resentment.

For leaders in any context, it is essential to build rapport and create trust between themselves and their followers, if they are to bring them on board to support projects or achieve goals. When the context is increasingly complex and uncertain, as is the case in global and remote workplaces, building those relationships becomes at the same time more important and potentially more difficult. A leader needs to invest considerable leadership time in getting this right. Thinking through the Interaction Compass and the range of strategies that can be associated with the different 'directions' of the compass may help with this.

Leadership and ethics

Many would see leadership as being closely connected with ethics. For instance, Ciulla defines leadership from an ethical perspective:

> Leadership is not a person or a position. It is a complex moral relationship between people based in trust, obligation, commitment, and a shared vision of the good.[52]

So, we turn to the issue of ethics in the next chapter.

Key takeaways

Core insights	Applications for practice

• Leadership involves the interaction of four main elements: leader, followers, contexts, and goals.
• Handling the leader–follower interaction is crucial but challenging, especially when:
  o managing performance
  o giving feedback
  o handling communication styles
  o choosing communication channels and working remotely
	• Develop a clear sense of your own preferred way of managing performance.
	• Find out how your direct reports prefer you to do so and consider any adjustments you may need to make.
	• Pay attention to your communication style and seek ways to increase the range of styles you feel comfortable in using.

---

[52] Ciulla, J.B. (Ed.) (2014). *Ethics, the heart of leadership* (3rd ed). Santa Barbara, CA: Praeger.

- Appreciation of the context is crucial, and leaders need to dynamically vary their styles accordingly.
- The Interaction Compass offers valuable principles for planning and understanding how best to show that dynamic flexibility.
- Dynamic adjustment need not be seen as a threat to personal authenticity.

- Think through the pros and cons of the different communication channels available to you and plan how you will use them to best effect in your work.
- Looking at Figure 9.3 and Table 9.1, identify the different leadership strategies you use regularly. Consider what others you could try using.
- Practise varying your leadership styles according to context and need, accepting that each location on the Interaction Compass can play a valuable role.

10

How to handle ethical challenges and maintain integrity

Introduction

Everybody faces ethical issues—some big, some small—on a regular basis. Sometimes people are very consciously aware of them; sometimes they barely notice them. Yet in all cases, their responses to them can have a significant impact on their actions and the settings in which they act. The aims of this chapter are therefore to consider what Global Fitness means from an ethical perspective, particularly as it is influenced by diversity factors. Our aims in this chapter are to:

- Outline the types of ethical dilemmas global people may face.
- Consider ethical challenges from within the organisation.
- Elaborate on the ethical challenges from outside the organisation.
- Recommend steps for enhancing personal ethical Global Fitness.

Introductory case study

As usual, we encourage you to reflect throughout the chapter on how the issues and examples apply to your own contexts. We start with an introductory case study that concerns the ethics associated with an organisation and international marketing.

Case Study 10.1: IKEA and their Saudi Arabian catalogue[53]

A few years ago, IKEA, the multinational furniture retailer, hit the headlines over one of its catalogues: women had been skilfully removed from its Saudi Arabian catalogue. Superficially the catalogue looked fine, but careful examination showed that all women had either been airbrushed out or replaced with other figures. The catalogue was freely available online and soon the Swedish

---

[53] Miska, C., & Pleskova, M. (2016). IKEA's ethical controversies in Saudi Arabia. In C. Barmeyer & P. Franklin (Eds.), *Intercultural management. A case-based approach to achieving complementarity and synergy* (pp. 120–133). London: Palgrave Macmillan.

press discovered it. This led to a barrage of criticism from newspapers and government officials in Sweden and beyond, with headlines such as "IKEA erases women". IKEA quickly apologised and acknowledged that this version of the catalogue was contrary to their core beliefs and that they deeply regretted the mistake made on this occasion.

One comment published on the internet[54] reflected on the ethical aspects of this as follows:

"Some people may claim that IKEA should not be criticized, because it was only seeking to respect Saudi Arabia's strict social mores. Or, they propose that IKEA was following a rational business strategy, customizing products being sent to a foreign country where it knew that moral and cultural values were not the same as in Western societies—and certainly not like those in Sweden.

"But, there is another way of looking at IKEA's decision to make its catalogue palatable for a group of Saudi censors—that it failed to take into account how it would look when exposed as taking active measures to collaborate with a regime notorious for its policy of gender apartheid."

There is yet another ethical question raised by the case: to what extent is it good and right for IKEA to demand of Saudi Arabia that it accept IKEA's "core beliefs" and practices, which find expression in their 'uncensored' catalogue? Are there 'good and right' beliefs which transcend other equally firmly held beliefs and which therefore may legitimately be imposed on others?

Reflect

1. What was the ethical issue at stake here?
2. In your view, should IKEA have allowed the catalogue to be altered in this way? Why / why not?
3. If you were an IKEA executive, what personal challenges would you face in having to make or defend this decision?

Types of ethical dilemmas

In simple terms, ethics concerns the notions of right and wrong, yet identifying what that means in practice is actually very complex. This is partly because ethical questions emerge in a wide range of situations, as Table 10.1 illustrates. In other words, unethical behaviour is not simply a matter of breaking the law or violating a regulation; it also includes lack of care and consideration, or a lack of respect, for a wide range of issues—which people may consider more or less important. In the organisational and commercial context, these include consideration for the environment, for core values, for employees, for consumers, for people in the supply chain, and for competitors. However, even in these cases the requirement for ethical behaviour is often based on a law or the

---

[54] https://knowledge.wharton.upenn.edu/article/missing-the-picture-ikeas-women-free-catalogue-in-saudi-arabia-fails-to-protect-company-values-and-reputation/

notion of duty of care, namely the responsibility in one's actions to restrict the potential for harm to others and society.

Table 10.1: Range of ethical foundations and the issues they raise

Ethical foundations	Fundamental ethical issue
1. Respect for the law and organisational regulations	Uphold the law / company codes of conduct and procedures or bend them a little?
2. Respect for core values and beliefs	Uphold or ignore the core values and beliefs of our organisation and company?
3. Respect for the environment	Uphold or ignore environmental standards?
4. Respect for employees	Treat employees well (e.g., equality in hiring & promotion, health and safety at work) or ignore or overlook these issues?
5. Respect for consumers and customers	Offer consumers and customers a fair deal or try to maximise company benefits, even if it is to others' disadvantage?
6. Respect for other stakeholders and interested parties	Consider or ignore the welfare and interests of those less directly involved in our business? (e.g., those in the supply chain or the sources of investment capital)
7. Respect for competitors	Treat competitors fairly (e.g., through refraining from espionage or copyright / patent violation) or ignore such matters?

The complexity of acting ethically becomes even more challenging when working in diverse contexts. This is because notions of right and wrong are significantly shaped by a person's socialisation and sense of identity, and as such are influenced by culturally-based beliefs and principles. These are potentially different (and in conflict with one another) not only from person to person but also from one setting to another, and not only in the abstract but also in the decisions and actions they trigger and justify.

As we go through the chapter, we'll consider many of the ethical dilemmas that individuals may face at work in different types of situations, in different roles, and at different levels of hierarchy. First, though, we encourage you to reflect on your own past experiences and consider which of them you have faced personally in your work.

Activity 10.1: Reflecting on past experiences of ethical dilemmas		
Ethical foundations	**Have you experienced this type of ethical dilemma?**	**If yes, briefly recall it and note the key issues that made it a dilemma for you. Use the 3R Review tool to help you, especially if you now view it differently**
1. Respect for the law and organisational regulations	Yes / No	
2. Respect for core values and beliefs	Yes / No	
3. Respect for the environment	Yes / No	
4. Respect for employees	Yes / No	
5. Respect for consumers and customers	Yes / No	
6. Respect for other stakeholders and interested parties	Yes / No	
7. Respect for competitors	Yes / No	

Acting with ethical Global Fitness within the organisation

Organisations typically require their employees to be compliant with the law and to act ethically, and yet a range of situations can serve to undermine this, usually unintentionally. We consider some of these in this section.

Averting ethical mishandlings and abuses

Organisations are naturally concerned about employee performance and take various steps to maximise it, including setting targets and reviewing performance. From a Global Fitness perspective, there are particular ethical issues in relation to this that leaders and managers need to consider: the proportionateness and fairness of the targets and reviews for all employees, especially when there are differentials in power, such as through role and majority / minority status (i.e., ethical foundation #4, Table 10.1). For instance, it may be especially challenging for staff who see themselves as a member of a minority group and who may already be feeling marginalised because of their identity character-istics (e.g., their ethnicity or gender) to negotiate targets; for them, to resist pressure from above to accept an unreasonably high target can be especially stressful. Similarly, for those who feel particularly obliged to obey those in authority (e.g., because they hold high power distance values—see Chapter 3), it can be especially hard to resist doing what the boss seems to want or explicitly orders.

Research findings offer evidence of the differential treatment that can arise from this. For instance, one study[55] analysed the performance ratings for employees of a large U.S. corporation, in which performance was measured in two ways: objectively and subjectively. Comparing the ratings for different ethnic groups, they found there were no significant differences in the objective measures, but major differences in the subjective measures and that these were linked to ethnicity. The authors report this as follows:

> The effects of race on subjective evaluations are dramatic. For example, a 35-year-old white, married, male employee with 10 years of company experience and 2 years of tenure within his current job who reached 100 percent of his sales goal has a 12.0 percent chance of receiving an "outstanding" rating. A black employee with the same attributes has a 5.7 percent chance of receiving an "outstanding" rating.

It is hard to judge how conscious or unconscious such differential assessments may be. Either way, it is unethical practice that shows disrespect for certain employees. People thus need to be particularly mindful of this and be actively on the lookout for any failings of this kind, in their own practice or that of others.

Activity 10.2: Appraisal and ethics

Reflect on the following questions:

1. Consider the appraisal schemes in your organisation.
   (a) In what ways do they encourage or discourage ethical behaviour?
   (b) What procedures are in place to ensure fair treatment for all, irrespective of background?

---

[55] Elvira, M., & Town, R. (2001). The effects of race and worker productivity on performance evaluations. *Industrial Relations, 40*(4), 571–590.

> 2. Have you ever felt any pressure or been incentivised in your organisation to perform in a way that you felt was unethical in some way or that made you feel uncomfortable about whether it was the 'right and good' thing to do?
>   (a) If so, what were the circumstances and why did you feel concerned?
>   (b) How did you handle the situation and how did it work out?
> 3. Have you ever noticed some unethical behaviour among your colleagues or superiors?
>   (a) If so, what were the circumstances and how did you feel about it?
>   (b) How did you handle the situation and how did it work out?

Ethics and codes of conduct

A widespread organisational strategy to minimise legally non-compliant and unethical behaviour is to institute codes of conduct. These specify what is and is not allowed, and covers matters such as financial procedures, conflicts of interest, procurement policies, and so on. These are very important and valuable, but they are not necessarily foolproof. Ironically, it can lead people to focus on what is legal (or allowed by the rules) rather than what is ethical.

This has come to light twice in recent years in relation to the behaviour of British Members of Parliament (MPs). In 2009, there was public outcry because it emerged that significant numbers of MPs were submitting high and dubious claims for the reimbursement of expenses resulting from their work as MPs. They justified their behaviour in terms of the law (it was technically allowed according to the code of conduct), yet most of their constituents (i.e., the people who had elected them) felt the expenses associated with the claims were completely unjustifiable (i.e., a conflict between ethical foundation #1 and #5, Table 10.1).

So, one of the dangers is that codes of conduct can encourage people to check whether the letter of the law allows them to do something, rather than consider the broader ethical issues associated with doing it. Nevertheless, codes of conduct are clearly important, especially when dealing with external clients, as we discuss in the next main section.

Acting with ethical Global Fitness with external stakeholders and interested parties

In the previous section, we focused on ethical dilemmas within the organisation. Very often, however, the ethical challenges come from outside the organisation. These can stem from different interpretations of what constitutes unethical behaviour as well as concerns to 'get business done'. Here we focus on four such contexts: gifts and bribery, stakeholder ethics, the supply chain, and corporate social responsibility (CSR). In each of these, cultural differences can play a particularly significant role.

Dealing with gifts and bribery

In many countries, gifts are an important element of building a relationship (see Chapter 5) and are not regarded in any way as bribery; in other countries, however, the giving and receiving of gifts can be highly problematic and there are strict laws (e.g., UK Anti-Bribery Act, the US Foreign Corrupt Practices Act) and company regulations about the legality and disclosure of such matters, including the value of gifts that are allowed. This difference in attitudes towards gifts reflects several differences in the Cultural Perspectives and Practices (see Chapter 3) that people uphold and influence their behavioural choices, including the following:

- Universalism–Particularism (scope of rule applicability): whether rules apply to everyone in all contexts, or whether they vary according to the particular relationship and particular situation.
- Rule rigour: whether rules always need to be firmly adhered to or can be applied flexibly.
- Task–relationship focus: whether priority is given to achieving the task or to building and maintaining a relationship.

Such differences can give rise to significant challenges for all those engaged in international business, and numerous problematic cases have been reported. For instance, the Germany-headquartered multinational company NES AG experienced this when trying to establish a holding company in Beijing.[56] The application for permission dragged on for several years and the European leaders were advised by their Chinese advisor that they should build connections with government officials by inviting them to dinner and giving them gifts. The Europeans refused, regarding it as bribery. However, their Chinese advisor explained that gifts cannot be equated with bribes, pointing out that according to Chinese law they only become bribes when the officials are given "money or property" for the purpose of obtaining "improper benefits". "Improper benefits" are defined as benefits that derive from a breach of "the law, regulations, administrative rules or policies".[57] So to the advisor, inviting people to dinner

---

[56] Lane, H.W., Distefano, J.J., & Maznevski, M.L. (2006). *International management behavior*. Oxford: Blackwell. Case study 18.

[57] https://www.globallegalinsights.com/practice-areas/bribery-and-corruption-laws-and-regulations/china

and giving them gifts with the intent of speeding up an approval process for a completely legitimate and legal initiative was not in any way a matter of bribery.

This indicates that in considering these complex situations, it is important on the one hand to gain PESTLE knowledge (legal, in this case) as well as to consider cultural differences around the importance of relationships. In relation to the latter, deciding what is or is not ethical is often challenging, as Case Study 10.2 illustrates.

Case Study 10.2: Kindness or a conflict of interest?

Helen, an academic and head of department at a top British university, was planning to take her whole family (husband and two sons) on a summer holiday trip to China. They were ending their trip in Shanghai, and senior staff at the university where she had worked for 7 years were keen to welcome and host them all, covering the costs of hotel accommodation, some meals together, and pick-up and departure transport. When Helen mentioned this to an administrator at her British university, she was advised that she should not accept this hosting as it could be seen as a conflict of interest.

Helen was surprised. Being familiar with Chinese culture, she felt this was a very normal way of saying 'thank you' for her contribution to teacher training in China over a number of years. But the administrator felt it could open the door to future pressure to provide favours for the Chinese university concerned, and that it was therefore unethical to accept.

Reflect

1. In your view, would it be ethical for Helen to accept the hosting? Why / why not?
2. If she refused, how might that affect her relations with senior staff at the Chinese university?
3. If she accepted, how might that be (a) beneficial or (b) detrimental to her British university in terms of future academic collaboration?

Paying attention to the ethical position of stakeholders

Another potential source of ethical dilemmas is the ethical behaviour and stance of (potential) stakeholders, including of donors, investors, and customers. Two recent examples are:

- The British Chancellor of the Exchequer (i.e., finance minister) called on companies to pull out of Russia following the Russian invasion of Ukraine. However, it then emerged that his wife's family company, from which they earn large sums of money, refused at the time to withdraw from Russia.[58]

---

58 https://www.theguardian.com/politics/2022/mar/28/sunak-under-pressure-over-wifes-russia-related-blood-money-dividends

- The Saudi Arabian-led takeover of a leading UK soccer club raised ethical questions: whether it is ethical to accept investment from a country/leader who has allegedly been linked with human rights abuses.

It is very senior managers who make such decisions, but grassroots (i.e., bottom-up) sentiment can also have an influence, especially when large numbers of supporters or purchasers of a brand are involved. Failure to consider ethical issues can backfire if leaders are not careful, as was demonstrated very clearly for IKEA (Case Study 10.1).

Probing ethical issues in the supply chain

There has been increasing concern in recent years about the rights of people who help produce the products that are sold to people in wealthier countries (i.e., ethical foundation #6, Table 10.1). It challenges us to consider all our responsibilities regarding this, both as consumers and retailers, and Case Study 10.3 provides an example from the food industry.

Case Study 10.3: Slave labour and the prawn industry[59]

In 2014, following a 6-month investigation, The Guardian newspaper reported a very serious problem with slave labour in the prawn/shrimp industry in Thailand. They found that migrants were being held against their will in horrific conditions on fishing boats off Thailand. The fish caught by these boats is turned into fishmeal, which is bought by CP Foods and fed to its farmed prawns. These prawns are then sold to major supermarkets such as Walmart, Carrefour, Costco, Tesco, and Aldi.

The Guardian reports the UK Managing Director of CP Foods as saying that while he knows there are issues with the prawns that come into port, his company has no clear picture of the extent of the problem. When the Guardian spoke with representatives from the various supermarkets, they all condemned slave labour, some saying they were working with CP Foods and/or the Thai government to address the issue, while Carrefour said they had tightened up procedures but admitted that it did not check right to the end of its complex chains.

The Thai government says that combating human trafficking is a national priority, while human rights activists say that the government has little incentive to address the problem because cheap labour is so important for the prawn market. Instead, they say that pressure from consumers and international retailers to deal with the issue would be the most effective form of action.

---

[59] https://www.theguardian.com/global-development/2014/jun/10/supermarket-prawns-thailand-produced-slave-labour

> **Reflect**
> a. Who do you feel has ethical responsibility in situations like reported in this case study? Give reasons for your answers
>   • The original producers (e.g., the fishing industry)
>   • The processors (e.g., CP Foods)
>   • The wholesalers (e.g., the supermarkets)
>   • The consumers (e.g., households)
> b. Does the level of ethical responsibility vary and if so, in what way?
> c. What would you do if you were an executive for any of these companies?

In this case study, we can see that awareness is a major factor. Supply chains can be long and complex and human rights abuses can therefore be difficult to check comprehensively. Information from different sources is thus of critical importance because it helps key people notice and start raising questions.

Some countries (e.g., Germany) have recently passed laws (and other EU countries are due to do the same) making it obligatory for companies of a certain size to protect the human rights of people who produce goods for the German market.[60] In 2021 the Thailand Department of Labour Protection and Welfare started partnering with seafood industry groups in an effort to eliminate the use of forced labour in the sector. However, they also pointed to cultural factors that could lead to a misinterpretation of figures. For instance, the Thai Labour Minister, Suchart Chomklin, downplayed the U.S. estimate that around 177,000 children aged five to seventeen are engaged in child labour in Thailand, saying "Sometimes business operators do not intend to use child labour, but children follow their parents [to work] and photos are taken, for instance, of children picking up shrimps and are seen as using child labour."

> **Activity 10.3: Supply chain and ethics**
> 1. How familiar are you with your organisation's procurement of products / services that enable it to function?
> 2. How confident are you that ethical issues have been satisfactorily explored and addressed in the procurement process?
> 3. What more could be done by organisations and individual executives?

Ensuring the ethics of Corporate Social Responsibility (CSR)

Corporate social responsibility (CSR) is of great importance nowadays to most organisations and they typically address it by avoiding harm on the one hand

---

[60] E.g., Germany's Supply Chain Act: https://www.bundesregierung.de/breg-en/news/supply-chain-act-1872076

and doing good on the other. The former can include steps such as guaranteeing product safety and respecting the requirements of environmental sustainability. The latter (i.e., doing good) is carried out in a variety of ways, including the following:

- Raising money for local concerns.
- Sponsoring local sports clubs or after-school activity clubs for children, teenagers etc.
- Volunteer schemes whereby organisational members are given time off to work with their local community or even further afield.
- Linking with communities in developing countries to provide consulting services or other knowledge-exchange programmes.

However, such 'doing good' initiatives have also been criticised as being more of a public relations exercise than a means of providing lasting value, and the environmental projects are often labelled 'greenwash', on the basis that their real aim is to contribute to marketing and employer branding.

When CSR initiatives involve developing countries, the situation can be extremely complex. Often a company may undertake a range of well-intentioned projects, perhaps as compensation for the disruption their business may cause, yet these are not always well received. For instance, Barrick Gold, a major mining company, was involved in a controversial project in northern Chile. Barrick signed a memorandum of understanding (MoU) with fifteen Diaguita—indigenous South American—communities and maintained that this MoU set a new standard for mining companies around the world in their relationships with such local indigenous communities. Yet the local people saw things completely differently, with one person claiming that her indigenous identity was being regarded as a commodity and exploited for commercial purposes.[61]

Sadly, this kind of situation is by no means unusual. In such cases, it is of vital importance to spend time truly trying to understand local people's preferences, wishes and needs, rather than pre-deciding what would be best for them. Only when there has been genuine dialogue and when mutual understanding has been built can such initiatives count as truly fulfilling corporate social responsibilities. Activity 10.4 provides the opportunity to reflect on CSR issues in your organisation.

---

[61] https://mccottawaoffice.wordpress.com/2015/09/30/another-canadian-gold-mine-barrick-gold-and-the-indigenous-communities-of-huasco-chile/

Activity 10.4: CSR and your organisation

1. What CSR projects is your organisation involved in?
2. What ethical principles do they uphold?
3. What steps have been taken to check how 'beneficiaries' of the initiatives feel about the project?
4. What guidelines does your organisation have with regard to receiving donations or working with investors?
5. To what extent do they guard against unethical practice?

Growing in personal ethical Global Fitness

The previous sections have identified a range of situations where ethical challenges may arise, especially in contexts of diversity. The choice to act ethically (or not) ultimately lies at the individual level and so a fundamental starting point is personal sensitivity to ethical issues. In line with transformational learning theory outlined in Chapter 1 and elaborated on in Part 2 of the book, the development of ethical Global Fitness, involves several of the steps of our E4A tool.

Step 1: Attend: pay attention and become aware of an ethical issue

We may think that it is easy to notice (potentially) unethical situations and sometimes it clearly is. However, this is not always the case; in fact, it is surprisingly easy to overlook ethical issues in certain situations. For instance, in the case studies we have considered in this chapter, we saw that IKEA overlooked the impact of adjusting their catalogue (Case Study 10.1), Helen and her administrator were not sure of the ethical acceptability of receiving free hosting from her previous Chinese university (Case Study 10.2) and major supermarkets failed to Attend to slave trade issues in their supply chain (Case Study 10.3). Sometimes we need another person to draw our attention to an ethical issue, even when we hold strong ethical principles, as Case Study 10.4 illustrates.

Case Study 10.4: Wording in a job advert

A Church of England church was planning to open a café and to recruit two part-time staff to help run it. The trainee clergyman asked Jane, a newly appointed church official, to look at the draft job advert for the jobs to be filled and to give some feedback. Jane (who until recently had held a leadership position in a not-for-profit organisation) noticed that the posts were identified as permanent, yet the church committee had only approved initial funding for 6 months, because of uncertainty as to how successful the venture would be.

Reflect

a. What is the ethical issue at stake here (see Table 10.1)?
b. Why do you think the trainee clergyman might have worded the advert in this way?

You might ask: why did the trainee clergyman not pay attention to these issues himself? There could have been several reasons. For instance, he might have been pre-occupied with other matters and not given sufficient thought to the issue; or he might have been goal-focused, fearing that advertising a temporary position might reduce the likelihood of receiving applications from good candidates. Alternatively, he might simply have had little or no experience of recruiting staff and so was unaware of the associated issues he needed to think about.

In this case, it was not difficult for Jane to draw attention to the issue. In many situations, however, people may hesitate to mention such matters, especially in situations of power inequality, in which one party is dependent on the other. The more powerful the transgressing individual(s) and the more widespread and ingrained the malpractice, the harder and the more dangerous it is to challenge the unethical behaviour and the greater the risk of negative consequences, such as losing one's job.

Attending is therefore not always easy, and nor is following up. Factors that can affect the likelihood that people will notice and raise ethical issues include:

- Pre-occupation with their own goals.
- Workload and stress, such that they may become too self-absorbed to notice.
- Assumptions as to whether it is their role to concern themselves with such matters.
- Concerns over power imbalances.
- Ability to empathise with others.
- Sense of affinity with the affected person(s).
- Prior experience of dealing with similar matters.

In addition, cultural factors can contribute significantly to the 'Attending' process because of the different principles and values that people uphold. In international business, behaviour that is considered ethically required in one country may be brought into question in another—sometimes surprisingly or shockingly. This is particularly common with regard to gifts and bribes, where there can be subtle (or not so subtle!) differences in legal/regulatory requirements, and / or where there are value differences in universalism–particularism, rule rigour, and task–relationship balance. (See also Chapter 7 on gifts and relationship building.)

Attending is thus an important first step in developing ethical Global Fitness. Activity 10.5 thus encourages you to reflect on your own experiences of noticing ethical issues.

Activity 10.5: Attending to ethical issues

1. Have you ever noticed an ethical issue that needed addressing? What was it, and how did you handle it?
2. Have you ever had to draw someone's attention to the ethical issues associated with something they were considering doing? If so, describe what the situation was and explain why you felt it was unethical?
3. Has anyone ever had to draw your attention to the ethical issues associated with what you were considering doing? If so, describe what the situation was and explain why the other person felt it was unethical?

Step 2: Ask and Analyse: Explore and balance the issues at stake

Once people have become or been made aware of an ethical issue, sometimes they may be very clear about what needs doing. On the other hand, at other times they may need more information and need to think things through very carefully. For instance, in a supply chain issue, a lot of investigation may be required, or in a gift / bribery case, it may be necessary to learn more about the local legal situation. Those involved may have to balance different cultural principles and values, and consider what is flexible or negotiable, or what is a red line for them or their organisation. During this stage, it is good to seek the opinions of others and consider their perspectives. However, other people's advice can be variable, so ongoing reflection is needed.

In considering the different options, individuals may consider the moral intensity or significance of the decision, taking account of the following factors:[62]

1. Magnitude of consequences: their perception of the degree of harm or good for the people concerned that may arise as a result of the decision taken.
2. Social consensus: the extent to which an individual believes others would act similarly in the same circumstances.
3. Probability of effect: an individual's assessment of how likely it is that the perceived outcomes of the decision will actually occur.
4. Temporal immediacy: the length of time before any negative outcome of the decision is likely to be experienced.
5. Proximity: the extent to which the individual is close to those involved.
6. Concentration of effect: how many people are affected, and to what degree, by the individual's decision.

---

[62] Jones, T.M. (1991). Ethical decision making by individuals in organizations: An issue-contingent model. *Academy of Management Review, 16*(2), 366–395.

Yet it is still not easy. As the leadership expert, Donna Ladkin, comments, there is no definite right answer:

> There is no 'right' answer that will suddenly make itself known, no matter how much you analyze the situation. What *is* important from an ethical perspective is the *process* used for coming to a decision.[63]

Step 3: Apply: Take ethical decisions and accept the consequences

Eventually, the deliberation needs to come to an end and a decision taken. The consequences can sometimes be challenging, as not everyone may agree with the action decided upon. Case Study 10.5, which concerns a Hong Kong bank official, illustrates this point. He faced quite a lot of opposition from colleagues when he made an ethical decision that could have a negative impact on profit. He reports it in his own words.

Case Study 10.5: Clients and money laundering

"Some months ago a client of ours was involved in money laundering. It was a very important client and the bank wanted us to hush the matter up because we made a lot of money from him. However, I decided to exit the client. The people in China were very upset with me; when my colleagues met me, they literally turned their backs on me. But I knew I had done the right thing; it comes from my faith, I am a committed Christian. I spoke to my boss and I explained why I did it; my boss was happy. I brought these Chinese bankers together and explained why I had made that decision. They understood; they still disagreed with me but I never doubted that I did the right thing."

Reflect
a. What type of ethical challenge did this banker face? (see Table 10.1)
b. What were the risks for this banker in acting as he did?
c. What would you have done in this situation?

In this particular case, the individual had sufficient status and confidence simply to make his decision. Sometimes, however, it is junior staff who have the difficult task of handling unethical behaviour among their colleagues or the people above them. The ideal way may be to find some kind of non-confrontational means of handling the situation. One option that can sometimes be feasible is to check the code of ethics of the company, the relevant industry or profession, and any associated laws or regulations. These

---

[63] Ladkin, D. (2015). *Mastering the ethical dimension of organizations. A self-reflective guide to developing ethical astuteness*. Cheltenham: Edward Elgar.

ethical standards could be discussed initially with trusted colleagues, with the aim—wherever possible—of gradually opening up a dialogue on business ethics generally and what it means for individuals and colleagues in a particular context. This would be a Low Control High Connection strategy (see Chapter 9).

Case study 10.6 illustrates a variation on this. It is reported by Sifa, a female leader in the finance sector in Kenya who found an amicable resolution to an abuse by people above her in their use of company vehicles.

Case Study 10.6: Managing ethical abuse among seniors at work[64]

"Once when I was in charge of administration, people who were senior to me were misusing vehicles, they were abusing their position. It was tricky, because I did not want to confront them, but at the end of the day—during an audit—I would be responsible and held accountable for it. Ultimately, I proposed to senior management the introduction of procedures that would make staff accountable. This was accepted and became the new policy and managed to stop the misuse. I thus managed to solve the situation amicably and without personal confrontation."

Reflect

a. What do you think gave rise to the ethical dilemma in the first place?
b. How did Sifa address the situation? (Refer to Table 10.1)

We see from both these case studies the importance of personal integrity. In other words, people need to think through and be clear about their own moral code. They then need to find appropriate ways of putting it into practice in their contexts. Activity 10.6 offers some reflection questions to help with this.

Activity 10.6: Taking ethical decisions

Think of a situation where you needed to make a decision that was difficult ethically.

1. What different needs and/or issues did you take into consideration?
2. How did you weigh them up for relative importance?
3. What decision did you eventually make and why?
4. What happened afterwards?

---

[64] Mutooni, K., Ng'weno, B., & Jordans, E. (2020). Changing leadership perceptions: Leaders in the private sector in Kenya. In E. Jordans, B. Ng'weno, & H. Spencer-Oatey (Eds.), *Developing global leaders. Insights from African case studies* (pp. 211–257). London: Palgrave Macmillan.

Key takeaways

Core insights	Applications for practice

• Ethical dilemmas can stem from many different sources and can be made more complex by cultural factors.
• Ethical challenges occur both within organisations and with external partners or clients.
• It is not always easy to notice ethical challenges; others may need to point them out to us, or us to them.
• Ethical decision-making is often not easy; it requires time and reflection and may have personal consequences.
	• Familiarise yourself with the different ethical foundations that may be relevant to your work (Table 10.1).
	• Check your organisation's code of conduct and identify areas where challenges may occur when working globally.
	• Always check any new initiative by:
	  o Attending to any potential ethical issues
	  o Asking key questions and analysing responses/data provided
	  o Applying your insights to your decision-making

Part 3

Moulding the context: Global Fitness Environment

Introduction to Part 3

Moulding the context: Global Fitness Environment

In Parts 1 and 2, we have focused on Global Fitness at the individual, interpersonal and group levels. Part 3 deals with a crucial third piece of the jigsaw: the context. We call this the Global Fitness Environment. It functions at multiple levels, as indicated in simplified form in Figure P3.1.

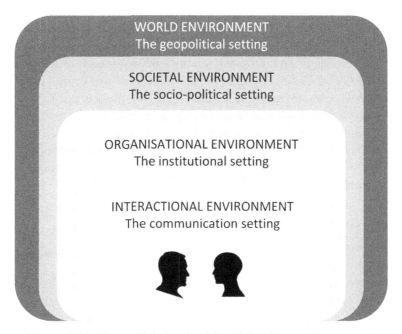

Figure P3.1: The multiple levels of the Global Fitness Environment

People develop and learn as a result of interactions with others in the very varied range of contexts they encounter in their socialisation—the family, school, workplace—indeed in any institution or environment in which people come together. These contexts can be favourable or unfavourable for learning and developing particular skills and attitudes. What is more, these contexts can be consciously and deliberately shaped to support the development of certain competencies.

People are also influenced by the society in which they live, as well as the broader world environment. To take an example related to the subject of this book, in 2015 the German state, civil society and individuals took steps which together became known as the *Willkommenskultur* (culture of welcome) to handle the settling of large numbers of refugees from Syria. These policies and actions not only facilitated the socialisation of newcomers into German society but in turn also resulted in fostering what were in effect Global Fitness skills and attitudes in the German population as a whole. This, however, didn't prevent an increase in xenophobia among some parts of German society.

As Figure P3.1 indicates, the Global Fitness Environment exerts its influence at multiple levels. In Part 3, we concentrate not on the World or Societal Environments, important though they are, but on the Organisational Environment. We explore how this context, in its framework conditions, policies and actions, can be deliberately moulded to help develop the Global Fitness of people encountering cultural diversity at work. We cover four main areas.

In Chapter 11 we focus on the fundamental need for psychological safety and how well-being can be fostered among employees, both of which affect growth in Global Fitness. In Chapter 12 we consider how organisations can be shaped to promote learning and innovation and thus leverage the cultural diversity of its people and interactions. In Chapter 13 we argue that organisations need to gather concrete information in order to identify the Global Fitness development priorities of their organisation, departments and individuals. In the final chapter of this part, Chapter 14, we consider how to plan, manage, and implement Global Fitness development programmes.

11

Ensuring well-being: How to establish the essentials

Introduction

Well-being is an essential foundation for developing Global Fitness and, certainly in the Global North, employers are more and more recognising it as one of their key responsibilities. This chapter focuses on the characteristics of an organisation / department / division that can significantly influence levels of employee well-being and its relationship to tackling the challenges global people and global organisations face in managing cultural diversity.

One of the main benefits well-being brings is a reduction in the fear and anxiety that uncertainty and stress may cause, and it thereby allows people to focus on their work, learning and growth (see Chapter 12). To return to the metaphor running through this book, in order for Global Fitness to be developed, the gym—the organisational setting—needs to be designed and fitted out in a development-friendly way. Well-being is an essential element of this and in this chapter, we focus on the following aspects:

- The nature and importance of well-being.
- Factors that influence levels of well-being in the workplace.
- The potential impact of cultural factors.
- Applications to your own organisation / department / division.

Our goal is that your reflections on well-being from a global perspective will help you fit out your 'organisational gym' in a way that supports the development of Global Fitness among all employees.

Introductory case study

We start by considering a case study example.

Case Study 11.1: Culture and re-organisations[65]

A U.S. distribution company experienced a decrease in profits and an increase in costs and so decided to reorganise. As part of the reorganisation, they replaced many older white, male employees by younger workers from India who were willing to work at the same location for lower wages. The new Indian workers and the retained U.S. employees worked next to each other in small- to medium-sized cubicles and had the benefit of a room next to their work area where they could take breaks and where they could heat their food in a microwave.

Reflect

a. How would you describe the feelings, worries, and concerns the retained U.S. workers were likely to have about their work situation?
b. What complaints do you think the U.S. workers might raise about the new Indian workers?
c. What feelings, worries and concerns do you think the Indian workers might have about their work situation?
d. What complaints do you think the Indian workers might raise?
e. What steps do you think senior management could take to address / help prevent such problems / concerns?

Broader considerations

As well as reflecting on the case-specific questions above, you may also want to consider the case from a broader perspective and in the light of the ethical issues discussed in Chapter 10:

f. How ethical was the distribution company's staff replacement procedures?
g. How far would it comply with the code of conduct of your organisation or labour law in your country?

All of these questions are associated with the issue of well-being and as we move through this chapter, we'll discuss the various factors that can undermine well-being, particularly those associated with cultural issues. We'll relate them to this case study step by step.

The unexpected and unfamiliar behaviours of members of different cultural groups, as well as problems of inclusion and sense of belonging, can easily cause feelings of exclusion, uncertainty, and confusion, along with a diffuse sense of unease and reduced well-being. Such feelings hinder high performance and need to be planned for and addressed by senior management. In this chapter, we consider ways of dealing with these issues.

---

[65] Hannum, K., McFeeters, B.B., & Booysen, L. (Eds.). (2010). *Leading across differences*. San Francisco, CA: Pfeiffer. Case study: The scent of difference.

Well-being: What is it, why is it important and how is it underpinned in the workplace?

The United Nations agency for the world of work, the International Labour Organisation (ILO), considers workplace well-being as part of Occupational Safety and Health and writes:[66]

> Workplace well-being relates to all aspects of working life, from the quality and safety of the physical environment, to how workers feel about their work, their working environment, the climate at work and work organization. The aim of measures for workplace well-being is to ... make sure workers are safe, healthy, satisfied and engaged at work.

The ILO goes on to underline the importance of well-being to the economic success of an organisation:

> Workers' well-being is a key factor in determining an organisation's long-term effectiveness. Many studies show a direct link between productivity levels and the general health and well-being of the workforce.

The laws of the country in which an organisation is located governing health, safety and the environment set the minimum framework within which measures related to these topics are implemented in organisations. Knowing that legal standards are adhered to provides a minimum of security and safety for employees and lays the foundation on which further instruments build. Codes of conduct and policies, value statements and vision statements may also prioritise well-being and factors contributing to it; employees may refer to these instruments if they feel a lack in this area.

Common well-being measures include programmes designed to counter alcohol and drug abuse, mental health issues, stress, bullying, discrimination, and sexual harassment. Others aim not at reducing negative factors impacting well-being but at actions that actually enhance well-being, such as sport and exercise. Many companies, connect three concepts: inclusion, safety, and well-being. For example, W H Smith, a leading global retailer for newspapers, books and convenience items, identifies three aims:[67]

- Be an inclusive employer with a workforce representative of the communities that we serve.

---

[66] https://www.ilo.org/safework/areasofwork/workplace-health-promotion-and-well-being/WCMS_118396/lang--en/index.htm
[67] https://www.whsmithplc.co.uk/sustainability/people

- Provide a safe working environment and support the mental well-being of all our employees.
- Advance well-being and livelihoods in our supply chain.

Inclusion is an especially important characteristic of an organisation aiming at developing global people and so we deal with it as a separate topic below.

To sum up, well-being in the workplace is a wide-ranging concept, covering the characteristics of both the physical and psychological environment. It is beneficial not only to the employees, but also to the organisation. It is not merely a way of improving organisational branding in the war for talent and customers in the western world, as some doubters would have it, but also as a key indicator of business performance. We explore these issues in more detail below, focusing particularly on a diversity or Global Fitness perspective.

Physical and mental well-being

The ILO sets many international standards for positive workplace environments, including the promotion of rights at work, decent employment opportunities, the enhancement of social protection, and the strengthening of dialogue on work-related issues. Nevertheless, different countries have many country-specific requirements that need to be adhered to. For instance, the UAE has a midday break rule which prohibits anyone from working directly under the sun between 12.30 pm and 3 pm during its blazing hot summers.[68] In China, women cannot be asked to work under certain conditions (e.g., working high above the ground, at low temperatures or in cold water, or anything involving hard physical labour) when they are menstruating.[69]

Given the extensive variation across countries in health and safety standards, a frequent challenge for companies headquartered in one region of the world is ensuring that health and safety standards laid down by HQ as standard for the whole company are adhered to in another region and indeed conform to local legal minimum standards.

The extent to which worker representation is implemented and listened to is a key concern, especially in potentially hazardous industries such as mining. For instance, a project funded by the Institution of Occupational Safety and Health (IOSH)[70] compared worker representation in the mining industry in Australia, Canada, India, Indonesia, and South Africa. The study found that in Australia, mineworkers were more able to make effective representations to

---

[68]   https://www.adphc.gov.ae/en/Public-Health-Programs/Injury-Prevention/Safety-in-Heat

[69]   http://english.mofcom.gov.cn/aarticle/lawsdata/chineselaw/200211/20021100050536.html

[70]   https://iosh.com/more/news-listing/developing-countries-miners-face-substantial-risk-inequality/

management on health and safety matters and stop dangerous work without fear of reprisal than miners in other countries, especially those in India and Indonesia.

A more individual angle on this is whistleblowing. The National Whistle-blower Center (NWC), headquartered in the USA, comments that there has been a growing global interest in establishing whistleblower laws and that whistleblower protections have been enacted in at least 59 countries. However, it also points out that many laws still fail to support effective whistleblowing.[71] It is also possible that Cultural Perspectives, such as collectivism and a high degree of power distance, may affect employees' willingness to raise any breaches of the law. This also relates to their possible fear of reprisal, an issue we consider in more detail later in this chapter.

Work-life balance

In terms of mental well-being, a wide range of factors can have an influence. One issue that is widely referred to in prosperous countries is work-life balance. Recently—especially following the Covid-19 pandemic—the issue of working from home and its link to work-life balance and well-being has come to the fore. Of course, many people cannot work from home, just because of the nature of their jobs. For those who can, many people find it better for their well-being to work from home at least two or three days a week.

However, two dangers can be associated with this: the risks of over-working and reduced human connection. As we have repeatedly mentioned, good relationships at work have both personal and professional benefits and are vital for Global Fitness. The businessman, Barry D. Moore, comments as follows:

> Now here is one of the biggest drawbacks [of working from home], the human connection. There are no workarounds for this. Being in the office means you will, over time, develop relationships with certain people that turn into friendships. You will even have professional rela-tionships where you gain a mentor or simply someone to bounce your work issues off. This does not happen for telecommuters, or at least the opportunities are far fewer.[72]

The importance attached to work-life balance and how it is (or is not) achieved varies from individual to individual and also from country to country. It needs to be remembered, however, that employees of high-achieving organisations

---

[71]   https://www.whistleblowers.org/whistleblower-laws-around-the-world/
[72]   https://www.greatworklife.com/pros-and-cons-of-working-from-home/

may not always be able to afford the luxury of placing the demands of work-ing life in an acceptable relationship to private life. The norms of corporate culture or professional culture, such as in many consultancies or the finance sector, may make this difficult. Work-life balance is hard to reconcile, for exam-ple, with the demands of the 996 working hour system in Chinese internet companies (i.e., working from 9 am to 9 pm Monday to Saturday) something deemed illegal by the Chinese courts in 2021 but fostered by hi-tech corporate culture, not only in China.

Uncertainty at work

Many people also face considerable job insecurity, and this brings us to a second key influence on mental well-being: uncertainty (see Chapter 2). Uncertainty can arise from numerous factors, for example, from working in precarious or unstable employment situations or being dependent on two or more jobs. Restructuring resulting from economic measures or mergers typically leads to employees fearing they may lose their jobs and when cultural factors are added to the mix, negative emotions can be even stronger.

For instance, uncertainty, fear and annoyance resulting from a merger with a German company were mentioned by two English managers: one spoke of his "resentment that although the German company had been losing a great deal of money and, despite it being a 'merger', the Germans took control"; the other com-mented "initially, at the start of the merger, I felt German dominance and power struggle before our jobs were defined, because I feared I would lose my job."

This was also the situation described in Case Study 11.1. In this par-ticular case, the U.S. employees resented their former colleagues' positions being taken over by 'outsiders' (the Indian workers), while simultaneously worrying that they themselves may be next in line to lose their jobs and be replaced. The Indians, on the other hand, experienced several formal com-plaints against them. They tended to speak among themselves in their native language in the hallways and the U.S. employees did not like this, perhaps fearing the Indians were talking negatively about them. There were also com-plaints about the smell of their food, as the Indian workers heated curries and other fragrant food in a microwave next to the work area. Even more prob-lematically, the Indians perceived race to be a salient issue. One commented: "If you are white / Caucasian, that is good, and if you are not, then you have to work harder."

Psychological safety and a sense of being included and belonging are also critically important to mental well-being. We explore them in turn in the following sections. First, though, we encourage you to reflect on your/your organisation's current situation.

Activity 11.1: Your organisation		
Personal reflections		
1. To what extent do you notice in your workplace that your organisation prioritises the following issues? 2. To what extent are they important to you?		
	Prioritised by your organisation on a scale from 1 low to 10 high	Important to you on a scale from 1 low to 10 high
Safety of the work environment		
Quality of the work environment		
Work-life balance		
Job security		
Feeling included, integrated, and belonging		
Working climate		
Questions for senior management		
3. What steps have you taken / could you take to find out the viewpoints of the employees in your organisation / department / work unit? 4. What issues emerge as priorities for management to address?		

Inclusion, integration, and well-being

An aspect of workplace life that has a major impact on well-being and that can also affect employees' sense of psychological safety (see also below) is the inclusion or exclusion and integration or marginalisation of members of different social groups. People belonging to different cultural groups within an organisation and possessing different identity characteristics (e.g., age, gender, race, religion, etc.) can feel excluded and threatened for a number of reasons. We touched on this in Chapter 5; here we consider it from a senior management / organisational perspective.

Cultural discrimination

Sometimes people's sense of exclusion may stem from feelings or experiences of discrimination. For instance, in the case reported in Case Study 11.1, and as mentioned above, the employees from India felt disadvantaged because of their race. This could lead to what we call a cultural glass ceiling—a barrier that comes from conscious and sub-conscious discrimination in a range of situations, including in job appraisals, promotions, new work opportunities, and so on (see Chapter 12).

Many companies have Equality and Diversity policies in place or codes of conduct that highlight the importance of such policies. These, in turn, may reflect statutory obligations and are obviously of very great importance. However, in themselves, they are insufficient because we all have patterned ways of thinking (often referred to as 'unconscious bias') that can lead us to make assumptions and judgements which are based less on 'facts' than on pre-conceived viewpoints and attitudes. These need to be addressed, as failure to do so can lead to negative attitudes and cynicism. An HR consultant comments as follows on this:

> In my experience with clients, organizations who say they value inclusion but *don't* do the hard work of living that value create much more cynicism and skepticism than engagement. On the other hand, organizations who are very clear about how they value inclusion and how that is reflected across the Talent Lifecycle and employee experience are vastly more successful. Ultimately, inclusion lives not only as a beautiful statement in the annual report or on the website, but in the behaviors and actions of the organization's people at every level.[73]

Developing a culture of inclusion

Developing a culture of inclusion and integration is the responsibility of everybody, including all in senior management. Of course, one important aspect is policy—the development of a suitable diversity and inclusion framework. Yet according to a 2022 white paper,[74] reporting on the responses of 367 HR professionals from across a wide range of industries and different regions of the world, the maturity of many companies' diversity, equity and inclusion (DEI) policies is not very advanced. Less than one-quarter of respondents reported that their organizations have "advanced" (18%) or "expert" (4%) DEI practices; the remaining 78% fell into less mature stages.

The paper also reports that most companies fall short in the areas of metrics and training. Only 42% of respondents reported any evaluation of diversity within leadership ranks and even fewer (23%) reported measuring diversity goals related to succession planning. Employees also had limited DEI-related learning and development opportunities and only 9% rated their organization's

---

[73] Fuller, P., Murphy, M., & Chow, A. (2020). *The leader's guide to unconscious bias*. London: Simon & Schuster.

[74] The future of diversity, equity and inclusion 2022. HR Research Institute white paper, sponsored by Affirmity. https://www.affirmity.com/wp-content/uploads/2022/03/Affirmity_the_Future_of_DEI_2022_Research_Report_hrdotcom.pdf

DEI initiatives as highly effective. So, while DEI policies often set diversity targets, such targets—important as they are—are insufficient on their own.

Cultural factors can play a role here. As mentioned in Chapter 9, research from Africa[75] has shown, women and young people often feel their ideas and viewpoints are not valued, because of cultural traditions that give status and power to older men, and they are pushing for change and greater inclusion.

Real implementation and change require reflection followed by action. This includes reflection both on one's own behaviour as well as that of the employees in one's team / department / organisation. Activity 11.5 offers a few suggestions of ways in which leaders can start to address this process.

Activity 11.2: Reflections[76]

1. Write down the names of your direct reports and if you have none, your key colleagues.
2. For each one, consider how your own identity characteristics (e.g., age, gender, race, religion etc.) could be influencing how you see this person, the type of relationship you have with them, and how you make decisions with or regarding them.
3. How positive or negative are the influences and how might they affect the person's sense of inclusion and integration within your team / department?

Language and a sense of exclusion

Language can play a major role in influencing people's sense of inclusion / exclusion. This is particularly the case for those who are less fluent in the working language, such as migrants. Care needs to be taken to support them through patience and mindful communication (see Chapter 4), thereby helping them develop their proficiency and move from peripheral new members to established core members of the workforce. If that is not done, creative and innovative ideas may be lost, as we noted in Chapter 8.

Feelings of language exclusion, however, are not limited to members of minority groups; members of the majority culture can also feel excluded on this basis. For instance, as mentioned above, this happened with regard to Case Study 11.1. The U.S. employees—who were already feeling uncertain and stressed since many of their colleagues had recently lost their jobs—disliked the Indian recruits speaking in their native language in the hallways. They couldn't

---

[75] Jordans, E., Ng'weno, B., & Spencer-Oatey, H. (Eds.). (2020). *Developing global leaders. Insights from African Case Studies.* London: Palgrave Macmillan.

[76] Based on material in Fuller, P., Murphy, M., & Chow, A. (2020). *The leader's guide to unconscious bias.* London: Simon & Schuster.

understand what they were saying, and feared they were speaking negatively about them.

We also noted a similar situation in Case Study 4.9 where there were complaints that members of certain language sections were speaking too loudly. Case Study 11.2 provides some additional information on this case, particularly from a discrimination perspective. As noted in Chapter 4, Noriko worked in the Japanese section of the marketing department of a multinational company based in the UK. Some British employees complained that her team were talking too loudly.

Case Study 11.2: Multilingual companies and language policy

Noriko's line manager thought the complaints against them could be because they were not speaking English and came across to others as loud, simply for this reason. Those complaining also wouldn't be able to tell whether or not the teams were discussing work matters and so that may also have influenced them. The HR manager checked up on the issue regularly and whenever he came to the Chinese and Japanese sections, he made comments like "So are the Chinese staff and Japanese staff quiet today?" Concerned about this, the manager of the two teams asked them to talk only in English—yet he was afraid to make that official in case it was regarded as discriminatory. Needless to say, both Chinese and Japanese teams did indeed feel discriminated against (other teams were not required to speak in English) and they also felt it was less efficient for work purposes. Not long afterwards, Noriko left the company.

Reflect

a. Why do you think the Chinese and Japanese departments were singled out?
b. How acceptable or unacceptable were the HR manager's comments?
c. What language policy would you recommend for a company with a multicultural workforce? What factors would you consider in drawing it up?
d. How far do language factors influence people's sense of inclusion / exclusion, integration / marginalisation in your own workplace? What evidence do you have to support your views?

These examples (Case Studies 11.1 and 11.2) also suggest that the well-being of the minority group members may be negatively affected by pressure from both colleagues and superiors to assimilate to the majority group. This can include the expectation that they should communicate in English even amongst themselves. This expected assimilation, whether communicated implicitly or explicitly, as in Case Studies 11.1 and 11.2 respectively, can be experienced as a threat to the social identity of groups and their members and can be very discomfiting. It may thus also affect employees' performance and goal achievement.

One of the top priorities, therefore, for an organisation aiming to develop its Global Fitness and that of its employees will be to take steps to reduce possible feelings of exclusion, particularly on the part of members of minority cultural groups, and thereby increase well-being. Possible measures that could be taken include:

- Raise awareness across the organisation of the damage caused by language that makes people feel excluded.
- Encourage all employees to be sensitive to the way in which they use language and the impact it may have.
- Avoid imposing any rules for language use because they are often counter-productive.

Psychological safety and well-being

Several times so far in this chapter we have mentioned the concept of psychological safety. This concept is much talked about in many parts of the western world and has been variously defined. We find global leadership consultant Timothy Clark's definition particularly helpful:

> Psychological safety is a condition in which you feel (1) included, (2) safe to learn, (3) safe to contribute, and (4) safe to challenge the status quo—all without fear of being embarrassed, marginalised, or punished in some way.[77]

We explain Clark's four stages as shown in Table 11.1.

Table 11.1: The four stages of psychological safety (based on Clark)

Inclusion safety	Inclusion safety is created and sustained for you when you are admitted to a new group and receive repeated indications of acceptance.
Learner safety	Learner safety occurs when you feel safe and supported to explore any new job, position, or task you may have, such as by asking questions, experimenting, and even making mistakes.
Contributor safety	Contributor safety occurs when you have acquired competence in your new job or position, and you feel safe and accepted as an active, fully-fledged member.
Challenger safety	Challenger safety occurs when you feel able to challenge others' ideas without fear of being punished or without the risk of damaging your personal standing or reputation.

---

[77] Clark, T.R. (2020). *The 4 stages of psychological safety. Defining the path to inclusion and innovation.* Oakland, CA: Berrett-Koehler Publishers.

Our discussion of inclusion in the previous section links with the notion of inclusion safety, as well as with aspects of learner safety. In this section we focus on contributor safety and challenger safety.

Contributor safety

As the explanation in Table 11.1 implies, contributor safety refers to trust by line managers in their employee(s) that they are competent to carry out their role. As a result, they are not overly micro-managed and they do not fear that they will be immediately reprimanded if things don't work out as intended.

Needless to say, this is a risk for senior management and so prior to granting the employees contributor safety, they will need to have first provided learner safety, supporting their employees in building up their competence. Then, to transition to contributor safety, there may be formal procedures, such as qualifying examinations, or other less formal processes that organisations and sectors may use to help confirm that the risk of greater autonomy is low enough for contributor safety to be granted. This means accepting that problems will not necessarily be solved immediately, that mistakes may be made, and that help from others may be needed. Then employees can feel confident about carrying out their role to the best of their ability.

Unfortunately, however, there can often be a tendency for senior management to expect high performance while simultaneously hindering contributor safety. This may occur, for example, because of failure (unintended or otherwise) to allow or encourage individuals to put forward their ideas (e.g., see Chapters 4 and 8 on turn-taking) or through their critical response to any lack of immediate success, as Case Study 11.3 indicates. This case study comes from an HR Consultant, commenting on his experiences working with hospital employees.

Case Study 11.3: Leadership blindness to psychological safety[78]

"Some organizations proclaim to be open to making mistakes and "failing fast", but their practices and the experiences of their people tell a different story. I worked with a hospital that holds innovation as one of their core values. To this end, they engaged us to create and execute a development program designed to foster greater innovation.

I had a candid conversation with the client, who shared the challenges she foresaw in building competency around innovation. Principal among them was the fact that creating opportunities for innovation was limited because of the very cautious culture and intolerance for error or mistakes. In other words, there was very little psychological safety.

---

[78] Fuller, P., Murphy, M., & Chow, A. (2020). *The leader's guide to unconscious bias*. London: Simon & Schuster.

> Subsequent conversations with several employees confirmed what she had told me. One employee said, "They tell us to be creative in our approach to problem solving. But if we try something new and the problem isn't resolved immediately and perfectly, we're reprimanded, sometimes publicly!" The organization's bias for avoiding risk overtook the need for innovation in daily practice.
>
> For people to give their best efforts, they need to know they will be supported, even when they occasionally miss the mark."

In this example, top management in the hospital were trying to foster innovation (see Chapter 12), yet their handling of psychological safety, especially in terms of contributor safety, was seriously undermining their goals. Their attitude to mistakes—that is, their lack of contributor safety—was making their employees perceive innovation as a risk. This is because it could easily result in a reprimand, which might be given in public. This in turn could lead to embarrassment, a negative assessment of their performance, and/or the possibility that their future career could be affected.

Challenger safety

In Case Study 11.3, the organisation wanted to achieve innovation, but they granted neither contributor safety nor challenger safety. As we discussed in Chapter 8, new ideas emerge from the stimulation of difference. When different ideas are rejected or not seriously considered, creativity is stifled or supressed and little innovation occurs (see Case Study 8.1). Clark explains it like this:

> Where there is no tolerance for candor, there is no constructive dissent. Where there is no constructive dissent, there is no innovation.

Lack of opportunity for sharing ideas freely can undermine motivation and reduce a sense of involvement and well-being. Clark advises two key things to enhance challenger safety and promote innovation: seek out differences and reduce the risk of ridicule. This involves building a diverse workforce on the one hand and encouraging divergent thinking on the other. The latter requires leaders to eliminate all ridiculing behaviour (i.e., not to engage in face-threatening behaviour—see Chapter 5) both in their own behaviour and also by creating a norm that does not accept it in others. This is sometimes easier said than done as Clark admits with a personal example:

> I remember being in a meeting with my team in which our chief financial officer (CFO) openly ridiculed our chief marketing officer for some of his marketing ideas and the way he wanted to allocate his budget. Rather than intercede and call out the CFO right then and there, I let it go. [...] I tolerated the ridicule and my inaction that day [...] opened the door for more ridicule and closed the door on more innovation.

Cultural differences can affect the way in which this is handled, and some people may disagree about dealing with it publicly. Nevertheless, it is too simplistic to assume that challenger safety cannot be achieved in strongly hierarchical contexts. Clark gives another example in which he explains how his Japanese boss was superb at nurturing a culture of enquiry. His boss made it clear from his manner of interaction that there were no stupid questions and no questions or topics that couldn't be raised. Not all senior management can manage that yet will need to do so if they want to significantly enhance creativity and innovation.

Lack of challenger safety not only affects level of innovation; it can also affect staff turnover. Case Study 11.4 illustrates this. It comes from a study of U.S. American-owned assembly plants in Mexico (maquiladoras) and are the words of one of the researchers.

Case Study 11.4: Psychological safety and staff turnover in Mexico[79]

"Employee turnover is often a major issue that contributes to increased costs in training and lost productivity. The following description of what one manager describes as very typical may help in understanding ways that communication influences this process. He said, 'Workers will not tell you when they're unhappy, they will just quit. On their termination form, they will write: "Oh yes, I was very happy, I would work here again." and they just quit!'. When I asked him, 'How can you tell when workers are unhappy if they don't tell you?' he responded:

> You have to watch them at work. Look at how fast they move on their job, look for the brilliance in their eyes, ask them questions, ask them for feedback about their job—is there anything they need? Ask how you can help your employees.

In this description, it is clear that the assembly-line worker who has recently terminated their employment is obeying the cultural norm of 'face-saving' and not stating their complaints directly. [...] it is the nonverbal cues, including pace of work and 'brilliance' in eyes, that the manager needs to be able to understand in order to then solicit [ask for] feedback from the employee through verbal channels. [...] When the manager interprets these nonverbal expressive behaviors, solicitation of [requests for] employee feedback is stated in a positive manner, honoring the face of the other—'How can I help you?' demonstrates respect for the other's capabilities in fulfilling their work roles, and the interdependency of the manager–employee relationship in working together to achieve corporate goals."

In this example, the employees were very reluctant to express any dissatisfaction explicitly; instead, they showed it much more implicitly (see discussion of

[79] Lindsley, S.L., & Braithwaite, C.A. (1996). "You should 'wear a mask'": Facework norms in cultural and intercultural conflict in Maquiladoras. *International Journal of Intercultural Relations, 20*(2), 199–225. pp. 210–211.

directness / indirectness in Chapter 4). So, the manager recommends that in contexts such as this, leaders should:

- Pay very careful attention to subtle signs.
- Talk with the employee in an appreciative manner.

Summing it up, Clark maintains that senior management need to "reduce social friction while increasing intellectual friction." This links with the argument we made in Chapter 8 that when teams have positive interpersonal relationships (i.e., low social friction) they are better able to use different ideas (i.e., intellectual friction) to generate innovation.

Activity 11.3: Psychological safety and organisational culture

1. Reflect on your own organisation. How similar or different is it to that described in Case Study 11.3 and/or Case Study 11.4?
2. What evidence do you have for your assessment?
3. What strategies have you used / could you use to promote greater contributor safety? What difficulties have you experienced or do you think you might experience?
4. What strategies have you used / could you use to promote greater challenger safety? What difficulties have you experienced or do you think you might experience?
5. How might cultural differences affect the ease or difficulty of achieving contributor safety and challenger safety and ways of doing so?

Performance management, motivation, and well-being

Another factor that influences employee well-being—albeit interconnected with the issues discussed so far—is an organisation's performance management policy. This can have a major impact on staff motivation, which in turn can influence well-being. However, from a Global Fitness perspective, there are often cultural differences in people's responses to performance-management policies and these can influence the extent to which the policies enhance or undermine staff motivation. The classic approach of rewarding individual performance may be unsuitable in country and organisational cultural settings which emphasise group-oriented Perspectives and Practices.

Cross-cultural management scholar, Terence Jackson,[80] argues that differences in fundamental values are key to understanding varying attitudes towards

---

[80] Jackson, T. (2002). The management of people across cultures: Valuing people differently. *Human Resource Management, 41*(4), 455–475.

performance management policies. He stresses the importance of the notion 'locus of human value'—the value that management attributes to employees—and distinguishes between an instrumental orientation and a humane orientation. This is an additional Cultural Perspective to those we introduced in Chapter 3. Jackson maintains that organisations that take an instrumental orientation see employees as a means to an end; in other words, they regard them as the route to achieving the strategic objectives of the organisation. On the other hand, organisations that take a humane orientation see employees as having value for who they are, rather than for what they can do for the organisation. These value differences give rise to different approaches to performance management as indicated in Table 11.1.

Table 11.1: Performance management priorities according to Human Value Orientation

Human value of employees to senior management	
Instrumental Orientation	**Humane Orientation**
• Job measurement • Pay for performance	• Job commitment • Person development

Jackson goes on to point out that when there are mismatches in senior management versus employee performance management preferences, as well as organisational rhetoric and practice, this typically results in low motivation among employees, a sense of alienation, leading to low productivity and problems in labour relations. Needless to say, all these elements undermine well-being and weaken the conditions for fostering Global Fitness.

It is really important, therefore, for senior management to spend time with their staff, finding out their performance management preferences and working with them to develop and implement policies and procedures that are as widely accepted as possible. This will involve reconciling possibly very diverse personal and cultural preferences.

Activity 11.4: Performance management priorities

1. How does performance management operate in your organisation?
2. How satisfied are you with it and why?
3. Which human value orientation is closest to your viewpoint?
4. How far does your human value orientation match your level of satisfaction with your company's performance management system?

Key takeaways

Core insights	Applications for practice

• In many economies in the Western world, physical and mental well-being is a fundamental ingredient of the health and safety at work requirements laid down in law and a pre-requisite for acquiring Global Fitness.
• A suitable work-life balance contributes to well-being, but a reasonable balance is often put at risk from precarious employment conditions and overly demanding corporate cultures.
• A sense of inclusion is vital to well-being and the performance of both employees and the company. It can be undermined when:
   ○ there is a cultural glass ceiling for certain employees
   ○ people feel excluded for language reasons or other reasons
• Psychological safety is of vital importance and occurs in stages as people feel:
   ○ included
   ○ supported in learning
   ○ trusted to work independently
   ○ able to question and disagree
• Effective performance management / reward procedures can be affected by the cultural values that employees hold.
	As a senior manager:
	• Familiarise yourself with your organisation's health and safety policies and check their suitability for your workforce and the pressures they are under.
	• Find out your employees' viewpoints on physical and mental safety and well-being and act on them.
	• Find out your employees' experiences of inclusion / exclusion: what helps enhance a sense of inclusion and what undermines it.
	• Involve employees in developing a set of procedures to promote inclusion which they can willingly follow and implement.
	• Find out how far your employees experience contributor safety and challenger safety. Plan ways in which you could increase both.
	• Examine your organisation's performance management /reward procedures and consider their suitability in light of feedback from employees on their preferences and take them into account.

12

Promoting learning and innovation: How to leverage cultural diversity

Introduction

In Chapter 1 we described the concept of transformational learning, pointing out the importance it attaches to people moving out of their comfort zones and engaging with difference in order to gain new insights, ideas and ways of doing things. In Part 2 of the book, we showed how that learning process can be applied to a range of different functional situations that you as an individual might face. In this chapter, we consider how senior management and decision-makers can and, we believe, should promote and support the process of learning, maximising the development of an innovative and dynamic workforce.

The aim of the chapter is to help you:

- Maximise innovation through minimising groupthink.
- Increase diversity through effective recruitment.
- Enhance Global Fitness development at work.
- Retain talent and knowledge through offering (if possible) attractive career pathways.

Fostering an open atmosphere—minimising groupthink, maximising innovation

In the previous chapter we considered the impact of workplace culture on well-being, and we noted in passing that too much uncertainty and stress can hinder people from focusing on their work, with the result that it can reduce their learning and personal development. Here we consider another angle on the issue—the importance of an open atmosphere and the need to minimise groupthink. This is essential if creativity, innovation and problem-solving are to be maximised.

In line with this, the CEO of Novartis, Vas Narasimhan, identifies organisational culture as the major determinant of performance, and argues that leaders need to foster a workplace culture that gives people a sense of purpose, stimulates them to be curious, and allows them the freedom to challenge existing ways of doing things and to come up with new ideas.[81]

As we noted in Chapter 3, one definition of culture is 'ways of doing things around here'. When people from a similar cultural background have worked together for a while, they can easily start thinking and acting in similar ways; in other words, they start creating their own small culture, which may have advantages. However, this can also make it difficult for newcomers to feel part of the group; what is more, it has the risk of encouraging groupthink. This can be dangerous, limiting open discussion and challenge and thereby reducing effective problem-solving.

A British parliamentary report[82] on the UK government's Covid-19 policy pointed to groupthink as a major factor that, in their view, led to the country's worst ever public health failure. Case Study 12.1 quotes from the report.

Case Study 12.1: The danger of groupthink

In October 2021 a report was published on the UK government's handling of the Covid-19 pandemic. It says, "The UK did not take enough advantage of the learning and experience being generated in other countries, notably in East Asia" and it identified groupthink as a key contributor to this. For instance, the report quotes the former Chief Medical Officer for England, Professor Dame Sally Davies, as follows:

> Quite simply, we were in groupthink. Our infectious disease experts really did not believe that SARS, or another SARS, would get from Asia to us. It is a form of British exceptionalism. We need to open up and get some more challenge into our thinking about what we are planning for [...] In thinking through what could happen, it would be well worth bringing in people from Asia and Africa to think about that as well, to broaden our experience and the voices in the room.

In light of this and other evidence, the report concludes that groupthink had a significant negative impact, resulting in the government not being open to approaches being taken elsewhere. In their recommendations for the future, they advise that the scientific advice given to the government through official channels should be published within 24 hours of it being given "to ensure the opportunity for rapid scientific challenge and guard against the risk of groupthink".

---

[81] *Novartis CEO, Vas Narasimhan: How to be a boss in an 'unbossed' company.* Video available on Youtube: https://www.youtube.com/watch?v=hsgi9CJ61wg&t=39s

[82] House of Commons Health and Social Care, and Science and Technology Committees Coronavirus: lessons learned to date Sixth Report of the Health and Social Care Committee and Third Report of the Science and Technology Committee of Session 2021–22. Retrieved from https://committees.parliament.uk/publications/7496/documents/78687/default/

While the report oversimplifies the input provided by scientists, underplaying the range of viewpoints and evidence presented to the government, it seems nevertheless that groupthink definitely played a negative role in handling the crisis.

How then can it be prevented? The former Chief Medical Officer's advice is to:

- Open up.
- Encourage different opinions to be expressed by different people in order to challenge a group's thinking and planning.
- Bring in 'outsiders' who can offer new perspectives and experience.

An atmosphere of psychological safety is vital for the first two points—an issue we considered in the previous chapter. The third point above draws attention to the need for input from a variety of people, including those with very different backgrounds and experiences. It also points to the value from the business point of view of a culturally diverse workforce and the importance of including a wide cross-section of people in the discussions. In Chapter 8 we considered how individuals and teams can leverage their differences and increase their creativity and innovation. Here we are considering it from a strategic management point of view—how to create the environment that fosters and encourages such growth. Part of this relates to recruitment and so we consider that next.

Diversifying the workforce through recruitment

Ensuring fair and creative recruitment

There are frequent reports in the media about recruitment inequalities associated with various identity characteristics, especially ethnicity and gender. Clearly, this is an important ethical issue, but here we are focusing on its impact on business success. A culturally diverse workforce has the potential to bring numerous benefits, as Figure 12.1 shows. If people from diverse backgrounds work well together, so that all can engage in constructive discussions, this can lead to enhanced goal achievement on the one hand, and to a more engaged and motivated workforce on the other. This in turn can result in stronger business performance, reduced employee turnover, enhanced employer branding and a better company reputation. So even for business reasons alone, it is an important policy to pursue.

Recruiting fairly and successfully is not always easy. Some organisations—aware that they are failing to recruit effectively and fairly—have introduced the automated screening of online applications and CVs, which selects first-round applicants on the basis of strictly job-related keywords. Subsequent selection

Figure 12.1: The potential business and management benefits of a culturally diverse workforce

steps filter out social identity features (e.g., age, gender, ethnicity) in the information on applicants so that possible prejudice does not influence the decision as to which applicants are invited for the final online and face-to-face steps of the recruitment process.

However, this does not necessarily solve the problem. This is especially the case for multinational organisations if they have a standard recruitment procedure because their system may be unfamiliar to those who are used to a different process. Recruiters may therefore fail to recruit or may miss out on some excellent candidates for this reason.

Case Study 12.2 illustrates this. The comments are made by a British director of a third-sector organisation working in Tanzania, who was supposed to follow the recruitment process set by UK headquarters. She describes the kinds of problems she faced when attempting to do so.

Case Study 12.2: Culture and the recruitment process

"A big area I have trouble with is recruitment. I think the sort of language we use is very Eurocentric. That's very off-putting. I think the elaborate process we have for interview is also very off-putting and intimidating. Here is an example.

I've been recruiting for a finance manager, and we advertised in an English-speaking daily newspaper because English is such an important requirement for the post. In the first round we got maybe 400 applications. It was very clear on the advertisement that applicants should not just send a cv, they must complete and submit the application form. We gave them different ways of getting the application form. So, the first round was really quite quick. We ignored everybody who hadn't filled in the application form and had just sent in their cv. But the quality of the applications that we got were appalling. We invited a relatively small number to come in for a briefing. We discussed the competencies and the approach with them and then we asked them to go back and re-do their application forms. And that in itself narrowed down the process. However, we weren't successful in finding the right candidate in that round so we went to a second round. The second time I just asked for cvs and I just ignored our internal process, which would have me hanged, but it's just so alien to the local culture that I decided that in order to get the sort of person I wanted I would have to meet them on their terms and not to try and persuade them to meet me on my terms."

As you can see from the account, the director received a very poor set of applications initially and despite giving people the opportunity to resubmit their applications, she still failed to recruit. She thus had to go to a second round and this time she ignored her organisation's internal process and used a system that she felt was better suited to the local context in which she was working.

On a generic level, this case illustrates the conflicting demands placed on expatriates (and others) by the culturally diverse context they are working in. On the one hand, they are subject to the standardisation and formalisation required by headquarters, often located far away and in a very different cultural setting. On the other hand, their context requires a flexible response (see Chapter 6 and Chapter 9). This tension, which needs to be balanced in some way, can be a source of considerable stress for global people. It demands resilience of the expatriate if the goal-orientation typical of the high-performing manager—in this case, finding the best qualified person for the job—is not to be compromised by not reacting flexibly to the context.

Activity 12.1: Reflecting on recruitment processes

Consider a recruitment process you are familiar with in your organisation.

1. What steps are involved?
2. How successful have they been in enabling you to recruit the calibre of staff you need?
3. How successful have they been in enabling you to attract culturally diverse applicants?
4. What difficulties do you think some applicants may have in fulfilling your application requirements?
5. What steps have you taken, if any, to check on this?
6. What recommendations, if any, do you have for improving the recruitment process?

Targeted hiring

Sometimes a company may choose a targeted new-hire approach in order to buy in the Global Fitness attribute that is lacking in the company but urgently required. For instance, in a Sino-British project, it was initially assumed that

English would be the working language of the collaborative project teams. Phase 1 of the project proceeded on that basis, but it soon became clear that this added very significantly to the workload of the Chinese partners and was leading to resentment. As a result, the British partners decided to recruit Chinese speakers with relevant professional expertise for Phase 2 of the project.

In this case, the type of missing Global Fitness expertise was relatively easy to identify and recruit for. However, trying to recruit for Global Fitness more generically begs the question as to how it can be reliably assessed in the recruitment process. Demanding it as a required qualification for the position is one thing; being sure that it has been demonstrated is quite another, as intercultural competence is notoriously difficult to assess reliably and objectively.

Many pencil-and-paper or online self-assessments only fulfil a low level of reliability, which may be acceptable when the instrument is used for development purposes but hardly for selection; few people have the expert knowledge required as an observer to assess such competence in an interview situation or assessment centre; and the mere demonstration of experience in a culturally diverse setting is in itself no proof of competence. This means that those involved in the selection procedure need to have a thorough understanding of the notion of Global Fitness and how to recognise it in applicants from different cultural backgrounds.

Other potential strategies

Apart from formal recruitment, there can be other opportunities for developing a diverse workforce. One option is the use of interns from groups outside the conventional pool of recruits or from abroad. In universities around the globe, thousands of students are required or keen to gain professional experience abroad. Relatively cheap, relatively flexible and themselves often equipped through their university studies with the intercultural skills which the receiving organisation is interested in fostering, foreign interns can bring about active engagement by the host company with other cultures in relatively unthreatening contexts, which are also not necessarily business-critical.

Building a Global Fitness talent pool is, of course, not just a matter of bringing diversity into the workforce. Existing staff need to be offered valuable work experience, attractive development opportunities, as well as a clear pathway for career progression. We turn to those various elements in the next few sections.

Maximising learning on the job and from the job

Opportunities for active engagement with cultural difference can result from simply doing business. If the workforce itself is diverse, then a wide variety of workplace experiences 'at home' (i.e., without international travel) can challenge the status quo through being unfamiliar and unexpected and can thereby have the potential to stimulate new thinking and learning. However, mindful reflection is needed for that learning to occur, as we have explored in Part 2 of the book.

The short visits to and from subsidiaries, suppliers, and clients abroad, which in the pre-Covid world were inevitable, offer further occasions for development. The decrease in international travel because of the pandemic and climate considerations is expected to continue post-pandemic and lead to an increase in the use of virtual media in the coming years. This will make grappling with different organisational and country cultures even more difficult but, at the same time, all the more crucial for successful collaboration. It remains to be seen if the prospects offered by augmented reality in the coming years may compensate for the deficiencies of current virtual communication media and the lack of face-to-face interaction.

Mentoring

If such visits abroad are to lead effectively to sustainable professional development, they need to be systematically supported. A formalised approach to tap into this experience is to use a mentoring system, whereby the more experienced, not necessarily older, member of staff is assigned a mentee. This person can turn to the mentor at regular or irregular intervals to profit from the mentor's greater knowledge and experience.

Diversity mentoring may be especially appropriate in this context. A mentor from a cultural minority within the organisation (for example, an inpatriate—see below) paired with a mentee from the cultural majority can lead to considerable learning and an incidental increase in the status of the minority culture. Professional bodies, such as the European Mentoring and Coaching Council, set standards and give guidance on procedures.

However, many companies may be unable to implement such a mentoring system for various reasons and alternative support mechanisms need to be found. One way is to combine visits overseas with formal training (see Chapter 14). This is the route taken by the company described in Case Study 12.3 and proved to be extremely effective.

Case Study 12.3: An SME's Internationalisation journey

Company X is a small, long established, family-owned, and partly family-run hidden champion,[83] part of the SME backbone of the German economy. The company has for many years been a respected and significant economic and social factor in its two rural locations in southern Germany. In the more than hundred years of its existence it has repeatedly re-invented itself to occupy today a niche with few competitors and an increasingly global client portfolio.

Reacting to the global nature of the demand for its products some years ago it embarked on a process of internationalisation by acquiring a competitor in Denmark, building a new production plant in Poland, and buying a plot of land for a further plant in India.

In the space of a few years, the company was faced with the task of encouraging a workforce with little experience of cultural diversity to engage with people in the very diverse, new foreign subsidiaries, who were often equally inexperienced at the interface of cultures.

As the Managing Partner drily pointed out, "Many of the German staff had never left the valley they live and work in." The talent pool was small and the reservoir of cultural knowledge and understanding very limited and so informal learning from rich, past experience was not a real possibility. Nobody could be found in the company to take up the expat positions deemed necessary to push ahead the internationalisation process.

The Managing Partner noted, "There were people we could have sent to Denmark who were technically qualified, but they were unwilling to take this development path". The company decided in the first instance to rely on frequent visits and began a slow process of intercultural professional development. Staff were encouraged to improve their English and intercultural training was initiated for all those with contact with the subsidiaries.

Informal learning

Many organisations, especially large ones—and unlike the company in Case Study 12.3—have a huge reservoir of knowledge, including knowledge of cultures and cultural differences. In these cases, a very valuable approach is strongly to encourage informal follow-up discussions after an intercultural event with experienced colleagues. This knowledge and understanding held by the experienced can be passed on informally in workplace tasks—for example, preparing meetings and negotiations—to the less experienced and thus remove or reduce the uncertainty connected with engaging with cultural differences. Such informal learning opportunities can be supplemented by 'lunch and learn' briefings and the like, which can be organised relatively easily and cheaply.

---

[83]   https://en.wikipedia.org/wiki/Hidden_champions

Expatriates

For large organisations, another development opportunity for both individuals and the organisation itself, is expatriate (expat) assignments. Organisations that have a sizeable talent pool may be able—and wish—to send somebody with expert knowledge to a location abroad for two or three years or longer. This can often be a promising development measure. The expat is often relatively young and being prepared for future leadership tasks. Engagement with cultural differences is necessarily a result, at least in the foreign workplace if not in the expat bubble, into which cosy and stimulating refuge from foreignness can be found.

In the best of cases, positive intercultural learning takes place, and with it professional and—implicitly—organisational development. Case Study 12.4 reports how this was the case for a senior UK project manager, Duncan, who spent several years in China in two separate assignments.

Case Study 12.4: An expatriate's development journey

"I was a senior project manager, and after 5 years working on a particular programme, I was looking for the next large programme role, and the new international programme roles offered an exciting role and career opportunity. So, I took up a placement in China.

I was hoping to enhance my experience and reputation as a programme leader, and to gain experience working in an international business. The position meant working closer with the leadership team and operating across all parts of the business. There were also significant financial incentives to encourage people to move and work abroad.

In fact, I ended up completing two separate assignments in China. I feel that both helped to build a strong sense of self-confidence in my own capability to go into a foreign environment and succeed in difficult circumstances. Without doubt this gave me the confidence to step into a new world of consultancy which has proved to be very successful."

However, the history of expatriate assignments since the beginning of internationalisation is full of stories of failure and these failures are one source of insights into what Global Fitness consists of.

One such key insight derived from the research and experiential evidence is that experience abroad and the enforced encounter with cultural difference alone are not a guarantee that Global Fitness increases. The expatriate and his / her family need to be prepared carefully before departure (see Chapter 14 for options) and ideally require ongoing and explicit support once in post. This can be provided by professionals but also by informal 'cultural informants'— locals and other expatriates who can make sense of the new world the expats are confronted with.

In fact, traditional expatriation (i.e., from global north to global south) is becoming less usual for a number of reasons besides the risk of failure. Why?

- It is an expensive approach, involving the transfer not just of the expatriate him / herself but often also of partner and children, the hiring of suitable accommodation, the provision of expensive international schooling and, on top of that, the payment of an overseas allowance.
- The rising educational level of local staff, who are in any case less costly, make it less necessary to bring in expert knowledge from headquarters.
- It is becoming increasingly difficult for companies to find people to stay in parts of the world with lower environmental standards and less effective (or in the case of Covid vaccination unavailable) anti-pandemic and other public health measures, as, for example, Beijing and Shanghai, are discovering to China's cost.

Economic migration world-wide has led not only to labour market flexibility but also to an increase in the country-cultural diversity of the global talent pool. One of the results of the freedom of movement of people in the European Union guaranteed by the E.U. treaties has led to increased economic migration within Europe itself—and incidentally contributed to the U.K.'s exit from the E.U. and a reduction in the diversity of its workforce.

Inpatriates

The larger scale of operations in already global companies also opens up a further path to engaging with cultural difference—namely the use of inpatriates (often known as inpats). The temporary transfer of people from foreign subsidiaries to headquarters (or to other subsidiaries) leads to an enrichment of cultural diversity in the host organisation. This is a place which is often mainly influenced by the cultural background of the organisation's founders and/or its immediate environment. Interestingly, cultural enrichment at headquarters is not usually the motivation for using inpats in this way; rather headquarters expects a greater familiarisation of the inpat with its own values, norms, and practices, which are then transferred back into the subsidiary on the return of the inpat. Organisations hosting inpats should, however, consciously take steps to encourage two-way learning through buddying activities, for example.

Volunteering

Yet another possibility concerns engagement with members of other cultures in CSR activities. For instance, in 2015 and subsequent years, volunteering to assist refugees and asylum seekers—and indeed integrating them into the labour market—brought about such contact for people in numerous companies in Europe. Whereas the intended and actual effect of such voluntary engagement on the part of business may have been something different (as the well-researched example of Austrian Federal Railways shows[84]), one inevitable side-effect will have been the active engagement with cultural otherness and the development of Global Fitness.

Whatever the method used to provide and promote opportunities for engagement with cultural difference, it is always important for people to reflect. Sadly, very often the sense of urgency prevalent in the business world means that time and space in the diary are not made available for such follow-up discussion or mentoring. As a result, important Global Fitness development opportunities are likely to be lost. When this happens, knowledge remains hidden and unused by people who do not 'own' it.

We encourage you to reflect on your own organisation in terms of strategies for enhancing learning from engagement with cultural diversity.

Activity 12.2: Learning on and from the job

Consider to what extent the measures described above and listed below are applicable to you or your current work situation.

Measure	A good idea for you personally / your team / organisation as a whole? On a scale from 1 low to 10 high	Already practised in your organisation? Yes / no / don't know	How to take it further; who to approach? Name / department
Short visits to foreign subsidiaries / clients / suppliers / partners			
Acting as a mentor			
Being a mentee			
Expatriate assignments			

---

[84] Einwiller, S., Ruppel, C., & Strasser, C. (2019). Effects of corporate social responsibility activities for refugees: The case of Austrian Federal Railways. *Corporate Communications: An International Review, 24*(2), 318–333.

Inpatriate assignments			
Hiring interns from culturally different backgrounds			
Short-term volunteering in culturally diverse settings			

Retaining talent, managing career progression opportunities

Throughout this chapter we have emphasised the importance of reflection and debriefing, so that both individuals and organisations can learn from the experiences gained and apply them to future work. Long since departed CEO of the massive German MNC Siemens, Heinrich von Pierer, once said words to the effect of "If only Siemens only knew what Siemens knows". Managing and using this implicit knowledge is a considerable challenge but also an asset which a company can all too easily lose, for example, when experienced and knowledgeable people leave the organisation.

Senior management needs to plan strategically to help retain this Global Fitness within the company, where an organisation is sufficiently large to make this planning meaningful. We acknowledge, though, that small and medium-sized enterprises are likely to have more limited possibilities for this. Moreover, company loyalty may be more widespread in some countries and contexts than others.

Nevertheless, it is important to bear in mind that when an employee is away in a different country, there can be a risk for head office to have an 'out of sight, out of mind' attitude, leading to problems when the person returns. For instance, Case Study 12.5 reports one expatriate's experience (personal communication).

Case Study 12.5: A problematic return experience

"I returned to headquarters after four years in a key market overseas. I gained really valuable experience during that time but was highly frustrated to find how badly my return had been planned. I didn't even get a mobile phone, let alone a desk, an office, or a real job. I was on the point of throwing it all in."

In this particular case, the person stayed and went on to receive a promotion. However, the opposite can easily happen, as Case Study 12.6 illustrates. This is the same person, Duncan, as reported in Case Study 12.4. He had gained a huge amount of very valuable experience and was able to work with very high levels of Global Fitness. However, due to poor repatriation arrangements on his second return, he left the company and has since had a very successful career as a consultant.

Case Study 12.6: Duncan's repatriation

"I had two assignments in China—the first as programme manager (I was promoted to programme director during this assignment). And the second as chief Integration Officer. So, I had two returns to the UK. One of the key differences between the two was senior sponsorship. I had strong sponsorship for my first return and was appointed to a very challenging and rewarding role which matched my aspirations. On the second, there had been significant changes in the UK leadership team and my return was less satisfactory. After a number of inappropriate roles, I decided to take a voluntary redundancy opportunity that arose."

The need for career advancement and the willingness to seek it by leaving one job for a more promising career elsewhere are factors which are fundamentally influenced (among other things) by personal circumstances and individual values (see Chapter 2, Activity 2.3) and indeed those common in country and professional cultures. We give an example below.

- Valuing stability and security in life may lead to less importance being attached to career advancement. In some settings, this inclination may be regarded positively as loyalty to the organisation; in others, it may be seen negatively as a regrettable lack of drive and dynamism.
- Valuing mental stimulation and self-actualisation may lead to greater importance being attached to career advancement. In some settings, this may be evaluated positively as enriching for the organisations; in others, it may be regarded negatively as egoistic and creating instability in the organisation.

Globally Fit HR management can ensure that such factors, which will vary from individual to individual, are taken account of in managing a career path. Career path management may be particularly problematic, however, for those with certain identity characteristics, because they may experience a 'cultural glass ceiling', a barrier to further upward progression, something that is neither good for them as individuals nor for their organisation.

For instance, a research study into the career experiences of Asian leaders reports that most roles filled by Asian leaders are those that benefit from local expertise (e.g., country management or senior sales and marketing functions). The author[85] argues as follows:

> A *cultural glass ceiling* comes into view for Asian leaders within these global enterprises. [...] Global human resource managers in various global enterprises headquartered in Asia, for example, have reported a leadership development pipeline well stocked with Asian junior-level management potential. At more senior levels where responsibilities expand to include regional or global scope, however, the flow appears to significantly lessen. The perceptions that have been created suggest that in order to advance, an Asian leader must adapt behaviors to those that reflect the culture of the headquarters. Other responses to cultural glass ceiling indicators often include a resigned acceptance of a perceived inevitable status or an exit strategy.

Similarly, another study reports on the career experience of a high-achieving minority woman manager—how her career advanced and then declined, leading her finally to leave her employment after investing seven years in the organisation. The authors conclude "the case reveals a discrepancy between the handling at corporate and individual levels of minority and women employees."[86] In other words, a gap existed in this organisation between corporate policies and how individuals were actually treated.

This evidence of unequal promotion opportunities is something that all senior managers should be concerned about and should address, for the benefit not only of the individuals but also of the Globally Fit organisation.

Activity 12.3: Repatriation

Thinking of your own organisation, reflect on the following questions.

1. If your organisation sends employees abroad for longer assignments (e.g., 6 months or more), what repatriation arrangements are in place for them?
2. To what extent have you felt concerned about diverse talent loss within your organisation? Why/why not?
3. If talent loss is a problem, what do you think are the underlying causes? In what contexts (e.g., levels, diversity groups) does it occur?

---

[85] Curran, K. (2020). *The cultural glass ceiling: Asian leaders navigating careers in global enterprises in Asia.* Unpublished PhD thesis, Fielding Graduate University.

[86] Bhawuk, D.P.S., & Anand, S. (2015). Cross-cultural management: Discrepancies between dealing with diversity at corporate and individual levels of employment. In E. Christopher (Ed.), *International management and intercultural communication. A collection of case studies, Volume 1* (pp. 77–89). Basingstoke: Palgrave Macmillan.

4. If talent loss is not a problem, what policies/strategies have been implemented that you feel have been successful?
5. How clear a career-progression route do employees in your organisation experience? How do you know?

Key takeaways

Core insights	Applications for practice
• Senior management and others with leadership responsibilities can foster the learning required to develop the Global Fitness of their people by ensuring that engagement with diversity is increased in a variety of ways.	As a senior manager: • Establish procedures for fair and creative recruitment. • Be aware that previous international experience is not a guarantee of Global Fitness. • Introduce opportunities to learn on and from the job.
• Not only for ethical but also for business reasons, recruitment needs to ensure fairness to members of all cultural groups.	• Encourage expatriation, inpatriation and volunteering as ways of creating a Global Fitness-friendly environment. • Take measures to manage and retain Globally Fit and diverse talent.
• There are severe limits to the practicability of the targeted recruitment of Globally Fit new-hires.	• Beware the disadvantages of a cultural glass ceiling.
• Work and HR management practices can be designed to maximise the development and retention of Global People.	

13

Identifying development priorities: How to monitor and benchmark performance and satisfaction

Introduction

In the previous two chapters, we have described how the organisational environment can—and we believe should—be shaped to foster the development of Global Fitness. We mentioned several times that it is important for senior management to find out about the status quo of Global Fitness in their organisation / division / department. This applies at three levels: the organisation as a whole, the group (e.g., a team, department or any set of people working together regularly), and the individual. In this chapter, we cover all three of these levels and consider the steps involved in identifying development priorities.

The aim of the chapter is to help you:

- Understand what preliminary work needs to be done in order to identify development priorities.
- Appreciate the importance of obtaining data so that planning is evidence-based.
- Draw on some case study examples to stimulate thinking around your own situation.

Getting started—clarifying your focus

The first step in identifying development priorities is to clarify your focus. This step helps to make more concrete what may well be no more than a somewhat vague impression that something is not quite as it should be. It involves exploring what exactly you are looking to improve and accomplish—in your organisation, within your teams, or among individual members of staff. In this section, we share some examples of how senior leaders in different contexts identified their focus at these three levels.

Identifying your vision for organisational performance and development

Here we present two examples of performance aspirations at an organisational level. The first is from a large organisation, the second from a network of universities.

Our first example concerns ambitions for a cultural shift within a very large multinational company. Vasant (Vas) Narasimhan, the CEO of the pharmaceutical company Novartis, is very aware of the complexity of leadership—that it involves high levels of uncertainty and requires senior managers to lead in such contexts by leveraging the differing and complementary strengths of a wide range of staff. Steven Baert, Chief People and Organisation Officer at Novartis, explains this as follows:

> Artificial intelligence helps us deal with everything that is predictable, that can be automated, but the real value of human capital is the ability to innovate in extremely complex situations.[87]

Senior management wanted to use the full potential of their teams and believed the best way to do this was to move away from a more directive style of leadership to one that empowers people (compare Chapter 9, on leadership). They truly believed that "the answer to any problem is within the room, it is within the broader team"[88] and that senior management needs to learn to provide the type of workplace context, including psychological safety (see Chapter 11), that facilitates the emergence of innovative ideas and solutions. The Novartis senior management wanted to bring about this kind of shift in the company's culture—a process they call 'unbossing'. The next step (see our next section) was to gather data and to check on the suitability of bringing about such a change.

Our second example comes from the Coimbra Group of European universities. In 2017 rectors and vice-rectors from across this network of leading universities, agreed at a high-level education policy seminar that there was a need to better understand and address the many and various challenges of internationalisation at their respective universities.[89] A key aim was to create conditions

---

[87] https://www.gallup.com/workplace/349589/unbossing-leaders-novartis.aspx

[88] https://www.myhrfuture.com/digital-hr-leaders-podcast/2021/6/22/how-is-novartis-reinventing-performance-management

[89] Donoghue, D., Thilly, L., Spencer-Oatey, H., Dauber, D., Pidgeon, N., & Barkhoff, J. (2020). Measuring internationalisation: A new approach for benchmarking within the Coimbra group network of European universities. *Internationalisation of Higher Education. Policy and practice, 3*, 5–21.

which would support the development of global students and global staff. The participants in the seminar therefore decided to run a benchmarking survey study with the following aims for each institution:

- **Evaluate** the current internationalisation strategy and reveal strengths and weaknesses.
- **Track** staff engagement, global curriculum development and international collaborations.
- **Enable** a programme to create global students, improving their employability prospects.
- **Prioritise** effort, optimise resource allocation, and enhance satisfaction.
- **Compare** against peers and best-practice benchmarks.

Their ambition was to identify areas for policy implementation that would enable them to enhance the following: the social and academic integration of international and home students, global curriculum development, international exchanges and collaborations, and programmes to create global opportunities for students, thereby improving their employability prospects.

They also hoped that the whole initiative would encourage more sharing across the participating institutions of their challenges and good practices. (It is interesting to note that using the international character of the network as a resource to generate synergistic, *new* practices was not explicitly on their agenda—something that we discuss in Chapter 8.)

Having identified their focus so clearly, the members of the Coimbra Group Executive Board were then in a position to seek out the best ways of gathering the data they needed.

Activity 13.1: Reflecting on your organisation

Think of an aspect of organisational performance that you are interested in or concerned about.
1. What are the issues you are interested in and / or concerned about?
2. What evidence do you have that these issues are salient?
3. What are your objectives in learning more about them?

Identifying your vision for group / team performance and development

Both the examples in the previous section concern development priorities at the organisational level. Often, however, top management's concerns are at a more localised level, such as at departmental or team level. Here we consider two examples.

The first concerns a design project manager at a Chinese electronics company who was concerned about the Global Fitness of the 110 staff in her department. The company develops apps for a worldwide community and were working on the design of an operating system to be used by around 300 million people around the world. The staff responsible included user-experience designers, graphic user interface designers, animation designers, and several project managers. The majority of them were Chinese, but there were also a number from Indonesia, India and the USA.

The design project manager described her motivation and goals as follow:

"As we are designing the apps for our worldwide users and also work with many international partners and colleagues, we think that being a global people [sic] is very crucial for us. Thus, we would like to test the current level of our members' global competence and intercultural awareness so that we could accordingly offer more constructive suggestions on how to improve it." [Personal communication]

She hoped that this would better enable them to deliver the products that met the wishes and requirements of their global audiences. So in this particular example, the purpose of identifying the development priorities was closely focused on the product design goals of her department: to find out how well the department was functioning in terms of global requirements.

Our second example concerns an alternative—or more accurately, complementary—goal for a group or team: how effectively team members are working together. It is common for managers to receive complaints about the functioning of their teams, with rapport difficulties having a negative impact on the achievement of project goals (cf. Chapter 8 where we deal with it from a team rather than senior management perspective). In such cases, we believe it is important to identify the root causes of the difficulties, which may well not be primarily cultural in nature, as well as to identify the aspects that are working well. This was the goal of a communications team leader, who commented to us as follows:

"Teamwork is crucial in every project we work on, so feedback highlighting what is working well and where improvements can be made, will benefit us all."

Both these latter two examples focused on identifying development priorities at the group level (department and team, respectively), but their concerns were slightly different. The design project manager in the electronics company was focused on the company's customers (i.e., an external focus) and wanted to be sure that her department members were sufficiently global in their outlook to meet their needs. The communications team leader, on the other hand, was more concerned about her team members' needs (i.e., an internal focus) and wanted to examine her team's perceptions of their experiences of working together. They therefore each needed to seek out tools that could meet their respective differing goals.

Activity 13.2: Reflecting on your department/team

Think of an aspect of department / team performance that you are interested in or concerned about.
1. What exactly are the issues you are interested in and / or concerned about?
2. What evidence do you have that these issues are salient?
3. What are your objectives in learning more about them?

Identifying your ambitions for individual performance and development

The third level at which development priorities may need to be established is at the individual level. Leadership development, for example, fits into this category, where senior management wants to enhance the performance of their current or future leaders. However, other foci are possible at this level. For instance, if personnel (or students, in the case of universities) are being sent abroad or are working in a pluricultural setting, the aim may be to prepare them for the adjustments they are likely to need to make and to foster the skills and qualities they are likely to require. (We discuss the management of expatriates in Chapter 12 and describe particular approaches to developing such competencies in Chapter 14.)

Our first example here concerns a Japanese pharmaceutical company, headquartered in Tokyo, which was partner in a joint venture with a Swiss multinational healthcare company. As a result of the Japanese–Swiss collaboration, many of the leaders in the Tokyo office needed to communicate regularly with teams in Switzerland. The HR department in Tokyo found that many of the Japanese leaders were having difficulty with this, not only for English language proficiency reasons, but also because of cultural differences in communication styles and ways of operating. They therefore decided to initiate an intercultural training programme for those leaders who interacted with staff in Switzerland.

Our second example concerns a newly established university in China that has the ambition to become a world-class research university. It has received major investment from its provincial government and has succeeded in attracting a very large number of world-class researchers from different parts of the world. The university management then became aware that there were a large number of adjustment and integration issues for these international staff, and so realised that they needed to plan various initiatives to help these individuals fit into the educational system of this Chinese university.

Obtaining top-management buy-in—the importance of data

Having identified a developmental vision, we believe the next step is to obtain robust data to guide the planning process.

A key element of this involves convincing top management of the importance and need for the initiative. All ambitious development projects require the buy-in of top management and budget holders and also of experts and decision-makers in Human Resources (HR) and Learning and Development departments. They need to understand the benefits of any changes and be convinced that they will address business needs. This is important not only for providing the visionary direction and conceptual support needed for bringing about change but also for approving the financial investment that will be needed.

Activity 13.3: Obtaining executive buy-in

Think of an HR / organisational development project that you have tried / have been trying to initiate at your organisation.
1. Were you / have you been able to obtain executive buy-in?
2. If yes, what strategies did you use to achieve this?
3. If no, what do you think the problems were, and what other ways do you think you could try / could have tried?
4. What evidence would have helped you make your case?

A key first step in obtaining this buy-in is gathering data. Steven Baert of Novartis comments as follows:

> I now jokingly refer to it that HR is evolving from being King whisperers to data Kings. There was a time that the power of any HR professional was that special relationship they had with their client [...] Too often we went on the basis of our connectivity, proximity to people to say, here is how the organisation thinks or feels about this. So, it was important to get a more data driven approach.[90]

In Novartis, once they had clarified their ambitions and knew the direction they wanted to move in, they undertook a period of large-scale data collection,

---

[90] https://www.myhrfuture.com/digital-hr-leaders-podcast/2021/6/22/how-is-novartis-reinventing-performance-management

gathering both quantitative and qualitative data. So, this raises the question: how to formulate the most suitable data-collection plan.

Most fundamentally, it is essential to identify tools or mechanisms that can offer meaningful information on the ambition foci we discussed in the previous section. This needs to be balanced against availability, as well as a number of other criteria, the key ones of which are as follows:

- Focus—what facets need researching (as discussed in the previous section)?
- Availability—what diagnostic tools are available?
- Suitability—do the available tools suit the audience and purpose?
- Design—what format(s) do the tools use?
- Quality—how valid and reliable are the tools?

There is a plethora of tools available on the market, covering a wide range of assessment foci, including the following:

Table 13.1: Indicative foci of intercultural assessment tools

Level	Focus
Organisation	• Global fitness • Internationalisation
Group	• Trust • Teamworking
Individual	• Intercultural competence • Global leadership • Cultural adaptability • Cultural identity • Prejudice and racism

As Table 13.1 implies, more tools seem to be available to probe the development needs of individuals than of groups or of the organisation itself. In many ways, this is understandable because professional development is typically aimed at individuals.

However, individuals do not function in isolation; they interact with others, and this creates a dynamic that results from each influencing the other. For this reason, when the focus is on people working together, ideally the tool should probe their interaction, not just their individual skills or competencies. This reveals development priorities for enhancing their functioning and performance as a team or group. At the organisational level, the aim is to gather information that will help shape organisational policy to drive culture change through revealing employee experiences and attitudes that need to be addressed if the organisation is to achieve its ambitions.

To illustrate how this can work, we provide some case study examples in the next section. We report on tools that we ourselves have used with clients, not because they are the only ones available or necessarily the most suitable for your situation (which, of course, we cannot judge without specific knowledge), but because of our familiarity with them and our access to data that might otherwise be unavailable for commercial sensitivity reasons.

Identifying development priorities—case study examples

Benchmarking internationalisation using the Global Education Profiler[91]

This case study example relates to the internationalisation initiative taken by the Coimbra Group of universities, introduced in the section above. They decided to use the *Global Education Profiler (GEP)*, which was developed at the University of Warwick, U.K. There are two versions of the *GEP*: the student version and the staff version. Both were used in the benchmarking study but for reasons of space we report here on the student version only. We first explain the tool design and then show how it helped the Executive Board draw up priorities for achieving their internationalisation ambitions.

Tool design

The student version of the *GEP* probes five factors: social integration, academic integration, global opportunities and support, communication skills, and foreign language skills.[92] Each factor is measured by a set of statements that students rate twice on 6-point scales: once for 'importance to me' and once for 'my actual experience' (i.e., how often they are experiencing it in their situation). This dual rating offers three types of key information: the importance that students attach to the internationalisation factors, the degree to which they have the opportunity to experience and engage with those factors, and the size of the gap between the two ratings. The insights from these three types of data can then be used to identify key development needs.

---

[91] https://www.i-graduate.org/global-education-profiler-gep

[92] For more information along with findings from another set of universities, see Spencer-Oatey, H., & Dauber, D. (2019). Internationalisation and student diversity: Opportunities for personal growth or numbers-only targets? *Higher Education, 78*, 1035–1058.

Findings and development priorities

The Coimbra Group universities that participated in the study received detailed results on their own findings, but naturally these are confidential to each university. In terms of the Coimbra Group's benchmarking priorities, summary information has been published[93] and a very clear picture emerges. For every university, the mean scores for each of the factors were high for importance which is positive insofar as the student respondents attached importance to each of the factors. However, there were three factors for which students reported low levels of experience—social integration, academic integration, and global opportunities and support.

These findings gave the Coimbra Group Executive Board a very clear message on development priorities for their network: their focus needed to be on providing students with more Global Opportunities and Support and to enhancing their Academic and Social Integration (i.e., for there to be more mixing and interaction among students from culturally diverse backgrounds). At the time of writing, they are now considering how they can promote this at a network policy level and individual universities are planning how to respond to their own specific results.

Mapping Global Fitness using the Global Fitness Profiler (GFP)[94]

This case study example relates to the Chinese electronics company referred to above. Given their worldwide customer base, the head of one department wanted to check how 'Globally Fit' her department was and therefore decided to run the *Global Fitness Profiler (GFP)* with her staff.

Tool design

The *GFP* is an online survey tool that explores the three core areas of the Global Fitness Development Cycle:

- Global Fitness in Practice: The attributes of Global Fitness that people need to demonstrate in their work.
- Global Fitness Engagement: The routines that people need to engage with in order to build and strengthen their Global Fitness.

---

93 Donoghue, D., Thilly, L., Spencer-Oatey, H., Dauber, D., Pidgeon, N., & Barkhoff, J. (2020). Measuring internationalisation: A new approach for benchmarking within the Coimbra group network of European universities. *Internationalisation of Higher Education. Policy and practice, 3*, 5–21.

94 https://globalpeopleconsulting.com/global-fitness-profiler

- Global Fitness Environment: The features of the organisation and host community that are important for fostering Global Fitness.

Each of these three areas is probed in the survey questionnaire via a number of factors, each of which has five component items. Respondents rate the items in two ways: "Importance to me" <u>and</u> either "My actual experience" or "Ease of handling"[95]. This means that, similar to the *Global Education Profiler (GEP)*, the tool goes beyond simple satisfaction measures, and crucially identifies the gap between:

- what people value and consider important and,
- what they actually experience and observe, or their skill strengths in handling the issues in their daily work.

The dual scales are important for revealing potential differences not only in people's experiences, but also in their underlying preferences.

The *Global Fitness Profiler* is modular in design so that organisations can select the factors that best meet their own particular needs. In the case of this company, they selected the factors shown in Table 13.2 for further investigation:

Table 13.2: The design of the *Global Fitness Profiler* with sample component factors

Global Fitness Environment Exploring organisational support	Global Fitness Engagement Exploring development routines	Global Fitness in Practice Exploring attributes
Elements for selection	**Elements for selection**	**Elements for selection**
• Global Opportunities (GO) • Equal Opportunities (EO) • Workplace Supportiveness (WS) • Foreign Language Learning Opportunities (FLO) • Intercultural Training & Support (ITS)	• Embracing the Unfamiliar (EU) • Mindful Reflection (MR) • Inclusion & Integration (INT) • Well-being (WB)	• GF Personal Qualities (PQ) • GF Knowledge & Understanding (KU) • GF Communication Skills (CS) • GF Relationship Skills (RS) • GF Leadership Skills & Qualities (LS) • GF Multilingual Management Skills (MM)

---

[95] This wording has since been adjusted following feedback on the difficulty of translating into different languages.

Findings and development priorities

The results are mapped onto a matrix with four quadrants, with those showing high importance and high experience ratings representing the most satisfactory situation. They are thus labelled flourishing. Summary results are provided as shown in Figure 13.1, where the development priorities can easily be identified, along with the areas that are functioning well.

In this particular case, there were many very positive factors. The departmental head found this encouraging, as they closely matched the areas they had been working hard on. However, it also enabled them to identify and prioritise the areas needing further work. These are summarised below.

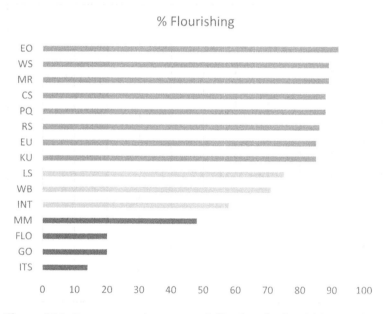

Figure 13.1: Percentage of responses falling into the flourishing quadrant

Development priority 1:
- 3 Global Fitness Environment factors:
  - Intercultural Training & Support (ITS)
  - Global Opportunities (GO)
  - Foreign Language Learning Opportunities (FLO)

- 1 Global Fitness in Practice factor:
  - Multilingual Management Skills (MM)

Development priority 2:
- 2 Global Fitness Engagement factors:
  - Inclusion & Integration (INT)
  - Well-being (WB)
- 1 Global Fitness in Practice factor:
  - Leadership skills (LS)

You may wonder why a factor that has 75% of responses in the flourishing quadrant (e.g., Leadership Skills in this case) would be identified as a priority for development, even if at a less urgent level. The reason is that 25% of respondents reported finding leadership difficult. Even though this is a minority, it still represents a noticeable proportion of leaders who are seeking more support and thus should not be ignored by senior management.

Clients received a detailed report, including a scatterplot showing the distribution of ratings along with interpretation for development purposes. Figure 13.2 on the next page provides an example.

Taking all the information into account, recommendations for organisational and professional development were generated, of the kind described in Chapter 14.

Probing teamworking dynamics using the Global Teamworking Profiler (GTP)[96]

Our third case study example concerns a small company whose staff are distributed globally. The company has a global mission, saying of itself that it 'works with clients to integrate corporate and brand language across all platforms and across different languages'. Its people cooperate in a small virtual team distributed across Germany, the UK, and the USA. Some team members have never actually met in person, so the challenges of such a team are—intuitively at least—considerable. The managing director of the company decided to run the *Global Teamworking Profiler (GTP)* so she could learn more about her team members' perceptions of working together and then plan how to address any issues that emerged.

Tool design

The *Global Teamworking Profiler (GTP)* is a diagnostic tool for professionals working in diverse teams which pinpoints where things are going well and where there are or may be problems. It explores the key, multiple factors that affect a diverse team's collaboration success: interaction and behaviour within the team

---

[96] https://globalpeopleconsulting.com/global-teamworking-profiler

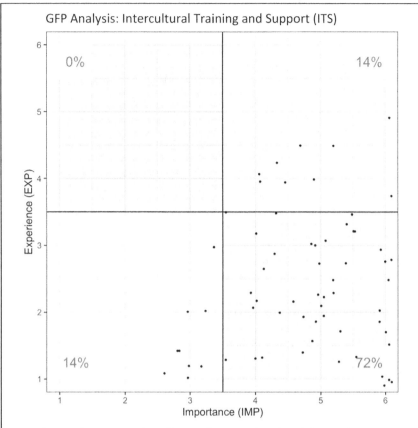

Figure 13.2: Sample feedback on one factor of the *Global Fitness Profiler*

(T level), team members' priorities and needs (M level), and issues for team leaders / senior management (L level). Feedback on team leader / senior management factors is provided only to team leaders / senior management themselves.

Each of these three areas is probed via a number of factors, each of which has five component items. Respondents rate the items in two ways: "Importance to me" <u>and</u> either "My Actual Experience" or "Level of Skill". This means that, as with the *GFP*, the tool offers insights into both what is important to team members and also how well they are experiencing them.

The *GTP* is modular in design, allowing organisations or team leaders to select the factors that best meet their teams' particular needs. This particular company chose to have all factors at all three levels investigated.

Findings and development priorities

For teamworking, it is important to understand if members' preferences over ways of working together are contradictory or aligned (i.e., compatible). For example, if some team members particularly want to meet socially, while others feel that is not important at all, their differing preferences may easily lead to tensions. In fact, even if just one person in a team of four or five has different work-style preferences from the others, that could be sufficient for that individual to feel isolated from the team. As we noted in Chapter 11, inclusion is important for well-being and psychological safety, and so if a finding like this occurs, more effort will need to be made to help everyone feel included. So, understanding the possible incompatibility of team members' preferences is a key first step in avoiding diverse team tensions and dysfunction.

Table 13.3 summarises the main findings from this particular company. As can be seen, there were very noticeable differences in both preference and

Table 13.3: Summary results from use of the *Global Teamworking Profiler* with one company's team

Flourishing factors	Factors needing some attention	Factors needing significant attention
Well aligned—functioning well	Somewhat misaligned— may be causing some problems	Very misaligned— may be causing significant problems
• Team support (T) • Member motivation (M) • Member communication skills (M)	• Team communication (T) • Team trust (T) • Teamworking procedures (T) • Team familiarity (T) • Leading & managing projects (L) • Leadership/ management support (L)	• Team relations (T) • Team familiarity— social (T) • Managing team cohesion (L)

Key: T = Team-level factor; M = Team member-level factor; L = Leadership-level factor experience in two of the Team-level factors and a certain amount of difference in four other Team-level (T) factors. For example, all team members felt good communication within the team was very important; however, four of them felt their team communication was functioning well, while the remaining two members felt it was functioning poorly.

The head of the company received detailed feedback along these lines (with care being taken to maintain the confidentiality of each individual's actual responses) and, with support from the consultants running the survey, was able to identify the developmental priorities for her team and to start planning ways of addressing them.

Key takeaways

Core insights	Applications for practice
• Development can be planned and implemented at different levels: organisation, group and individual.	As a senior manager, in order to support robust decisions:
• Whatever the level, development priorities need to be identified from data so that they are evidence-based.	• Clarify the performance area you want to focus on and what you want to achieve.
• The most suitable tools for obtaining the data will vary according to development focus and level.	• Obtain top-management buy-in for addressing the focus you have identified.
• There are many tools on the market, although far fewer probe organisational level and group level needs than individual level needs.	• Search for suitable tools that address your development focus.
• Probing both importance and experience yields valuable insights.	• Obtain 'buy-in' for use of the selected tool from key members of the target respondent group.
	• Use evidence from the tool to prioritise how and what professional development projects to initiate.

14

Managing development initiatives: How to plan and implement programmes

Introduction

In the first two chapters of Part 3, we described the organisational framework conditions for developing Global Fitness. In Chapter 11 we pointed out how well-being in the organisation can be generated by ensuring psychological safety and fostering inclusion and integration. In Chapter 12 we showed how organisations and the work done in them can be shaped to encourage engagement with cultural diversity, thereby supporting the process of cultural learning and the development of Global Fitness. Chapter 13 then described how diagnostic tools can be used to collect data to allow the identification of both strengths and development needs in organisations and teams. This chapter elaborates on how development needs can be satisfied.

The aims of this chapter are:

- To revisit the various reasons for implementing professional development initiatives.
- To propose important principles to be considered by decision-makers when initiating and planning professional development measures.
- To demonstrate the important role played by evidence- and needs-based methods to assure development measures are both effective and efficient.

Development initiatives: Why are they needed?

The CFO remarks to the CEO: "What happens if we invest in developing our people and they leave?" The CEO answers: "What happens if we don't, and they stay?"

This is a fictional exchange, but it reflects the sentiments of many senior managers. They may see expenditure on professional development as an unwanted cost that is difficult to justify rather than a wise investment in people.

In such situations and especially when resources are scarce, it can sometimes be difficult to make a persuasive business case for investing in the development of interpersonal skills, such as those associated with Global Fitness. Nevertheless, if the need for development has emerged clearly from diagnostic research, for instance as outlined in the previous chapter, it is risky to ignore the findings and the expenditure occurring can more soundly be regarded as an investment to improve business performance.

As we explained in Chapter 13, development programmes can be initiated by and focused at different levels and different people: the organisation as a whole may be the focus identified by top management, or it may be the work group (e.g., department, team or project) that is targeted, or indeed the individual. Table 14.1 below gives an overview of these targets, possible initiators, and participants in the development measure.

Table 14.1: Target level, initiators, and participants in the development measures

Target level	Initiators / Proposers	Participants
Whole organisation	Top management	Selected key position holders or multipliers
Work group (e.g., department, team, or project)	Work group leader or member; HR	Work group leader and/or members
Individual's work	Individual person; HR	Individual person

What considerations actually drive a professional development initiative may also differ by target level.

Development initiatives at the whole organisational level

Senior management typically has a strategic goal that they wish to achieve and that they believe is required for business success. Such goals will inevitably involve changing the organisation not only structurally but also by changing people's behaviour. For example, as we mentioned in the previous two chapters, senior management at Novartis wanted to achieve greater innovation in the company. They believed that the best way to do so was to move away from a directive style of leadership to one that empowers people. So in 2019 they launched their Unbossed Leadership Experience (ULE) development initiative.

Within the education sector, universities also have strategic goals. These are often intrinsically educational in nature, such as equipping students and staff with Global Fitness for the globalised workplace and improving research collaboration and quality. Accordingly, many universities see internationalisation as a means of achieving these key strategic educational objectives and as a result have instigated various organisational and people development programmes in support of that.

Similarly driven by top management are organisation-wide change and development initiatives, which are often instigated for compliance, ethical and / or reputational reasons. The justification is often clearly financial given the potential or actual huge loss in the value of companies which can be caused by violations of the law and the resulting corporate scandals. The business case here is obvious.

In many cases, these scandals are followed up by organisational culture change programmes which often incorporate specific HR development initiatives. For instance, massive corruption at the German engineering giant Siemens in the early part of the new millennium led not only to new corporate governance structures but also to compliance training for 15,000 employees and to the implementation of a web-based anti-corruption training programme for more than 120,000 employees[97]. Such programmes are often a mandatory part of the agreement reached between the corporate offender and the authorities.

In 2021, the Anglo-Australian mining conglomerate Rio Tinto responded to countless cases of bullying, everyday sexism, sexual harassment, and racism[98] by introducing an organisation-wide, cultural change programme. The independent report[99] into the scandal recommended a framework of dozens of measures at all levels of the organisation, guided by the principle of Caring, Courageous and Curious Leadership.

Activity 14.1: Ethically based or compliance-based development initiatives

Think of your own organisation.
1. What training / development opportunities have recently been offered to all employees to drive culture change or compliance? What do they focus on?
2. Are any of them compulsory? If so, what is the basis for them being compulsory?
3. How might cultural factors affect the ease with which they are implemented? For example, consider how power distance, rule rigour, universalism as opposed to particularism (see Chapter 3) or differences in preferred learning style (see below) may affect implementation.

Next, we turn to why professional development may be needed at the work group (e.g., department, team or project) level as the rationales may be very different.

---

[97] https://nerdyseal.com/siemens-change-after-corruption-scandal/
[98] https://www.theguardian.com/business/2022/feb/01/bullying-sexual-harassment-and-racism-rife-at-rio-tinto-workplace-review-finds
[99] https://www.ft.com/content/7a4b0437-ce29-44fb-a959-da414ef99884

Professional development initiatives at the work group (e.g., department, team, or project) level

At this level, the rationale for development typically stems from a more operationally motivated need. Very often there is an urgent problem that needs addressing. Case Study 14.1 describes one such example of a development measure implemented by one of the authors.

Case Study 14.1: Addressing the challenges of internationalisation in manufacturing

The internationalisation of a Swiss medium-sized manufacturing company has been in progress for a few years, with the establishment of production sites in eastern Europe and south Asia and sales offices around the world. Senior management at Swiss HQ has formed the opinion that the USP (i.e. Unique Selling Point) of the Swiss high-end manufacturer has been negatively impacted by this increased cultural diversity of the company and that this has given rise to frictional loss, delayed completions, budget overshoots and, particularly important for the company's high-end products, poorer quality. This perception has been increasingly confirmed by the experiences of those on the ground. At the company's regular, annual three-day management meeting at Swiss HQ, one day is now set aside to tackle the problems with the help of an intercultural expert. His brief is to create understanding and acceptance by those involved of the differences in work style which are thought to be the source of the problems and to generate ways to improve collaboration.

In this case, problems had already arisen, and it was only after this that the need for development was recognised and implemented. However, development initiatives are likely to be more effective if potential issues are anticipated and measures implemented before the problems arise or before they become serious or entrenched—provided, that is, that participants recognise as genuinely useful the development need identified.

A high-end retail company with specialist stores worldwide recently had the foresight to do just this. They wanted to make sure that their retail sales staff would provide their customers with excellent service, both interpersonally as well as in relation to their products, so one of the current authors was requested to run training specifically on building rapport with their customers worldwide (see Case Study 14.3 below).

Professional development initiatives at the individual level

In some organisations, having recognised a development need, staff are free to enrol in a development measure of their own accord. Or individuals are recommended to do so if they are about to take up a new position and they need to be prepared for the challenges involved as in Case Study 14.2.

Case Study 14.2: Preparing for expatriation

A German senior manager located in the USA at a US subsidiary of a German MNC is to become a member of the top management of a major subsidiary of the same German company in the UK. Because of the Covid pandemic his expatriation is delayed, and he starts his UK assignment while living and working from home in Germany. The intention is for him to be expatriated to the UK with his wife and two secondary school-aged sons.

Reflect

a. What areas of development do you think might be needed in this case? Consider which aspects of Global Fitness Qualities, Global Fitness Knowledge and Understanding, Global Communication Skills or Global Rapport Management Skills may need particular attention.

Much of what is known about the nature of Global Fitness has emerged from the years of increasing internationalisation and the investigation of what is known as expatriate failure or, more positively expressed, intercultural effectiveness. Living and working abroad, as we have shown in previous chapters, can be especially stressful. People may adapt to their new surroundings and their new job as the changed circumstances may demand—or they may resist adapting.

Either way, and at all points between these two extremes, the experience can expose them to considerable levels of stress. This stress can lead to people performing well below their usual standard and below the standard expected by their organisation. This is why companies relocating their employees to other countries, and the relocation companies which may be given the job of handling the logistics of the move, have long since recognised the value of expatriation preparation.

This preparation can be of various kinds, including:

- Country briefings focussing on information needed to handle everyday life and more specific PESTLE type knowledge (see Chapter 3) needed in the new workplace.
- Culture-specific (see below) awareness training.
- Culture-general coaching aimed at generating self-awareness and insights into individual personal qualities (see Chapter 2) which may help or hinder the person to adjust to the new environment and perform well in the assignment.
- Coaching to enable individuals to learn from their intercultural experiences (see the tools and approaches in Part 2).

Experience and research have shown that the negative experiences of the expatriate's family members may often contribute to the failure of the expatriate assignment as a whole, so including the expatriate's partner and children in the preparation is often wise. Some consultants and trainers have specialised in the needs of the children of expatriates.

Planning principles for professional development initiatives

Even if the aim of a development initiative is *organisational* development and change, its success ultimately depends on developing *individuals* in the hope of changing their behaviour and attitudes. Psychologist and intercultural guru Milton Bennett[100] memorably reminded us many years ago of the responsibility implicit in this undertaking: "Education and training in intercultural communication is an approach to changing our 'natural' behaviour. (...) This attempt at change must be approached with the greatest possible care." Indeed, it needs to be done with the informed consent and understanding of the people embarking on this journey of personal change and needs to be shaped by skilful 'guides'.

In this section we consider some of the broader principles that decision-makers need to take into account when planning development initiatives.

Professional development requires realistic objectives

Firstly, it is important not to set over-ambitious objectives as to what can be achieved within a given period of time. Consider, for example, Case Study 14.3 below, which describes the training brief sent to one of the authors by the learning and development manager of a major retailer.

Case Study 14.3: An unrealistic training brief

Participants: Senior trainers working for a major retail company

Length of session: 45 minutes

Structure of session:

- What is interpersonal rapport?
- Why trainers should build interpersonal rapport into their 'train the trainers' sessions & how to do it.

---

[100] Bennett, M.J. (1993). Towards ethnorelativism: A developmental model of intercultural sensitivity. In R.M. Paige (Ed.), *Education for the intercultural experience* (pp. 109–135). Boston, MA: Nicholas Brealey Publishing.

- Why rapport is important in selling to customers and how to handle it well.

Learning outcomes:
- By the end of the session, the senior trainers will be able to define and understand the importance of interpersonal rapport in 'train the trainer' sessions and between sales staff and customers.
- By the end of the session, the senior trainers will be able to run 'train the trainer' sessions with a conscious focus on enhancing interpersonal rapport.
- By the end of the session, the senior trainers will be able to run training sessions with sales staff so that the latter can demonstrate competence in building rapport with customers.

Reflect
a. How much of this do you think would be realistic to cover in a 45-minute session?
b. What would you recommend the consultant to agree to cover in response to this brief?
c. Why do you think the Learning and Development Manager wrote the brief in this way?

Professional development requires time

A quick-fix approach is unlikely to lead to success as practically all learning takes more time than may often be assumed. This insight applies particularly to developing Global Fitness because its various constituent competencies differ in their susceptibility to overt development measures. This means that some competencies can be developed as the result of a consciously applied development measure whereas others are less able to be developed in this way. Some may develop of their own accord as a result of experience—or may not develop at all.

The table below highlights the constituents of Global Fitness and the extent to which they can be developed or may or may not develop by themselves without overt external development influence.

The transfer, acquisition, and a certain understanding of PESTLE-knowledge of the kind described in Chapter 3 about an unfamiliar country culture can be done quite rapidly: a presentation, an article or a website can be digested quickly and relatively effortlessly. The full significance of Global Knowledge and Understanding, however, is only likely to occur after it has become salient in an intercultural interaction and self-reflection has taken place.

Understanding the role of Global Communication Skills (Chapter 4) and Global Rapport Management Skills (Chapter 5) may be a relatively quick process but actually acquiring or developing these skills will take longer—and they may be acquired to a certain extent intuitively through experience.

Changing your attitudes, for example, towards cultural diversity, and your values may need more time and experience, even if you understand that certain

Table 14.2: Speed and ease with which Global Fitness can be developed overtly through different measures and experiences

	Can be acquired consciously and quickly through learning and training	Can be developed consciously and more slowly through learning and training	Can develop unconsciously and more slowly through experience	Can develop consciously and more slowly through self-reflection and/or coaching	Tend to develop slowly, despite any conscious focus through self-reflection and/or coaching
Speed of development—fast to slow	faster--slower				
Knowledge and understanding	✓	✓	✓		
Skills and behaviours		✓	✓	✓	
Attitudes			✓	✓	✓
Values			✓	✓	✓
Personal qualities					✓

attitudes and values you hold may not actually support the building of Global Fitness. Attitudes and values may be underpinned not only by deeply held and explicitly communicable beliefs and convictions but may also be accompanied by similarly deeply experienced feelings.

How quickly, then, can you change the way you view the diversity you are confronted with? And do you even want to? How long does it take to understand and accept that a change of attitude would foster the development of greater competence? To what extent can you foreground certain Global Personal Qualities you may know are conducive to Global Fitness but which you may only barely recognise in yourself? Again, this is a process impossible to complete in a short time, if at all. Even if organisational and workload constraints may mean that it is difficult to conduct a development programme over a longer period of time, ideally it should be.

Professional development requires targeting

When it comes to professional development in Global Fitness, the 'one-size-fits-all' approach ultimately fits no one. Every person and every group brings a more or less different set of knowledge, skills, attitudes and personal qualities to the global setting; every particular global context, organisation or interaction situation demands a more or less different set of competencies.

Even if it is likely that a common core will form a part of many development measures, standardised, off-the-peg professional development programmes are unlikely to meet all the particular needs in question despite the claims of those offering such programmes. This means, for example, that pre-designed e-learning content is best used in a blended learning scenario, in which the standard digital programme is supported by group- and person-oriented, in-person training and coaching. This is not just a question of effectiveness but also of efficiency—scarce resources need to be targeted in the best possible way.

Very often the need for professional development becomes obvious because the intercultural house is already on fire and there is an obvious crisis in intercultural cooperation. Here are two cases from the authors' recent practice:

- An international R & D team fails to make the progress desired. Some of the team members think it is because of the obstructive behaviour of a key knowledge-owner.
- A Chinese team working virtually with a UK team, led locally by a German, breaks off communication with the British team for unclear but obviously important reasons.

Collaboration problems were obvious in both of these cases. Sometimes, however, the need for providing learning opportunities emerges as a diffuse feeling that something is not going as smoothly as hoped, or as normally as it 'should' be going. On other occasions, the development need becomes a strategic priority because of a decision to buy or merge with a foreign company (and the cultural due diligence, which sometimes follows).

These observations and perceptions need to be examined carefully and elaborated on in more detailed discussions. They are the initial trigger for development action to be taken. But in themselves they are, of course, not a sufficiently firm basis for deciding on the range of possible development actions, finally selecting exactly how to proceed and not least the budget to be made available.

For this to happen, an evidence- and needs analysis-based approach, which identifies the development needs by collecting data from and about the development candidates and their global tasks and challenges, is obviously essential. Remarkably, whereas this targeted approach may be among the repertoire of tools offered by some larger providers of such development measures, this is not necessarily the case with others or with all individual intercultural trainers hired directly by corporate clients.

In the previous chapter, we presented various diagnostic tools which can provide a very robust, evidence-based, data-supported foundation for taking decisions on developing Global Fitness. In the following section, we elaborate on the pedagogical advantages of a needs-analysis based approach and then present an easy-to-use pencil-and-paper needs analysis tool.

Professional development must aim to meet identified needs

In Chapter 13 we explored how professional development needs can be identified through diagnostic tools. When the tools target individuals and/or very small groups (such as the *Global Teamworking Profiler* does), the reports will provide the development information that is needed. In fact, filling in such a diagnostic tool is a highly valuable first step in the development process itself because it foregrounds issues and prompts people to think about important factors. In the best of cases, responding to the diagnostic tool initiates and supports a process of reflection.

However, such diagnostic information and preliminary prompting may not always be available to a provider. A broader assessment may have been carried out, providing development needs at an organisational level or multi-group level, or no diagnostic information may have been collected at all. A provider is simply contacted to address an internally perceived need.

In these cases, alternative steps need to be taken to identify the professional development needs of the participants and this is known as a needs analysis. A needs analysis will help the provider to identify the existing gap between:

- The requirements and demands of the culturally diverse contexts and situations experienced by the development candidate, and
- The lacks in the form of competencies identified in and by the candidate. It can also identify his or her personal preferences with respect to the professional development planned.

Such an instrument serves another important purpose: it increases the credibility of those conducting the development programme and the programme itself. It shows that the provider takes his / her job seriously, is interested in the experience and problems of the participants and wants to target the development to their particular needs and wishes.

A simple needs analysis, designed to be filled in by participants in a development workshop called 'Communicating and Collaborating across Cultures' and described in only very general terms, is reproduced in Activity 14.2 below. The needs analysis is intended to provide the workshop facilitator with more precise information to help determine the goals and content of the intervention.

Activity 14.2: A sample needs analysis

Think of a situation in which you have been dealing with colleagues or clients from cultural backgrounds different from your own. Then read through the questionnaire below and consider how you would answer the reflection questions given at the end of the activity.

Dear Participant
I am looking forward to meeting you at the first session of our Communicating and Collaborating across Cultures Workshop. As I would like to tailor our session to your needs, experience, and expectations, I would appreciate it very much if you could take the time to fill in the questionnaire below. Your answers, which will only be used in preparing the workshop, will be treated in strict confidence and will not be made available to third parties without your permission.
Yours sincerely

1. Family name: Given name:
2. What language(s) would you describe as your mother tongue(s)?
3. Of what country cultural group(s) do you regard yourself a member, e.g., Swiss, German, USA, etc.?
4. Which social groups (e.g., profession, religion, ethnicity) do you particularly identify with?
5. What is your job title?
6. In what kind of cultural / social group do you generally notice the <u>greatest differences</u> in communication and collaboration style?

   organizational culture   country culture   professional culture
   functional culture   gender   ethnicity   age   other

7. In what kind of cultural / social group do you generally experience the <u>greatest difficulties</u> in communication and collaboration?

   organizational culture   country culture   professional culture
   functional culture   gender   ethnicity   age   other

8. What communication channels do you use in your work? Please indicate approximate percentages.

   email =   % | face-to-face =   % | phone =   % |
   video-call =   % | instant messaging =   % | other =   % |

9. What is the main nature of the communication and collaboration you are / will be engaged in? Please indicate approximate percentages.

   meetings =   % | buying / selling = % | working in teams =   % |
   leading teams =   % | reporting =   % | training =   % |
   doing presentations =   % | dealing with everyday life abroad =   % |

10. Please describe a specific case in your current collaboration experience which you found especially challenging to deal with. Anonymise the case if you wish. Please indicate whether you give permission for this case to be discussed in the workshop.

   ☐ I grant permission to discuss this case in the workshop

11. Please complete this sentence: "From my point of view as a participant, this workshop will be a success if ....

12. Do you have any wishes for this programme which you would like to share with me? If so, please use this space!

Reflect

a. Do you feel that all your needs and wishes in the situation you are thinking of are catered for in the questionnaire?

b. What questions may be missing?

c. Are there any questions you'd find difficult to answer?

Professional development programmes must specify expected outcomes and appropriate content

Of special significance in deciding on the desired outcomes and content of learning opportunities are the actual or anticipated interaction situations of the development candidate(s) as we described above. Combined with information about the cultures / social groups they have contact with and the media used for such communication, the description of the most frequent interaction situations in the needs analysis used above, for example, will enable the person or organisation conducting the development measure more easily to pinpoint the knowledge, skills, attitudes, and personal qualities necessary for mastering these situations. In this way, they can identify the content of the development measure. Such information can be provided by predecessors in the job to be taken up, future colleagues and his / her superior, HR, and the development candidate him / herself.

In more concrete terms, the categories of outcome direct the attention of those responsible for the development intervention to the following questions:

1. What does a development candidate need *to know and understand* that he / she doesn't know and understand now, so that:
   • this person will be better able to handle the culturally influenced contexts and situations more effectively and appropriately and thus grow in Global Fitness?

2. What does a development candidate need to be able *to do* that he / she isn't able to do now, so that:
   • this person will be better able to handle the culturally influenced situation and setting more effectively and appropriately and thus grow in Global Fitness?

3. What attitudes and personal qualities does a development candidate need *to reflect upon and possibly develop* that he / she is currently less aware of, so that:

- they will be better able to handle the culturally influenced situation and setting more effectively and appropriately and thus grow in Global Fitness?

The answers to these questions are likely to ensure that the development measure meets the identified needs and thus assure its quality in terms of effectiveness and efficiency. Figure 14.1 describes the functions and features of the different types of content and how they are related to individual and organisational performance.

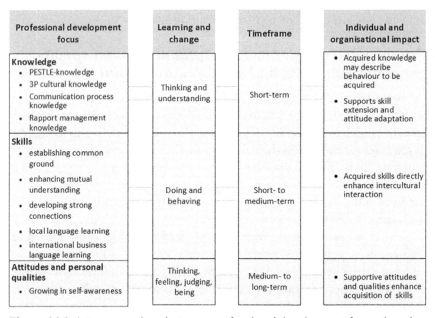

Professional development focus	Learning and change	Timeframe	Individual and organisational impact
Knowledge • PESTLE-knowledge • 3P cultural knowledge • Communication process knowledge • Rapport management knowledge	Thinking and understanding	Short-term	• Acquired knowledge may describe behaviour to be acquired • Supports skill extension and attitude adaptation
Skills • establishing common ground • enhancing mutual understanding • developing strong connections • local language learning • international business language learning	Doing and behaving	Short- to medium-term	• Acquired skills directly enhance intercultural interaction
Attitudes and personal qualities • Growing in self-awareness	Thinking, feeling, judging, being	Medium- to long-term	• Supportive attitudes and qualities enhance acquisition of skills

Figure 14.1: Interconnections between professional development focus, learning and change, timeframe, and impact on individuals and organisations

Approaches to and methods of developing Global Fitness

Even if you are not personally involved in conducting such professional development, but rather may be responsible for commissioning it from suppliers or freelance trainers, you will need to brief them or have a good understanding of what they propose. The route to qualification as an intercultural development specialist is often informal, there being few recognised courses offered by universities or professional associations. The designation 'intercultural coach / trainer' is not protected and entry barriers to the profession are therefore low and the market opaque. For these reasons learning and coaching offers and those implementing them need to be selected with great care by well-informed HR development decision-makers.

Activity 14.3: Approaches to and methods of Global Fitness professional development

1) Read through the following two descriptions of intercultural management situations for which a need for professional development has been identified. Choose the one which you find more interesting and/or relevant to your current situation. Consider and note down what development measures you feel would be appropriate.
2) Then go on to Activity 14.4 below.

Situation 1: The advisory board of the Hungarian subsidiary of a German SME is to take up its work in a few weeks. The board consists of two members of the top management team at the German parent, the Hungarian Managing Director, the Polish Managing Director of the Polish subsidiary and the Danish Managing Director of the Danish subsidiary, who is to be the chair of the advisory board.

Crucial interaction situations according to needs analysis: meetings, leading / working in teams, reporting, doing presentations.

Situation 2: A Swiss company is intending to expatriate at short-notice two internal auditors to its subsidiaries in Mexico and Malaysia respectively to lead a local team of locals. Their task is to audit the two subsidiaries concerned, according to new urgently applicable international regulations and to ensure that sustainable processes are put in place. Neither has previous leadership experience and only the auditor going to Mexico has experience of the country. Both have been on a look-and-see trip to the country concerned.

Crucial interaction situations according to needs analysis: meetings, leading people / teams, reporting, doing presentations, dealing with everyday life abroad.

When a decision-maker has to approve the design of the professional development measures proposed in any particular case, an understanding of contrasting guiding principles, methods and forms can be useful. Deciding whether the proposed development measure is appropriate can be facilitated by answering the questions above using the contrasting pair of guidelines below.

Activity 14.4: Criteria for deciding on approach and method to be used

Now revisit your answers to the question in Activity 14.3 above. Referring to each of the following, identify the primary Global Fitness aim you wish to achieve.

a. To enable the participant(s) to behave, act and interact effectively and appropriately in a wide variety of different cultural settings (culture-general content) OR in a particular country culture (culture-specific content)?
   Culture-general content vs. culture-specific content

b. To equip the participant(s) with knowledge and an understanding of culturally influenced unfamiliar behaviour, actions, and interactions OR to enable the participant(s) to communicate in such culturally unfamiliar settings?
   Values, norms, practices vs. intercultural communication

c. To enable the participant(s) to learn through the insights of the trainer or through experience of and guided reflection on authentic OR simulated intercultural interaction in workshops, role-plays etc?
   Knowledge transfer vs. experiential learning

d. To enable the participant to learn from the insights of others in a similar situation OR with the personally tailored support of an expert, perhaps on the basis of a self-assessment?
   Group learning vs. individualised learning

e. To present the participant(s) with solutions OR to help the participant(s) generate their own solutions?
   Training vs. coaching

f. To enable the participant(s) to acquire a very basic knowledge of the local language OR a more sophisticated knowledge of the predominant international business language?
   Local language learning vs. predominant international business language learning

---

Monitoring the quality and impact of professional development measures

It has become usual in professional development to assess the quality of the measures undertaken by asking participants to evaluate them against certain criteria. They may be asked to assess, for example, the applicability of the content to their own situation, the learning effect, and the qualification and performance of the trainer. Simply measuring participants' satisfaction in general terms with aspects of a development measure rather than asking more precise questions is unlikely to provide sustainably useful insights into the quality of the event.

Evaluation usually happens immediately after the development measure has ended although, in fact, some aspects of the quality of the development measure may only become obvious and be better assessed some months or even years later. This is especially the case in view of the insight that much learning and development is essentially a medium-term matter. What may be applicable to a job situation can't finally be judged in advance of its actual application, no matter how grounded that assessment may appear to be.

Perhaps more interesting from an organisational standpoint, not only for senior management and decision-makers, is to attempt to gauge the impact of a development measure on the organisation. In Case Study 14.4, Steven Baert, Chief People and Organisation Officer at Novartis, commented in June 2021 on its impact on their pilot group of 16,000 people.

Case Study 14.4: The 'unbossed leadership experience' initiative at Novartis[101]

"When we asked the 16,000 people [...] 96% of the population said we don't want to ever go back to the old system, we prefer this new system. That by itself is already, I think, very convincing. We have seen examples of these teams being more empowered during the pandemic in coming up with solutions for complex problems. Those are just anecdotal examples, but still this encourages us. And then across all the data and all the measurements we did, we saw a significant improvement in how people perceive receiving feedback, how people feel about the objectives that they are working on, how they are inspired by their work. All of that gave us confidence."

As can be seen from Baert's comments in Case Study 14.4, senior managers looked at leaders' reactions, their level of motivation, and their success in solving problems when deciding whether to expand the programme to a wider set of people. Interestingly, they were happy with some anecdotal evidence at this point, and there is no mention of financial ROI, although that may well come later.

Another approach to assessing the effects of a professional development measure was taken in the case of the Japanese pharmaceutical company mentioned in Chapter 13. The company ran a simple personal growth tool before training, immediately after training, and again several months after training in order to judge impact, at least from the perspectives of the participants. The results are shown below and make clear the advantage of not assessing a development measure only immediately after its completion but also after some time has elapsed when the participants have had the opportunity to put the learning into practice.

---

[101] https://www.myhrfuture.com/digital-hr-leaders-podcast/2021/6/22/how-is-novartis-reinventing-performance-management

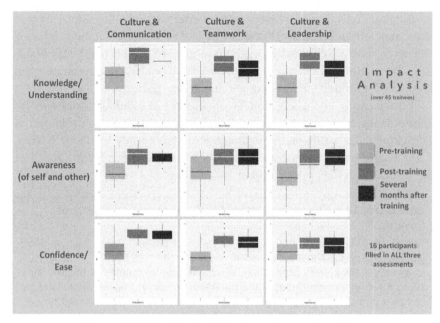

Figure 14.2: Longitudinal checks on impact of training

Key takeaways

Core insights	Applications for practice
• Global Fitness development measures can be initiated not only for operational but also for strategic reasons.	• Don't over-fill the agenda. Be realistic in what you can achieve within a given period of time.
• Decision-makers need to be aware of the principles, approaches, and methods of Global Fitness professional development in order to make robust decisions.	• Avoid the quick-fix. Learn from the psychology of learning that developing the multifaceted competence of Global Fitness will take time to develop.
• Robust decisions can result from consideration of the evidence generated by diagnostic tools and needs analyses.	• Avoid the one-size-fits-all approach. All development candidates bring their own personal set of competencies to the table.
• Development measures can be best evaluated not just immediately after the completion of the measure but also after some time has passed.	• Collect and act on relevant information so that the development measures actually meet real and perceived needs.

- Make sure that the course designer can explain to you—as the decision-maker—his / her reasons for selecting the goals and content of the development measure.
- Make sure that as a decision-maker you have a basic understanding of approaches and methods in intercultural professional development and the terms used to describe them.

Concluding reflections

15

Becoming global: A continuing need

At the very beginning of this book, we introduced the Global Fitness Development Cycle, explaining it in terms of three key elements:

- Global Fitness Goals (the qualities, understanding and skills needed for people to succeed in global contexts—described in Part 1).
- Global Fitness Engagement (the transformational learning steps which people need to engage in, in order to develop Global Fitness—explained in Part 2).
- Global Fitness Environment (the features of the context that affect both of the other two elements—covered in Part 3).

Our argument throughout has been that global people require Global Fitness so that they can better handle the complexity of the interactions taking place in culturally diverse settings. In concluding the book, we touch on a few remaining issues.

The process of globalisation: Is it coming to an end?

In Part 3 of the book, we considered the Global Fitness Environment in terms of an organisational context. However, as the introduction to Part 3 pointed out, the Global Fitness environment is a multi-layered phenomenon. Global people are not only influenced and affected by their immediate context, but by a wide range of broader contexts, including the societies and indeed the global community they are members of.

In the decades following the second world war, internationalisation and then globalisation progressed and accelerated. Ease of travel abroad, improved communication technology and social media—both for work and for pleasure—made the global appear more local and brought it closer to home. Global Fitness became more evidently necessary.

At the same time, the relatively homogenous nation states of the Global North became what the Global South had always been—more culturally diverse. This was the result, for example, of economic and humanitarian migration and the voluntary movement of people, such as within the European Union. The need for Global Fitness at this domestic, societal level simultaneously became more obvious.

However, the incessant globalisation that set in during the second half of last century and the beginning of this, has slowed since then and some would say is being reversed. People speculate that a process of deglobalisation has begun. So, if that is the case, some may argue that the need for Global Fitness is declining, and that Global People will no longer be such a critical resource.

The economic forces driving globalisation indeed lost some of their influence from 2008 onwards as a result of the banking and financial crisis and the subsequent economic slowdown. The Covid-19 pandemic starting at the end of 2019 brought further slow-downs first in Asia and then elsewhere. This led international business to question their dependency on what turned out to be vulnerable supply chains thousands of miles long and markets equally far away from headquarters.

The hopes of the liberal democracies, seeking support in modernisation theory that globalisation would lead not only to greater prosperity for all but also to the democratisation of autocratic and authoritarian states, were disappointed. The erosion of the multilateral, rules-based world order which had been assumed to be the pre-requisite for globalisation set in. Populism, nationalism, and inward-looking foreign and economic policies are now to be found in previously open and liberal societies.

This has changed the nature of the environment at the societal and global level which was hitherto supportive of globalisation to one which makes the continuation of the positive effects and opportunities of globalisation seem unlikely. But these developments do not lessen the need for Global Fitness and Global People. On the contrary, we would argue that it is even more vital.

The ongoing need for Global Fitness

World events in recent years—notably the Covid-19 pandemic and major conflicts in many parts of the world, including in Syria, Yemen, Afghanistan, and Ukraine—have made many reflect on the current state of intercultural relations which are burdened by so many problems, errors, and failures.

Yet there have also been positives. For example, impressive collaborations across various boundaries (e.g., national and sectoral) enabled the effective development of vaccines, if not in their distribution. Similarly, despite the horrors of the suffering of the Ukrainian people, hundreds of thousands of ordinary citizens in Western Europe opened their homes to refugees.

Yet, this latter outpouring of compassion and support raised other questions. Some have asked why there is so much greater concern for Ukrainians than for Afghans or for tragedies of war or famine in other parts of the world.

The head of the United Nations refugee agency, Filippo Grandi, commented that despite feeling humbled by the overwhelming expression of support, he was also concerned about the discrimination that has occurred:

> We also bore witness to the ugly reality, that some Black and Brown people fleeing Ukraine—and other wars and conflicts around the world—have not received the same treatment as Ukrainian refugees. They reported disturbing incidents of discrimination, violence, and racism. We can—and must—salute solidarity, while also resolutely condemning acts of discrimination and bias.[102]

He then called on people everywhere to unite around "our common humanity and speak as one for equality, justice and dignity for all."

Whatever the future of globalisation, we are still living in a world obstructed and marred by boundaries of all kinds—racial, social, economic—that need to be overcome. At the same time the common global challenges we face—in particular, the warming of the planet and the damage to our natural environment and ecosystems—require the sort of strenuous common effort and innovative global collaboration that is only possible through Global Fitness. We all have a role to play in this journey—a journey that includes our own personal and professional development, providing support for others, and helping build Global Fitness in the groups, workplaces, and societies we are members of. It's a challenging and meaningful endeavour—a crucial journey for us all to make.

---

[102] https://news.un.org/en/story/2022/03/1114282

If you would like any support in applying the insights from this book to your work situation, GlobalPeople Consulting Ltd., a company which counts among its founders two of the authors of this book, offers an extensive range of services, tools and resources related to cultural diversity at work. Amongst them are:

- professional development e-learning content and courses for licensing
- diagnostic profilers for purchase
- consultancy services, masterclasses and other professional development programmes and
- research services on all aspects of living and working in diverse contexts.

Our website has a large selection of resources and reports which can be downloaded free of charge.

https://globalpeopleconsulting.com/

Index

Note: References in *italics* are to figures, those in **bold** to tables; 'n' refers to chapter notes.

Made in United States
North Haven, CT
30 January 2023

31859047R00153